How to Be
A GODDESS

A Step-by-Step Guide to Becoming the Woman Men Dream About

JENN CLARK

Publisher: Expert Subjects, LLC
4775 Collins Avenue, suite 3206
Miami Beach, FL 33140

How to be a Goddess
An Expert Subjects' book, published by
agreement with the author

ISBN: 9780988676596
Printed in the United States of America

Cover design by Marija Vilotijevic

Expert Subjects, LLC

Dedicated To

Every "bad" guy who forced me to examine myself, even though they caused me to doubt that true love really existed.

And to my wonderful "L," who made me believe again.

Table of Contents

Prologue

There I was: recently divorced, battered from my reemergence on the dating scene, and totally broken-hearted. After over a decade… wait, scratch that… a lifetime of bouncing from relationship to relationship, guy to guy, and never fully comprehending what I was doing wrong, I found myself truly alone for the first time. No white knight was coming to rescue me. (Just a bunch of weirdos I'd reconnected with on Facebook.) No Prince Charming was on the horizon. (Just a bunch of Match.com freaks.) My fairy tale ending seemed highly unlikely.

Where was Disney when I needed it?!?

Even though I was the thinnest I'd been since my early twenties (mostly from lack of appetite) and my hair was longer than it had ever been, I could not have felt uglier. My self-esteem was so shot from all of the dating disasters I'd experienced, you'd have thought I was a hunchback with a mono-brow. It was most definitely a low point in this girl's life, let me tell you.

So I decided to write about it. I wrote about all my bad dates, all the worthless guys who'd treated me poorly, all the missteps and mistakes I'd made since my divorce. I started a blog called "Just Another Bad Guy" which I shared with a few of my closest friends. I wrote my stories. I wrote my single girlfriends' stories. I wrote and wrote and wrote. And as I wrote, I started to laugh. (Laughter is never a bad thing in times of crisis.) And more importantly, I started to learn. Patterns emerged and I was able to see what I was doing wrong and how my actions kept messing up my love life.

The blog that started off as a place to vent, eventually morphed into "Jenn X: 30Something & Single." And soon, a loyal readership followed. After I went public with my writing and started spouting my theories on relationships, I began to receive questions from women all over the globe. Even though thousands of miles separated us, we were all searching to find a solid relationship with a man who treated us well. We really weren't so different after all! It turns out what works for relationships in the United States works in every other part of the world as well. I take great comfort in that. And I feel a very special bond with my sisters everywhere.

It still surprised me how my "Relationship Advice" and "Reader's Question" posts resonated with the women reading them. I figured what I had to say was nothing more than common knowledge and common sense. And – at the end of the day – I think that's true. I think we all know, deep inside, how we are supposed to conduct ourselves in relationships. I think we know what works with men and what doesn't. I believe that women have an amazing intuition and sixth sense when it comes to matters of the heart.

Ever notice how you can give your girlfriends great advice about their love lives, but when it comes to applying it yourself... not so much? You're not alone. We'll be the first to tell our girls to dump that out-of-work, cheating bastard's ass, but if it's our guy who's no good? That makes things a lot harder, doesn't it?

So that's where I come in. Consider me your best girlfriend, your dating coach, and your champion. I'm here to give it to you straight and tell you exactly what you need to do to find, attract, and keep that great guy. You'll be challenged to live life differently and view relationships and yourself in a totally new way.

In short, I'm going to show you how to go from doormat to goddess.

But first, let me explain why I chose the word "goddess." In 2010, I moved back to Los Angeles after nearly a decade in Texas and I finally allowed the reality of my divorce and all of my dating fiascos to hit me.

And did they ever hit me full-force. I think I cried more than I had ever cried in all of my years put together. Some days I could barely get out of bed. The loneliness was – at times – unbearable. I couldn't help but wonder if I'd made a complete mess out of my life.

During those darkest days of not just my dating career but my life as a whole, my girlfriend sent me a quote by Pablo Picasso that says, "There are only two types of women - goddesses and doormats." Ouch.

Wait, it gets worse! Most of us are doormats. I know it sounds harsh but it's true. We let men (or our lack of one) dictate how we feel about ourselves. We chase after them. We compete with other women for their attention and approval. We accept bad behavior and disrespect. We'll continue in relationships where we are hurt, cheated on, and mistreated. When we allow a man to walk all over us, we are a door-mat. Plain and simple.

In contrast, when I think of a goddess, I think of a woman who is se-cure and confident with herself. A man doesn't dictate her self-worth. She doesn't fall all over herself trying to impress them. Instead, she lets men come to her. She is the picker and the chooser. She's not easily attained and the man who wins her feels like he has won an incredible prize. *Because he has to invest a lot to get her, he becomes invested in both her and in the outcome of the relationship.*

I wonder which woman Pablo Picasso – and every other male on earth – would want. If you were a man, who would you want to be with? How attracted are you to that overly-eager guy who calls you non-stop and always seems to place himself right next to you? Doesn't everyone want to be with someone they see as high status? Someone who isn't so easy to get? Someone who presents a bit of a challenge?

Instinctively, you want a man to view you and treat you like you are a special prize. *You want to be adored.* It's okay, girlfriend. When women are honest about what it is they truly want, we discover that deep down we all want the same thing. It's part of our genetic makeup. So I say be honest with your desires. And then work to make them a reality.

How to Be a Goddess

Your "Jenn X" was once a doormat herself and I know firsthand how badly that can suck. I know what it's like to feel manipulated, mistreated, and misused. But as soon as I read that quote, I knew what I had to do. I knew who I wanted to be and how I wanted to be treated. I knew the type of man and relationship I wanted in my life. So I began the process of evolving from doormat to goddess – from begging dog to dream girl.

When I wrote the article "How to Be a Goddess," I knew I was onto something. I had a strong feeling that the word "goddess" and the mentality and attitude that accompanies it would resonate with women. Yet, its success still surprised me. At the time of this writing, the article has gone viral with over half a million views. Even more importantly is how my readers responded to it. Many began to use the word goddess in their letters and comments to me.

"I want to handle this like a goddess."

"I'm trying to be a goddess."

"What would a goddess do in this situation?"

Soon, "goddess" and "Jenn X" were synonymous. How amazing is that?

Transforming into a goddess is a process; it takes time and practice. But it is so worth it. Not only will you see a dramatic improvement in your romantic relationships, but in your overall outlook on life as well. And by reading "How to Be a Goddess," you're taking the first step toward that goal. In fact, this book provides a series of steps – the building blocks to create a whole new you. It's a roadmap that will lead you through a journey to your new-found "goddess" status. And I'll be with you the entire way.

So kick back and enjoy. Get ready for some girl talk, radical honesty, and my personal keys to success. If I can transform myself from doormat to goddess, so can you.

XX

Step 1

Awakening the goddess within.
Before "he" even appears.

I love the relationship quote "Be the kind of person you want to date." It's true, right? So often, women think that just because we're... well... WOMEN... men should instinctively line up and treat us like we're princesses. And when they don't, we become incensed, indignant, and outraged.

"How *dare* he treat me like that?!?"

"How could *he* blow *me* off?!?"

"I deserve *much* better!!!"

Really? Do you?

Listen up, ladies. If you want men to respect, love, and adore you, you have to be worthy of their respect, love, and adoration. Imagine if you met a guy who was unattractive, broke, and a complete a-hole and yet he insisted that you treat him like he was the biggest prize on earth. Would you do it? I highly doubt it. You probably wouldn't even give him the time of day. So let's not demand the same of men, alright? Instead, let's forget about them for a bit and focus instead on ourselves. And the very best time to do this is when there's no potential man in sight.

I think it's wonderful to be single. When you're single, you are sailing your own ship. You have complete control over your life and, besides your parents and boss, you probably don't have many people you have to answer to. Yet we often hate our single-dom, don't we? We're so busy trying to find a mate that we often overlook the business of ourselves. This is the first big mistake women make in love.

So if you're single, relax for a minute! Don't be so eager to jump right into a relationship. Get yourself looking, feeling, and acting your best. Get your shit together, sister! The higher quality you are, the higher quality of men you'll attract. This is a fundamental dating rule. And if you want men to see you and treat you like a goddess, you need to be a goddess, my dear!

DATING RULE #1:
The higher quality you are, the higher quality of men you'll attract.

Even if you're currently in a relationship, there are still improvements you can make on your own and for yourself. Take the time to make them. The better you feel about yourself, the better you'll be for your significant other. Self-improvement and self-love are actually what make for a happier, healthier relationship. Women tend to think that if they try to make their partner "better" and change him into who they think he should be, that's the key to success. Not even close. The only changes we can ever really make are to ourselves.

So what is it we need to be working on right now? What are the attributes of a goddess? Here are her ten major characteristics.

Awakening the goddess within. Before "he" even appears.

A GODDESS IS...

- Confident
- Strong and Independent
- Emotionally Mature
- Optimistic
- Attractive
- Feminine
- Not Easily Attained
- Intolerant of Disrespect
- The Pursued (as Opposed to the Pursuer)
- Sexually Responsible

Reading the list of the goddess's characteristics is all very well and good, but until you put them into action, you haven't taken the necessary steps to improving your life. Let's break them down and see how they play out in day-to-day life.

A goddess is confident

What is confidence exactly? It's knowing who you are and, more importantly, liking that person. It's being sure of yourself. A woman who is confident carries herself upright. She doesn't look to others for approval. She won't dress or act in outrageous ways merely to get attention. She rarely notices if people notice her. Why? Because she doesn't need to.

True confidence is a rare quality. So it's no surprise that it is one of the things that attracts men the most.

DATING RULE #2:
Confidence is the most attractive attribute a woman can possess.

Men are used to meeting insecure girls. And they can spot them from a mile away. Actually, all of us can. Here are some tell-tale distinctions between the insecure girl and the confident woman.

THE INSECURE GIRL VS. THE CONFIDENT WOMAN

- The insecure girl dresses overly sexy and dry humps her girlfriends on the dance floor in order to get male attention.
- The confident woman realizes such attention is fleeting and won't flaunt herself just so guys will gawk at her.
- The insecure girl criticizes other females in front of men to make herself look better.
- The confident woman doesn't find it necessary to put others down.
- The insecure girl doesn't feel complete unless she has a significant other. Desperation is her middle name.
- The confident woman is happy if she's single or attached and knows it's better to be alone than in a mediocre relationship.
- The insecure girl tells everyone who will listen how fat her thighs are and secretly hopes they will tell her she's wrong.
- The confident woman doesn't need to elicit compliments from others.

My friend Trisha knows first-hand how damaging insecurity can be.

"I used to be obsessed with what people, and men especially, thought about me," she explained. "It got to the point where I would wear super revealing outfits so guys would look at me and think I was sexy. As they seemed to look less and less, my outfits would get smaller and smaller."

Eventually, Trisha realized she was seeking the wrong kind of "approval."

"I just looked in the mirror one day and realized that flaunting my body because of my insecurity wasn't getting me what I wanted. Men didn't take me seriously and my relationships were all short-term. So I just stopped. I stopped caring about getting that kind of attention and focused on building up my self-esteem instead. I took a class and learned French, which was something I'd always wanted to do. I even planned a vacation to France and took the trip by myself. It was wonderful. I realized that I could be alone and still be happy."

When Trisha focused her energy on improving herself and working on her self-confidence, she began to get the *right* type of attention and her relationships improved as a result.

"Suddenly, I was no longer the girl in the hoochie-wear who men labeled as 'good time only.' Guys were treating me better because *I* was treating me better. That's when I met the man who would eventually become my husband."

Confidence is not arrogance. In fact, when you meet someone arrogant, you can rest assured that they are actually over-compensating for their insecurity. The most confident people are humble. They don't need to brag or boast about themselves because they are secure with who they are.

DATING RULE #3:
The less you seek other's approval, the more confident you are.

So walk tall. Hold your head up and smile — it's a sign of confidence. (Side note: Flipping your hair and looking around to see who's looking at you is a sign of insecurity, by the way.)

How to Be a Goddess

A goddess is strong and independent

Very few men want a weakling for a partner. Women who are incapable of or reluctant to take care of their own lives are big time turn-offs. *Men want a woman to need them, but they don't want a needy woman.* If you look to guys to solve your problems and to serve as your be-all, end-all; it's time to rethink your motivation for being in a relationship.

Steven was married to a woman who he describes as especially needy when it came to finances.

"She refused to work. Simply refused. We didn't have kids so it wasn't like she was a stay-at-home mom or anything."

Even though he made plenty of money, Steven began to resent the fact he was the sole provider and he started to look at his wife as more of a burden than a joy.

"It made me feel like she was my dependent – which isn't very sexy. It's not like you want to be romantic with your child! She had no concept of money or appreciation for how hard I worked. I felt like I was a paycheck and only there to finance her shopping."

Steven's wife eventually ran them into nearly $200,000 of credit card debt. Steven got out of the marriage but the debt remained.

"I'm *still* paying for that mistake," he said with an eye roll.

Men don't find needy women sexually attractive or stimulating. Never make him your everything, depend on him to meet all your needs, or lose yourself in the relationship. Maintaining your independence means you maintain the spark.

Awakening the goddess within. Before "he" even appears.

QUIZ: ARE YOU STRONG OR ARE YOU NEEDY?

- Do you consistently ask others for their opinions and look to them for approval?
- Do you have trouble making decisions?
- Do you expect a man to take care of you materially and pay your way in life?
- Do you want others to do things for you because you don't want to do them for yourself?
- Do you have a career you enjoy and work hard at?
- Do you have personal goals you're trying to achieve?
- Do you have activities and interests you participate in which have nothing to do with men?
- Do you have a strong group of friends you won't abandon for a guy?
- Do you know how to do some of the basic things in life? Write a resume? Balance your checkbook? Get a car loan?

A goddess doesn't let life live her; instead she lives her own life. She has goals, dreams, and aspirations separate from her romantic relationships. She would never give up her friendships and ambitions just to be with a man. She knows what she wants to be when she grows up and works toward it. She is a whole person. Forget the line "You complete me," from the film "Jerry McGuire." A goddess is not half a woman looking for a guy to make her feel complete.

How to Be a Goddess

DATING RULE #4:
Men want a woman who needs them, not a woman who is needy.

A goddess is emotionally mature

Emotions are a tricky thing. If we let them, they can dominate us and control our behavior. I'm sure we've all made the mistake of letting our emotions get the better of us and done something stupid as a result. It totally happens. But a goddess strives to make this a rarity, rather than a regularity. She knows how to control her emotions.

I have a nephew who just hit the "terrible twos." When something doesn't go his way, he gets upset, red in the face, and might even cry. It's one thing when a toddler reacts to a situation like this, but women are expected to outgrow such behavior. Many of us haven't evolved past our temper tantrum years and still insist on acting like little girls instead of mature women. How do you conduct yourself when things don't go well?

THE LITTLE GIRL VS. THE MATURE WOMAN
- The little girl pouts, sulks, and/or whines when she doesn't get what she wants.
- The mature woman deals with disappointments gracefully.
- The little girl falls apart in times of crisis and needs to be taken care of.
- The mature woman handles herself and becomes the "eye of the storm."
- The little girl spirals out of control when upset or hurt.
- The mature woman remains calm even when dealing with difficult people and circumstances.
- The little girl insists things are done her way and on her time frame and gets pissed off when they aren't.
- The mature woman allows for compromise.
- The little girl has a temper.
- The mature woman knows how to keep her anger in check.

Men want a woman who is emotionally dependable and stable. He wants to know that if there ever was a crisis, you could be counted on to carry your share of the weight. The woman he wants next to him in the foxhole is the woman he wants to have as his partner.

DATING RULE #5:
A man wants a partner, not a daughter.

A goddess is optimistic

You know what? Life is tough. Some days it is downright horrible. People can be mean and hurtful. Some guys will break our hearts and move on without a glance back. However, I believe every woman has a choice of how she handles adversity. She can either become angry and bitter or she can choose to remain optimistic and hopeful.

In my opinion, one of the biggest turn-offs is a bitter woman. Personally, I can't stand them. And I can only imagine what a nightmare they are for men. Let me tell you a story about Paula to illustrate my point here.

Paula was my friend for over fifteen years. As life wore on and things didn't turn out as she planned, Paula became more and more cynical. Every aspect of her life was sheer misery – from her job to her relationships (or lack thereof). In fact, Paula was one of the unhappiest people I have ever known. You could literally see every line of bitterness on her once pretty face.

Did people want to be around Paula? No way. Many of my other friends refused to go out with me if she was going to be there. And I was always making excuses for her.

"She really is a nice person."

"She's going through a tough time."

Eventually I realized this wasn't a phase. She wasn't just down on her luck. Instead, she'd allowed negativity to occupy every part of her and it had now become who she was.

One of the few times when Paula actually seemed happy was after I told her I was getting divorced. I think she had it in her head she and I would ride off into the sunset and be miserable together. (And by that I mean we would be sitting on her sofa watching movies every Friday night.) I could think of nothing I wanted to do less. When Paula became upset when I went out and didn't include her or when she acted jealous that I was dating and she wasn't, I knew it was time to end our relationship.

As tough as it was to be Paula's friend, I cannot even imagine what it would have been like to date her. I think the men who met her must have felt the same, because that girl could not get a boyfriend to save her life. She wore her misery on her sleeve and her unhappiness was more than obvious.

A goddess is the opposite. She chooses to look on the bright side. She knows life isn't perfect, but she doesn't let it beat her down. Instead, she finds the good in her circumstances and keeps a positive attitude. As a result, people are drawn to her and like being in her company.

DATING RULE #6:
We can all be bitter about something. But a goddess knows that bitterness will only end up hurting her.

A goddess is attractive

I'm not going to be politically correct here. I'm not going to tell you what you *want* to hear; I'm going to tell you what you *need* to hear. Deal? Deal.

Wouldn't it be fabulous if we could look however we wanted and men were merely concerned with who we are on the inside? It sure would. In fact, I bet we'd all go eat a large pizza for dinner and never again get out of our pajamas. I know all about this. You see, from seventh through twelfth grade I went to a private, girls' prep school. Besides the "mean girls" of junior high, it was actually pretty fun. Very few of us bothered with makeup or doing our hair. We wore boxer shorts under our uniforms and didn't give a shit about how we looked. We were there to learn and boys were not part of the picture. There was something very cool about all of it.

My college years couldn't have been more different. I attended USC back when USC was *the* party school of the west coast. I was in a sorority and I'm pretty sure that at least 75% of the students – both male and female – ranged from very attractive to insanely hot. It seemed like every girl (or at least every girl I knew) tried to look good each time she stepped onto campus. And why not? With all of the gorgeous guys around, we had to look our best, right?

Here's the honest truth: Men are attracted to what they see. Try to spin it any way you like, but it won't change the fact they are visual. Their eyes go to pretty. Period. End of story. And we've all got to deal with it.

DATING RULE #7:
Men are attracted to what they see.

Crucify me if you want, but I promised you radical honesty, didn't I? Now for the good news. No matter how beautiful you are, there is always someone who is more beautiful. *Huh? How is that good news?* Because our job as goddesses is not to be the hottest woman on the planet (impossible), it's to be the hottest woman we can be. So stop comparing yourself to other women. From now on, you are only concerned with you. Got it?

Let's cut to the chase. If you want to attract men, you have to be attractive. Call me an anti-feminist, call me shallow, call me whatever you want. It is what it is. And we all know it's true.

Because of my work, I have the luxury of asking guys their opinions on women for my research and as a result, I've learned what they want. Very few guys are going to think it's hot if you dress sloppily and don't maintain good hygiene. Not many men dream about heading home after a long day at the office to a woman who's wearing a housedress and slippers. What do men fantasize about? Victoria's Secret models. The chicks in Maxim. The Dallas Cowboy cheerleaders. So I say give 'em the fantasy. Do your best to make it their reality.

Do you hate me yet? I hope not! But even if you don't, I can hear you groaning.

"But I'm no Victoria's Secret model!" you're probably saying.

Nor am I, sister. But I know how to work what I got. So let me teach you my tricks.

WHAT MOST GUYS FIND ATTRACTIVE

- **Pretty hair.** Seriously. I suggest growing it out to at least past your shoulders. Mine is almost to the small of my back at its longest parts and if I had a dollar for every time a random guy stopped to tell me how great my hair is, I could retire. You don't want to overdo your style, though. Big hair is a turn-off. Anything that looks intricate or like it's held together by 500 bobby pins is a no-no. It should be free and flowing.
- **A nice smile.** Here's a tip: Teeth whitening kits. They really do work and will be one of the best investments you can make in yourself. (I'm a big fan of the Smile Brilliant! products. You can find them at SmileBrilliant.com.) Once your smile is looking good, never miss an opportunity to use it. Coming across as friendly and open is a big turn-on.
- **A healthy glow.** I don't know many guys who think ghostly pale skin is sexy. But on the other hand, a little self-tanner goes a long way. You want to look sun-kissed, not orange. Those of you who have naturally dark complexions should consider yourselves very lucky. For the rest of us, a good bronzer is a quick fix.

- **A good physique.** Let's get this straight. If he wants a woman with the body of a twelve-year-old boy, he's got serious issues. Scary skinny, lollipop women are not attractive. Men *do not* like extremely thin ladies, okay? But the vast majority absolutely positively wants a woman who is in decent shape. I'm convinced that with dedication and determination 99.9% of us can get to a place where we are at a healthy weight. Sure, it takes hard work (and for some of us it takes more work than it does for others), but taking care of your body shows that you respect yourself. So it's super hot to a man on a variety of levels.

- **Natural makeup.** We all look better with a little enhancement. The key is to do it in a way that people notice you, not the stuff on your face. Earth toned eye shadows are always a good choice. And I'd suggest never leaving the house without a bit of concealer (when necessary), mascara, and a light lip gloss. You never know who you'll meet when doing your grocery shopping! And be sure to keep your hands and feet manicured. Guys really do notice them.

Again, this isn't about becoming something entirely different for "him." It's about being the best *you* can be. It's about being attractive on the outside so that he can fall in love with the inside.

A goddess knows that when she looks her best, she feels her best. And feeling good about yourself is critical to having a good relationship.

A goddess is feminine

Almost every man I've polled has put "femininity" on the list of qualities his dream girl would have. Okay, maybe most of them haven't actually used that exact word, but when they tell me what they want, that's the gist of it. They want a woman who is a woman. They want to partner with the yin to their yang.

I think femininity gets a bad rap. We think of feminine women as girlie and immature. This is so not the case. Being feminine is about embracing your womanhood. It's true that if you are feminine, you probably come across as more youthful. But that's because you don't let hardness age you by causing wrinkles on your face!

A feminine woman doesn't try to be a man. She can hang with the guys without becoming one. She enjoys the differences between males and females and knows how to let a man be the man. And although she is strong, she is also soft.

DATING RULE #8:
Real men want a woman who is a woman.

GETTING IN TOUCH WITH YOUR FEMININE SIDE

Women today have been told that we can do anything and everything a man can do. And probably better. It's hard not to succumb to the thinking we really don't even need men anymore. Maybe we technically don't. But if you are like me, you still want one.

Femininity should be seen as the female equivalent of chivalry. If you want a man who is a gentleman, you need to be lady-like. The following tips should help you to "woman up." If you're single, be sure to practice them with your male friends and any other guys in your life.

- Let him be the one to say "table for two" when entering a restaurant.
- Guys love it when you cling to them during the scary parts of a movie. In addition, kill no bugs when in a man's presence. Seriously. Bug killing is their job.

- Don't cuss around them. Save the F-bombs for lunches with your girlfriends.
- Don't try to compete with a man. If you tell him you can "kick his ass" at air hockey, you've just engaged him in battle. He'll see you more as a friend (competitor) than a girlfriend.
- No man ever needs to know about your bodily functions. Ever. There is such a thing as being "too close." (Outcome: He will no longer see you as sexy.)

DATING RULE #9:

If you want a man to behave like a gentleman, you have to behave like a lady.

A goddess is not easily attained

Part of human nature is we want the things which are not easy to get. As women, we covet designer handbags and expensive shoes. Likewise, men want the women who are somewhat "out of their league."

Have you ever noticed one of the highest compliments a man can give another man goes something like, "Wow. Your wife is incredible. How did a loser like you get such a great woman?"

And then the lucky guy will shrug and laugh. But inside, he is beaming with pride.

Anything which comes too easily is not prized. Imagine if you just graduated from college and a Fortune 500 company offered you a job as their CEO. Although I'm sure you'd be excited at first, it wouldn't be long before you wondered what was wrong with them. Don't you have to start close to the bottom and work your way up? Doesn't anything that's worth something require energy, effort, and hard work?

The same goes with relationships. When a woman meets a man and attaches to him immediately, he may be flattered at first. But very quickly he'll wonder why she's smitten so easily. Doormats don't require a man work for her attention and approval. Goddesses do. Doormats get involved without ensuring a man is up to her standards. Goddesses don't.

Players, spoiled brats, and immature boys want women quickly and easily. But chances are they aren't really looking for a true relationship. Real men, however, *want* to work for their reward. Yes, that's right. They *want* you to challenge them. They *want* you to give them the opportunity to step up and show you how great they are. They *want* you to wait and get to know them before you start picturing them as the guy of your dreams. So why deprive them?

DATING RULE #10:
Men who are relationship material want a woman who is a bit of a challenge.

A goddess is intolerant of disrespect

Part of challenging men is showing them what they can and cannot get away with. And it's crucial you set boundaries from the very beginning for the type of behavior which is acceptable and the type which isn't. In fact, this doesn't just apply to men. Boundaries are necessary in any relationship.

People who disrespect you and treat you badly are bad people. And they should be avoided as much as possible. In some cases, it may not be realistic to avoid them completely. (Who hasn't had a nightmare boss or two?) But no one should sign up for a relationship with a toxic person; be it friend or boyfriend.

As I've grown older, I've become a firm believer in calling people out on their intentional bad behavior. If someone tries to hurt you, I think it's a lot better to confront them than sulk in a corner and let resentment fester. Doing so has definitely caused my list of friends to shrink, but I believe a true friend wouldn't do things they know would cause you grief.

I recently dealt with this exact situation with Taylor. Taylor was one of my oldest and best friends and when I found out that she was saying bad things about me and spreading false rumors, I was devastated. She even went so far as to try to sabotage my writing career. It didn't take a genius to realize Taylor was no friend. Although she denied her actions when I confronted her, I knew I couldn't trust her. And I had to make the painful decision to cut her out of my life.

People who truly love and care for you do not intentionally try to hurt you. Instead, they treat you with dignity and honesty. They care about your feelings because they care about you. *Real friends do not want to inflict pain. And neither does a man who loves you.*

DATING RULE #11:
A quality man who loves you will always try to treat you with respect.

DISRESPECT THAT'S A DEAL BREAKER

It doesn't matter if it's a girlfriend or boyfriend who acts in these ways, if anyone does the following to you – RUN, SISTER, RUN!

- Gossips about you or talks smack behind your back.
- Tries to put you down in front of others. Or at all.
- Undermines you and your goals. (Beware of the jealous office bitch!)
- Blatantly lies to or about you. Side note: "No, your ass doesn't look fat" isn't a lie. That's just common courtesy.
- Cheating. Listen up. If he's cheating on you in the beginning, he'll keep cheating on you until the end.
- Repeatedly ignores you when you tell them that something they're doing is hurtful.
- Abuses you emotionally, verbally, or physically. That is the ultimate sign of disrespect and a complete deal-breaker.

Of course, all of us are imperfect and from time to time we're going to unintentionally do something which causes another pain. Goddesses make mistakes, too! However, a goddess knows the difference between accidental and intentional disrespect. If she's the offender, she owns up to it and apologizes immediately. If she's the offended, she forgives the contrite and never brings it up again. But if someone intentionally mistreats her, she has the strength to end the relationship.

DATING RULE #12:
A goddess has the strength to stand up for herself… even if it means walking away.

A goddess is the pursued (as opposed to the pursuer)

Something has seriously shifted in male-female relationships over the last century or so. I like to picture how it was in "the old days." Can you imagine what it must have been like to sit in your parents' living room waiting for all of the eligible, young men to come a courtin'? I guess I'm old-fashioned, but that doesn't sound half bad to me.

These days, women chase after men like they're starving dogs and the guy is a morsel of kibble. We hit on them, buy them drinks, call them first, and ask them out. Heck, some women are even the ones to ask them for their hand in marriage. I honestly cannot even imagine that.

Guess what's happened as a result? Many men have become L-A-Z-Y. They don't feel the need to put forth much effort into a woman because…well…because they don't have to! Gee. Thanks, ladies.

But here's something interesting. Even though most guys will gladly accept an invitation to have dinner or sex, when they find a woman worth going after (and one who encourages them go after her), they instinctively know how to pursue her. Why? *Because it's in their nature.* Just like women want to be adored, men want to conquer.

Awakening the goddess within. Before "he" even appears.

DATING RULE #13:
It's in a man's nature to want to pursue a woman. And it's in a woman's nature to want to be pursued by a man.

I don't know why it's so wrong to say this. In fact, I receive more criticism for this way of thinking than for anything else. Women are all too eager to tell me the "rules" have changed and we are now free to pursue men if we feel like it. I'm sorry, but I just don't believe this is the case. And it doesn't make me outdated or an anti-feminist to embrace this view.

Deborah, a woman I know, used to disagree with me about this. Deborah considered herself a "modern" woman who thought it was perfectly acceptable to go after a guy if she was interested in him. "Why wait for him to make a move if I want to?" was her thinking.

Deborah began to change her tune after a long talk with one of her girlfriends.

"She asked me how many of the guys I approached ended up calling me or asking me out. I had to admit not too many. I began to assess how my best relationships were with guys who pursued me and the worst, shortest-lived were with guys who I chased after. Usually, those guys would end up losing interest pretty quickly."

Chasing after a man is unattractive. It actually causes them to move in the opposite direction. Like I said earlier, they may indeed find the attention flattering at first. And maybe to some women, winning a guy over might feel like an accomplishment. But here's what inevitably happens. The man values her less because he didn't have to work for her. And the woman becomes more and more insecure with her place in the relationship. She wonders if he really does love, cherish, and adore her the way she longs to be loved, cherished, and adored. Since he never had to prove himself – since she never challenged him – she never knows true security with this man. Sure, you might get the relationship and maybe even the ring by being the pursuer, but is it that really the kind of relationship you want?

How to Be a Goddess

A goddess would never chase after a guy. Instead, she relaxes and waits to see who comes to her. If a man isn't interested, she lets him move on and is confident that another guy will be.

DATING RULE #14:
A goddess never chases after a man.

CHERISE'S RUBBER DUCK THEORY

I've had the luxury of having some amazing girlfriends. One of those ladies is a woman named Cherise. When we were in our twenties, Cherise said the most incredible thing to me and it completely opened my eyes to men and relationships.

"Picture yourself sitting in the bathtub with one of those yellow rubber ducks," she told me. "You know how if you push the water toward you, the rubber duck moves away from you? But if you push the water away from you, the rubber duck comes toward you?"

I told her I could visualize it.

"Men are like rubber ducks, Jenn. The harder we move toward them, the farther away from us they move. But if we push them away slightly, that's when they come right to us."

I think my mind exploded when I heard Cherise's "Rubber Duck Theory" for the first time. Is she a genius or what?

A goddess is sexually responsible

The second most common criticism I receive is that women are now free to have casual sex, just like guys. College-aged girls have written to inform me they "hook-up" first and figure out the dating stuff later. You think it's really so different from when I was in college? It's exactly the same, chica.

Awakening the goddess within. Before "he" even appears.

Dear Jenn,
I think you are completely outdated. Here's what happens these days:
We meet and have sex. If we like each other, maybe he'll take me out
on a date. Or we'll have sex a few more times. If I never hear from him
again, oh well. What's so wrong with hooking up right away?
Lori

I will give you that these days very few men will annul a marriage if he discovers you weren't a virgin on your wedding night. Yes, times have changed in that respect. I will also concede that unless you have religious beliefs which preclude it, it's entirely acceptable for an unmarried woman to have had a few lovers in her past. In fact, it's somewhat expected.

But here's what hasn't changed: Women who put out frequently and indiscriminately are still viewed negatively. There has always been and there will always be a double standard when it comes to women, men, and sex. Men can get it on with whomever they like, as often as they like, and they are "studs." Promiscuous women are still called "sluts." That's just the way it is, my dear. And thinking that a guy will see you differently – merely because he's Gen Y – is utter nonsense.

I really think much of this boils down to biology. If you think about the act of sex itself, it's much more personal for a woman. You are actually letting a man into your body. If a stranger walked up to you on the street and wanted to stick his finger in your mouth, would you let him? Doubtful. Yet many women will let a strange man's penis into her vagina as long as he's cute and she's had a few too many fruity martinis.

I don't condemn this. And if all you're looking for is a booty call or a friends with benefits-type of situation, then by all means go ahead. It's your life and those are your choices to make. I'm much more concerned about the girls who think sex is a gateway to a relationship. It's not. And a guy won't be more inclined to see you as a potential girl-friend if you sleep with him right away. In fact, it has the opposite effect. I suspect most who disagree with me are simply young and naïve. Have a bunch of guys use you for your body while offering nothing in return and then let me know how you feel, alright?

A goddess knows that great sex becomes great sex when the connection is both physical and emotional. And she waits to consummate her relationships until security, trust, and commitment are established. By waiting, she shows a man that she values herself and her body.

DATING RULE #15:
Sex is truly great sex when the connection is both physical and emotional.

Feeling a bit overwhelmed? Don't worry, it's really not as hard as it may seem. And consider this chapter to be the launching pad for what follows. We'll explore all of this in greater detail as we go along. For now, remember it boils down to self-respect. If you treat yourself with respect, others will be much more likely to do the same.

Achieving goddess-status may take some work, effort, and practice, but it is absolutely attainable. Just look at how far I've come

DO AS I SAY, NOT AS I DID
(My Own Journey from Doormat to Goddess)

When I was in my early twenties, I spent four years with a man I'll call "J." Very few people know how insecure I felt during that relationship, but in the interest of complete disclosure, let me highlight some of the low points and illustrate a few of the mistakes I made.

Awakening the goddess within. Before "he" even appears.

- Mistake #1: The second time I met "J," *I* was the one who asked *him* out. Although he said, "Sure," I still knew it was the wrong thing to do. If he really wanted to see me, he would have made it happen on his own.

- Mistake #2: On our very first date, "J" told me how his ex-girlfriend broke his heart. Tears actually began to form in his eyes! Here's the deal, ladies. If something like this happens to you, don't think he's getting all emotional because he's a sweet and sensitive guy. IT'S BECAUSE HE'S NOT OVER HER YET! Although I had a hunch that this was the case, I ignored my instincts and continued to date him anyway.

- Mistake #3: After going out for a few weeks, *I* initiated "the talk" and asked *him* for exclusivity. He agreed. Maybe not all that enthusiastically.

- Mistake #4: Even though I saw a condom wrapper sitting on top of his trash can, I believed his excuses and lies it wasn't his. He said a friend had borrowed his bedroom one night and added, "Would I be that stupid just to leave it there for you to see?" My gut told me he was being dishonest but I decided not to listen to it.

- Mistake #5: *I* asked *him* to move in with me. He agreed. Maybe not all that enthusiastically.

- Mistake #6: I knew I was never really "J's" type. He liked petite brunettes and I am a 5'8" blonde. I couldn't do anything about my height, but I dyed my hair brown hoping he would be more attracted to me. (Can you say big time doormat?)

- Mistake #7: Throughout our four years together, I knew "J" was still in love with his ex and wanted to be with her and not with me. When we eventually broke up, they got back together.

How to Be a Goddess

It was at that moment I decided to try to never ignore my gut, pursue a man, or change myself to impress him. I haven't been perfect at this (my big post-divorce slips will follow later), but since embarking on my journey to goddess-hood, I've worked to never get to that horrible place of doormat-land ever again.

XX

30

Step 2

Every goddess deserves a god.

I no longer believe in those crazy lists where you write down all the qualities you want in a guy. Yep, the "doormat" me made them. And my bet is you probably have too. They usually go something like this:

Dear God,
Please bring me a man. He must be:
  At least 6 feet tall.
  He must have (insert hair color here) with (insert eye color here).
  He must love animals, want 3 kids (2 boys, 1 girl), and make me laugh.
  He must be athletic, sweet, sensitive, outdoorsy, rich (or at least rich enough), have a great job, be musically and/or artistically gifted, affectionate, drive a nice car, have at least one degree (preferably two), enjoy fine dining, be fun, be stable, dress well, have a credit score of

31

at least 810, be able to rescue puppies out of tall trees, treat me like I'm perfect, agree with everything I say, and want to do everything I want to do.

Thank you in advance,
(Insert your name here)

Here's the deal with those "lists." They usually end up being pure fantasy (no man will ever be that great). And more often than not, they are a mirror image of the person *you* want to be. I say throw away your lists. Does it really matter if he's 5'11" instead of 6'2"? Would you rather date a douche bag in a Mercedes or a great guy in a Honda? Do you really think there's such a thing as a rock star who will be faithful and treat you well? Let me be honest with you: they don't exist. And holding out for the impossible (or at best, the highly improbable) is a sure-fire path to a lifetime of singlehood.

DATING RULE #16:
Throw away your fantasy lists and focus on what's really important in a guy!

The "must-haves"

I'm not suggesting you compromise yourself just to be with a man. No way. Instead, let's get another type of list going. Let's look at a man's true "must-haves." Let's figure out what makes a guy a good or a bad candidate for a relationship. Doesn't that make a lot more sense? Eye color and height are negotiable. His character isn't.

A MAN'S TRUE MUST-HAVES

- He must have integrity.
- He must have empathy.
- He must be strong.
- He must be respectful.
- He must be encouraging.
- He must be loyal.
- He must be giving.
- He must be successful.
- He must have self-control.
- He must have a sense of humor.

All too often women meet a man and think that just because he's cute and has a good job, he's husband material. In our minds, we can go from stranger to boyfriend in about 2.2 seconds. Add a little sex into the mix and poof...we're smitten! Never mind that he doesn't call when he says he will, insists on always splitting the check, or disappears for a week at a time. And then the headaches and heartaches set in.

When you first meet a guy, you've got to fight the urge to spiral. You need to keep your wits about you and go as slowly as possible with your emotions. You need to relax and watch him! Always, always check out his character.

DATING RULE #17:
He can change his haircut, his job, and his friends. But his character will never change.

Let's start by asking ourselves the following questions:

Does he have integrity?

If he is a real man, he will be true to his word. His yes will mean yes and his no will mean no. A guy with strong character realizes his reputation is meaningful. If he says he will do something, he does his best to do it.

My good friend Sarah recently dealt with a man who lacked integrity. When they first started dating, he had this very annoying habit of telling her he'd call her and then not following through. He also broke plans frequently and often flaked on her at the last minute. It literally drove her crazy! She kept wondering what *she* was doing wrong, what about *her* caused him to not keep his word. Eventually she realized it wasn't her – it was him – and she decided to move on. Thank goodness, because she now has a wonderful boyfriend who was a man of his word from the very beginning.

Here's the deal. If a guy breaks his promises to you in the beginning, it doesn't matter if they are "small" things. It's a sign of his character and it's a red flag you should not ignore. Paying attention to what he says is important. But what he does is even more significant. If he breaks promises to you in the beginning, he won't start to keep them later on.

DATING RULE #18:
You'll never find happiness with a man whose words and actions do not match.

Does he have empathy?

Here's an easy definition of empathy: The ability to identify with someone else's thoughts or feelings. Just the other night, my boyfriend said to me, "When you hurt, I hurt. Especially if it's because of something I've done." That, my friend, is empathy. Look for a man who has it.

Heather was involved with a man who was not empathetic. Whenever she needed him to be there for her, boyfriend would magically disappear as if he were David Copperfield.

Every goddess deserves a god.

"He couldn't handle it if I was having a problem. He'd completely shut down. And if I was upset with him? Forget about it. He'd sooner tell me I was wrong than admit to doing something that hurt me. The words 'I'm sorry' were *not* in that dude's vocabulary."

I, too, have dealt with empathy-deficient men. For example, "J" could never understand why certain things he did (such as rarely taking me out) hurt me. Nor did he make any effort to change them. Instead of ending things and moving on, I tried over and over to make him see the situation from my perspective which only frustrated both of us. I eventually learned empathy isn't a behavior you can teach.

Sadly, many people – both men and women – lack empathy. And it can take some time to determine if he's got it. If he's the type of guy who seeks to understand you and see where you're coming from, that's a very good sign.

Is he strong?

Physical strength can certainly be sexy, but it's much more important he's strong on the inside. Strong men are in control of their lives. They don't allow others to push them around and won't be emasculated. He draws boundaries and won't compromise himself or his beliefs.

When women get involved with a man who is a push-over, they very often test him to see how far he will bend. When we are able to run rough-shod over a guy, we lose respect for him. Just like a man doesn't respect a doormat, neither does a woman. Let's face it, weak men aren't sexy! So find a guy who doesn't let *anyone* – including you – bust his boundaries.

Once you've found your he-man, make sure he isn't a bully. Keep in mind anger and controlling behavior are always signs of weakness, not strength.

Is he respectful?

Have you ever dealt with a man who treated you rudely? Maybe he said inappropriate things or talked down to you. Maybe he was insulting or demeaning. When a guy treats a woman with disrespect, it's more than just bad etiquette or being distasteful. He lacks an appreciation for others and their feelings.

A man who respects you will try his best to be a gentleman around you. He'll work on his manners and he won't make you do anything you are uncomfortable with. Men treat us the way we expect to be treated. If we respect and value ourselves, a good guy will as well.

DATING RULE #19:
The more you show him you respect yourself, the more a man will respect you in return.

Is he encouraging?

A good man wants a good woman next to him. He wants a woman who believes in him and who he believes in as well. A good man will build you up and support your work, friendships, and anything else that's important to you. If a man ever tries to knock you down or undermine you, he's most definitely not an encourager.

Christina was involved with a man who did not support her.

"He didn't like my friends," she told me. "He was always trying to tell me I shouldn't hang out with them. He didn't like the way I dressed and he thought I should change that, too. When he tried to get me to change jobs, I decided it was time to change boyfriends."

DATING RULE #20:
Surround yourself with people who support you.

Is he loyal?

Loyalty is more than not cheating on you. A loyal man is true and honest with the people in *every* aspect of his life.

Think it's okay if a man you're dating cuts corners in areas of his life which don't directly affect you? Think again. If he isn't loyal and upstanding with others, he won't treat you any differently. Just ask Veronica. She dismissed the warning signs with her attorney husband Robert.

"When I first started dating Robert he admitted to me he often embellished his hours so he could bill his clients more money. He said it was common practice among lawyers and I didn't think too much of it. Fast forward fifteen years and he's being sued for malpractice. Even worse, I found out he had a whole other family I knew nothing about. He'd been cheating on me for years. I wish I'd paid more attention to the little things."

Veronica is right. As they say, the devil is often in the details. Never ignore the "little things" about him. They are often indicators of the "big things." For example, make sure he knows how to be a good friend. Try to determine if his business dealing are on the up-and-up. If he lies to people or seems two-faced, you can be sure he lacks loyalty.

Is he giving?

When a man is crazy about a woman, he will want to do things for her to put a smile on her face. He'll want her to be happy. Very often, women will stick around and try to encourage a selfish man to be more giving. It seldom works.

Dear Jenn,

I've been with my boyfriend for about six months. He never takes me to dinner or buys me anything – even on special occasions! He claims he is "broke," but he just spent $200 on a new iPhone for himself. He has no problem buying his friends drinks if they go out, but he won't do the same for me. In fact, it was my birthday last month and he said he was too poor to get me a present or take me to dinner. He could have fixed me a meal or something, right? I try to be understanding but it's hard. I just feel so neglected.

Taya

A good guy will want to give of his time, energy, and money because he enjoys being in your company. If he's stingy or selfish with any of these things, he's not a giver. And if he doesn't "give" with a Saturday night, a movie ticket, or a meal, how can you expect him to give the big things like friendship, love, and support?

DATING RULE #21:
Guys who are selfish with their time, energy, and money will also be selfish with their emotions.

Is he successful?

A man needs to feel that he's accomplished something career-wise, or is at least well on his way, for him to be a true partner in a relationship. If he doesn't and he's got the slightest bit of ambition, he's going to be much more focused on his work than on you. This is one reason why guys in their twenties are a lot less likely to settle down than those in their thirties. A quality man doesn't necessarily have to earn a big salary, but he has to be satisfied with his career.

A man who doesn't work, is always "in between jobs," or has a shady employment history is a disaster waiting to happen. It doesn't matter if he's about to inherit $100 million, a real man wants to earn his own way.

Does he have self-control?

Guys who lack self-control are – in essence – immature boys. They want to do what they want to do when they want to do it. Grown-up men know that delayed gratification is a sign of maturity and they live responsibly. Guys who don't plan for and think about their futures aren't really men.

Heidi was involved with Darren, a good-time boy to say the least.

"That guy loved to go out and drink," she recounted. "That was all he did. *Every night*. He was either at work or out drinking. He was always broke because he spent so much money at bars. He was always hung-over so his work began to suffer. He was fun for a couple of months, but I could never be serious about him. What kind of future would there be with a guy like that?"

Guys who drink too much, party too much, or take extreme risks may be fun for a while, but they seldom make good partners. A youthful attitude is a wonderful thing and being fun and outgoing is great. Being completely irresponsible isn't.

DATING RULE #22:
You can't have a mature relationship with a guy who is immature.

Does he have a sense of humor?

Who wants to spend an eternity with a guy you can't laugh with? He doesn't have to be a stand-up comedian, but he should be able to see the humor in life. Teasing each other good heartedly creates a bond and the ability to laugh at the inevitable speed bumps keeps things fun. Pessimists and gloomy guys will only bring you down. However, make sure your funny guy is laughing with you; not at you.

Whenever I think about men who supposedly have a sense of humor, I am always reminded of a guy I dealt with shortly after my divorce. Aaron was actually a comedian – a *professional* comedian – and he made his living by making people laugh. (And a good living at that.) "How could this guy *not* be a hoot?" I thought to myself when we first started seeing each other.

In reality, Aaron was one of the unhappiest people I have ever known. Not only was he a major bummer to be around, he was just plain angry and took the opportunity to express that anger every chance he got. After a couple of dates, I finally got the joke. Despite his profession, Aaron had exactly *zero* sense of humor in the real world. I soon learned that just because a guy might act like a comic at times, it doesn't necessarily mean he's got a sunny disposition.

DATING RULE #23:
Before you fall for what's on the outside, make sure he's good enough on the inside.

The "deal breakers"

Now that we've explored a potential man's "must-haves," let's look at the things we should never have to live with. Let's face it; some guys are just not boyfriend material. I like to call them "deal breakers." No matter how perfect they seem, if they fall into one of these "deal-breaker" categories, they simply aren't fit for a healthy relationship. And yet, women fall for these guys all the time. Part of the reason is they present a challenge. We think if we are able to "tame the beast," we'll have somehow won. Unfortunately, the beast usually ends up biting us in the ass.

Women also make the mistake of trying to "fix" men. We think if we are good enough or love him enough, we'll help him get to a place where he is a man of quality. Don't make this error! "Deal breakers" are always "deal breakers."

STOP! THE FOLLOWING GUYS ARE ALWAYS DEAL BREAKERS!!

- "Players," "Playboys," and "Peter Pans"
- "The Cheating Bastard"
- "Sir Lies-A-Lot"
- "The A-hole"

"Players," "Playboys," and "Peter Pans"

Don'tcha just love these guys? Or perhaps I should say *boys*. It doesn't matter if they are fifteen or fifty; a guy who acts like he doesn't want to settle down is one of the worst choices for a relationship. Women will waste years and tolerate all sorts of bad behavior hoping and praying he'll one day decide he's sown enough wild oats.

Guys who collect women like they are objects, have a booty call (or two) for each night of the week, and try to party like rock stars are total "deal breakers." Watch for the guys who brag about their sexual activities or who only seem to be interested in getting you into bed. Don't even bother trying to reform them. And whatever you do, don't believe their lies they'll "be different" with you. Yeah, right.

It's true that most of these guys eventually do grow up and get tired of the game. But when a bad boy decides to truly reform, he'll keep his past in the past and treat you completely differently.

DATING RULE #24:
If a player really wants to stop being a player, he will stop acting like one.

"The Cheating Bastard"

Very few men are going to come right out and tell you that they're a cheater. But I do think there are early warning signs which can be strong indicators of his level of fidelity (or lack thereof):

- If he has a solid history of cheating in the past.
- If he is always texting while out with you or is oddly possessive of his phone.
- If he scopes out rooms as if looking to better-deal you.
- If your gut tells you. It's usually right.

If he cheats on you in the early stages of a commitment, I believe you should walk away. Once that bond is broken, it's highly likely he'll do it again. And by staying with him, you've basically accepted his behavior.

DATING RULE #25:
If he cheats on you in the beginning of a relationship, he'll cheat on you until the end of it.

I think it's also important to mention that guys who cheat *with* you are also "Cheating Bastards." Anyone who is taken is a total "deal breaker." Married guys, guys with girlfriends, and – get this – guys who are still in love with their ex-girlfriends (they are "emotionally taken") are always going to be bad news.

As any woman who has ever gotten involved with a married man will tell you, it is one of the most heartbreaking things a woman can experience. I've had several friends who have made this mistake. One of them, Beth, explained the pain like this.

"It's a horrible combination of the unrequited love of wanting what you know you'll never have mixed with nearly intolerable guilt and shame. You feel like an awful, immoral woman for getting in this situation. At the same time, you want him to leave his wife even though you know deep down he never will. You feel guilty about that, too – wanting a family to break up. So you believe his lies about how horrible his wife is and how unhappy he is, mostly in an effort to justify what you are doing. In the end, you are left depleted and empty. Then comes the inevitable reality he was just using you to serve his own needs – that you actually meant very, very little."

Men who cheat with you are cheaters – plain and simple. No matter what you want to tell yourself, it wasn't because you were so special they couldn't resist. Mark my words, if you are ever unlucky enough to snag a taken man away from his significant other, eventually another woman will snag him from you.

DATING RULE #26:
If he cheats with you, he'll cheat on you.

"Sir Lies-A-Lot"
When people lie, they do it to cover up something they did or something about themselves they don't want others to know. Lying is very

cowardly and a sign of weakness. There is really no such thing as a "little lie;" all lies are betrayals. In my opinion, there are only two acceptable lies in any type of relationship:

- "No, you don't look fat."
and
- "That zit is barely noticeable."
That's it.

Strive to live lie-free and find a guy who does as well. A man with good character is upfront about himself and accountable for his actions. And that's the only kind of man worth having.

"The A-hole"

"The A-hole" is a generic, catch-all term for any guy who treats you badly. I'm not talking about a onetime mistake or some minor transgressions. I'm talking about that guy who continually acts like your feelings don't count, hurts you, disrespects you, or tries to control you. I'm talking about a guy who makes you cry way more than he makes you smile.

If someone causes you to feel insecure, unsettled, or unstable, they are bad for your physical and mental health. It's never worth it to be with someone who makes you unhappy. Just take a look at the letter I received from Cassie.

Dear Jenn,

About a year ago, I was with a guy who treated me terribly. Sometimes he would be super sweet and attentive and then he'd practically ignore me for weeks at a time. If he wanted sex or something from me – like notes from a class we were in together – he'd call and I would be there for him. I felt like I was always at his mercy and everything was on his terms. I thought I was in love with him and I couldn't understand why he didn't love me back. He would give me so little that I convinced myself I wasn't worth much. I felt so stupid and used that I ended up crying myself to sleep on a lot of nights.

After I found your blog and several of the articles you've written for "Girl's Guide To," I realized the only thing I was doing wrong was putting up with him. So I stopped returning his calls and started ignoring him. It took awhile, but he eventually got the hint. Since doing that, I feel so much better about myself! No guy is worth all those tears.

Thank you!

Cassie

DATING RULE #27:
Anyone who treats you badly, disrespects you, manipulates you, or continually hurts you — no matter how they do it — is a total "deal breaker."

"Mr. Wrongs"
In addition to the "deal breakers," there are also categories of guys who are bad choices when it comes to having a healthy relationship. At first glance, they may not be as flagrant with their flaws as the "deal breaker" gents. It may take a bit to see their true nature, but they are unacceptable nonetheless. They are the classic "Mr. Wrongs." Woe to the woman who tries to make one of these men her mate.

THESE GUYS ARE JUST PLAIN WRONG...
- "Mr. Hot and Cold"
- "Mr. Emotionally Unavailable"
- "Mr. Mother Issues"
- "Mr. Rerun"
- "Mr. Using You for Sex"

Every goddess deserves a god.

DATING RULE #28:
Never try to make a "Mr. Wrong" your "Mr. Right."

"Mr. Hot and Cold"

I'm sure most of us have experienced a guy who comes on strong - super strong, in fact - only to lose interest or pull away quickly. If he does come back around, this often becomes a cycle throughout our entire "relationship" with him. One minute he's hot, the next he's cold. One day he seems interested, the next he doesn't. Frustrating, right?

> *Dear Jenn,*
>
> *Why are guys so inconsistent? Right now, I'm dealing with this guy who will be super interested one minute and the next it's like he barely knows me. He'll text he wants to see me and if I say "no," he bugs me until I say "yes." When I do see him, it will be days and days before I hear from him again. Why does he act like this? How can I make things more stable with him?*
>
> *Crystal*

Faucets are supposed to have hot and cold taps. Men are not. Yet many of them have no trouble turning off the heat and going icy. When it happens to us, we are left to wonder what's going on and if we did something to put out his fire. The reality is we probably didn't. When a man runs hot and cold, it is usually because *of his own issues.*

What are those issues? It boils down to three possibilities:

Possibility #1 - Men who waiver between hot and cold often don't have the emotional equipment necessary for an adult relationship. They don't have the ability (or interest) in doing the work to sustain things over time. Maybe they like the chase and once you show you're into them, they lose interest. Maybe they don't want to be in anything "serious" and so they back off. Whatever the reason, these guys are not men of quality. They aren't able to be honest with you (nor with themselves) and instead they blow you off, stop paying much attention to you, or run away altogether.

Possibility #2 - Other times when a man runs hot and cold, it's because he's not "feeling it" with a particular girl. When a man is truly crazy about a woman, he doesn't want to pull away or avoid her for extended periods of time. I know this can be confusing because he was once all "hot" for you! We'll think to ourselves, "He *used* to like me! What's going on now??" Here's the truth: When a hot/cold man is running "hot," he's trying to get what he wants from you – whether it's sex, ego gratification, or whatever else. If he goes "cold" after he's gotten it (or after you don't give it to him), he's showing you how he truly feels about you. Sure, he might like you enough to not want to let you go totally, but he's not afraid to keep you on simmer while he explores other options.

Possibility #3 - Lastly, some guys are plain, old jerks. They get a thrill from playing with your emotions and causing you to be upset. When you reward his bad behavior by getting angry or acting needy, he feels like he's "won." In his mind, he is somehow "worthy" because he has a woman all bent out of shape over him. This man is a narcissist and unless you want to be at his mercy consistently (and therefore miserable), you should avoid him at all costs.

The hot and cold guy is major bad news. Why? Because he is so damn addicting. We know he was once "hot" and we think to ourselves we'll be able to get him boiling once again. And then we set out to change his feelings. We'll chase after him, get angry or emotional, use sex… anything to reignite his flames. Chances are he will give just a little bit, but it will rarely be anything more than a lukewarm interest. We keep trying to get back that initial high – that fire – but it doesn't come. Because we have invested so much, we have serious trouble letting go.

The hot and cold relationship is one of the most dysfunctional relationships a woman can have. Our basic need to feel cherished and protected isn't being met. We get caught up in a cycle of rejection and hope. ("Is he coming around?? Maybe?? Yes??.... Aaaah, wait... Nope.") We doubt his feelings for us and, as a result, we doubt ourselves. There's very little joy that results from hanging onto a man like this, but there is sure to be a lot of pain. Never forget that your mental and emotional health are the most important things. Don't sacrifice them for a guy who isn't certain about you.

DATING RULE #29:
If he's hot and cold, he doesn't feel more than lukewarm about you.

"Mr. Emotionally Unavailable"

Have you ever been involved with a man who always seemed to put up walls with you? Maybe he would only give you a small piece of himself. Maybe he would regularly act cold, distant, or aloof. Maybe he would refuse to commit despite the fact you'd been dating for a lengthy amount of time. If this sounds familiar, congrats – chances are you've been involved with an emotionally unavailable man.

What is emotional unavailability exactly? It's defined as a person who is unable to create lasting bonds of intimacy. People who are emotionally unavailable will usually say they want a relationship, but their behaviors prevent them from actually being able to have one. This disparity leaves the other person feeling confused, neglected, and unwanted. Fun, right?

As with any problem, the first step in solving it is to identify it. So if you're wondering if a guy is emotionally unavailable, the following will help you to figure it out. Keep in mind that even *one* of these traits can be an indicator of his emotional unavailability.

ARE YOU WASTING EMOTIONS ON AN EMOTIONALLY UNAVAILABLE MAN?

- **The relationship isn't going anywhere – because he doesn't want it to.** He won't introduce you as his girlfriend. He doesn't seem interested in making things exclusive. When you want to discuss "the relationship," you're faced with a brick wall. Rather than moving forward, you've become stalled. Sharing your life with this type of man often feels like you're stuck in relationship limbo, but that limbo is complete hell. Women waste time and suffer untold heartbreak on men who are incapable of or uninterested in moving things to the next level. We hope and pray his attitude will change, but it rarely – if ever – does.

- **He's involved with someone else.** Much like the "Cheating Bastard," if he has feelings for another, he's not going to be able to give you the emotional intimacy you need and deserve. In fact, it's impossible to have a true relationship with someone who is already spoken for. It's incredibly painful to become involved with a man who is attached and you will never feel completely loved by him. Why? *Because you aren't.* It's important to reiterate his involvement doesn't have to be physical. Just ask any girl who has fallen for a man who is still emotionally hung up on his ex.

- **His past relationships were short-lived.** Does the object of your affection have a sketchy history when it comes to his romantic relationships? Has there been a revolving door of women coming and going? Do the standards of what he's looking for seem so high that no woman will ever meet them? Emotionally unavailable men are often unable to sustain a long-term relationship. They move from woman to woman in an effort to prevent deep attachment.

Of course, they also lack self-awareness. So it's no surprise they blame the demise of their love affairs on the *other* person's faults.

- **He can't discuss his feelings. Ever.** It's not a huge secret many men are reluctant to talk about their feelings. But there is a difference between reluctance and refusal. The emotionally unavailable man doesn't just have difficulty with deep conversations; he completely shuts down, shuts up, or shuts you out. He becomes an enigma and it is nearly impossible to determine what he's thinking or how he's feeling. He will often seem like a stranger.

- **He backs off just as things get serious.** Since emotionally unavailable men can't handle the day-to-day aspects of a real relationship, they often get out as soon as the initial "high" of getting to know you has worn off. Very often, emotionally unavailable men are narcissists who are much more interested in *you* loving *them* than they are in loving you. As soon as you express disapproval with something they've done or when the inevitable conflicts arise, they can't handle it. And so they withdraw – or even exit – from the relationship and find another woman who once again makes them feel good.

Relationships cannot survive if they are one-sided. With the emotionally unavailable man, you will always be giving much more than you are receiving. There is no reciprocity, no fairness. So if you are currently spinning your wheels with a man who is emotionally unavailable, it's time to stop. Every woman deserves a man who is willing to share his entire self.

DATING RULE #30:
Emotionally unavailability means he is unavailable.

"Mr. Mother Issues"

I'm convinced one of the single most important factors which determine how a man will treat you is his relationship with his mother. And "Mr. Mother Issues" comes in so many forms. There's "Mr. Too Much Mothering" and "Mr. Not Enough Mothering." Let's not forget about "Mr. My Mother Was A Bitch And So Is Every Other Woman" and "Mr. My Mother Was Perfect And No Woman Will Ever Live Up To Her." My personal favorite experience with a "mother issues" guy was with a man I'll refer to as "Mr. My Mother Never Really Loved Me." Oh my, was that ever fun!

"Mr. My Mother Never Really Loved Me" was one of the most difficult men I have ever had the pleasure of knowing. Nothing I did was ever enough and I felt as though I constantly had to prove myself and my feelings to him. It was as if he set up a series of hoops through which I had to jump. And If I failed to be his one-woman circus act, he would accuse me of not caring enough about him.

"Mr. My Mother Never Really Loved Me" was at least self-aware enough to know his "mother issues" were the root of his need for total allegiance.

"It's because my mom abandoned my brother and me when we were young," he explained. "I haven't spoken to her in years."

I quickly realized I could not solve his problems with mommy. In fact, no woman would ever be enough to work out *those* issues.

Men's mothers can be tricky. You want him to love and respect his mother. But he should also be able to see her faults and have boundaries with her. If he can't and there's ever an issue between you and her, you will lose. Every. Single. Time.

DATING RULE #31:

Watch closely to how he treats his mother. It will probably be similar to how he treats you.

"Mr. Rerun"

It's pretty hard to have a serious relationship when you are constantly breaking up and getting back together, isn't it? One minute you're together, the next you're not. Fast forward five minutes and the two of you are yet again an item. You feel like you're in a state of constant flux – always waiting for the next blow-up and never completely certain of your relationship status. Friends and family watch from the sidelines and scratch their heads wondering if they should put both of your names on the invite to cousin Sally's wedding.

When you're dealing with a "Mr. Rerun" it doesn't matter so much *who* is instigating the endings and beginnings. The only thing that's really important is it's happening at all. On-and-off relationships are a sign things just aren't working and, most likely, never will. The same issues will continue to surface and break you apart again and again. Just ask Lexi…

Dear Jenn,

I've been dating this guy on and off for about three years. I've ended things several times over the course of our relationship because I think he flirts with other women too much. It really upsets me and he knows it, but he doesn't change even though he says he will try.

I love him and I keep going back to him, but it's the same problem over and over. Will things ever be different?

Lexi

A relationship with "Mr. Rerun" is much like watching a repeat performance of your favorite television show – *you already know how it's going to end.* That script has been written and the outcome remains the same. What keeps breaking you up over the course of your relationship will ultimately cause the final curtain call.

DATING RULE #32:
Reruns are for television, not for relationships!

"Mr. Using You for Sex"

One of the biggest relationship myths is a man will fall in love with a woman because of great sex. This might sound ridiculous, but given the common sex mistakes well-meaning women make every day, it's clear many of us fall into the trap of thinking it's true. Or, at the very least, that we are the exception to the rule. Have you ever done one or more of the following?

- Agreed to a "friends with benefits" or "booty call" situation even though what you really wanted was a serious relationship with the man?
- Dropped everything to go over to his house for a last-minute sleepover even though you hadn't heard from him in over a week?
- Spent weeks or months sleeping with a guy who showed no interest in taking you out on a real date, let alone in making things exclusive with you?
- Gotten physically involved with a guy who was taken and then hoped he would leave his girlfriend for you?

If you can answer "yes" to any of these questions, you have allowed a man to use you for sex. Let me be clear – if all you want is casual sex with no strings attached; go for it. The problem lies with "relationships" where all the man wants is sex and the woman wants more. Having a man use you for your body is one of the most hurtful things a woman can experience.

Not every situation where a man uses a woman for sex is as clear cut as the examples above. Very often there's some confusion involved. It might not be as blatant as a "booty call," but you have a sinking feeling he's not as serious about you and you'd like some help with seeing the warning signs. So use the following as a check list.

IS HE USING YOU FOR SEX??

- **He doesn't take you out.** A man who is interested in more than sex will take you on dates. It will be dinners and movies in public places, not just a beer and a DVD at his place. If the majority of your relationship is spent either on the couch or in the bed, he's using you for sex.
- **He doesn't seem interested in getting to know you.** A man who is serious about a woman wants to know everything about her. He cares about what kind of food you like, how you spend your weekends, and about your job. In the early stages of dating, he will ask you questions about yourself. If he doesn't make an effort to learn who you are, he's not thinking long-term.
- **He's not affectionate.** If the only time he touches you occurs when he's expecting sex or during sex, that's a serious problem. If he won't spend the night or can't get away fast enough after sex, that's a very bad sign.
- **He's inconsistent in contacting you.** If he doesn't initiate regular contact and only texts you when he wants a late-night "delivery," you can be certain he's using you. In the early stages of dating, a man who is crazy about you won't let more than a couple of days pass without sending you a text or calling. If you've been seeing each other for months, he should be in daily contact. If he's not communicating with you, he's not thinking about you. Except when he's horny.

■ **You suspect he's using you.** All too often, women ignore their guts when it comes to men. It's like we meet a guy, fall for him, and lose all sense of rationality. Most women have a strong intuition and we shouldn't be afraid to listen to it. If your gut tells you something about him isn't right and you think he might be using you for sex, he probably is.

We often don't like to face the fact a man can have sex without any emotional attachment. We want to think it will be "different" with us. But women get used sexually every day. It doesn't matter how beautiful, smart, or amazing we are – it can happen to anyone. So here's what I have to say: Protect yourself. See yourself as the goddess you are – a special prize. Wait to give yourself to a man – both emotionally and physically – until you're sure he's worthy of that gift.

DATING RULE #33:
If he's casually using you for sex, he'll never give you anything more than casual sex.

Think a good man is impossible to find? Despairing you'll never meet anyone who can satisfy all of these requirements? Never fear! Eligible, quality men are indeed out there. High caliber men of good character exist in the real world. Moreover, they're looking for a woman who is a goddess – a woman just like you. In the next chapter we'll explore the best ways to find him… Stay tuned!

DO AS I SAY, NOT AS I DID
(My Own Journey from Doormat to Goddess)

I've had more than my fair share of bad guys. I've been cheated on, lied to, manipulated, and disrespected. But my ultimate "deal-breaker" actually came right on the heels of my divorce. Those of you familiar with my blog know this gent as "K."

"K" was one of a kind, let me tell you. He was an old friend from college and, on paper, he had everything a girl could want. He was good looking, funny, smart, and successful - just to name a few of his attributes. In addition he was also a liar, a con artist, a user, and a shady character in almost every possible way. Why? *Because he was married.*

When "K" began his assault on me through Facebook, I was lonely and vulnerable from my marriage and divorce. And he played right into my weaknesses. Although our "relationship" never really evolved past nightly chats on FB, I became addicted to his attention. And he to mine. What started as "friendship" quickly turned into dysfunction.

I told "K" I would never have an affair with him, but that didn't stop him from trying. He played all the cards – his wife was cold, he was desperately unhappy but couldn't leave because of the kids, he had thought about me for twenty years, and on and on. It was all lies. The truth was "K" was a serial cheater. An adulterer plain and simple.

It wasn't long before I was tired of his games. I remember waking up one morning and thinking to myself, "What are you doing? You're better than this." And so I just stopped.

"K," of course, moved on. To a girl he knew from high school. I know because he told me this in an email. Apparently she was more sexually accommodating than I was. Yep, he mentioned those details, too. He subsequently made a few more attempts to contact me and I ended up blocking him on Facebook. Thank God for Facebook block!

Looking back on this, I feel such remorse. Getting involved with a married man, even only "emotionally," is without a doubt one of the most shameful experiences of my life. But I promised you honesty, didn't I? And hopefully you can learn from my mistakes.

I did gain some valuable lessons through my experience with "K." First and foremost, never ever get involved with a married man. Nothing good will come from it. Secondly, when you are vulnerable, you have to be very careful about the men you let into your life. When you are weak, you probably aren't making the best decisions. And last but not least, when on Facebook, it's always wise to keep yourself offline.

XX

Step 3

Location, location, location? It's not so much "where" as it is "how."

Let's go back to my earlier vision of the olden days when young ladies would patiently wait for the eligible gents to knock on the door of their parents' homes in order to woo them into marriage. My, how times have changed, haven't they? If a woman used that tactic now, she'd pretty much guarantee a lifetime of singlehood. Yet so many of us do exactly that, don't we? We are reluctant to get out there and meet people. We become intimidated and don't like to put ourselves in new situations. We hesitate when it comes to joining a group or expanding our social circles. It's like we expect our dream man will just magically appear on our doorstep one afternoon. Even if a UPS guy is your fantasy, this isn't likely to happen. In today's dating culture, you have to get out there and make an effort to meet men. It's just the way it is.

DATING RULE #34:
If you want to meet men, you have to put yourself in a position to meet them.

Even though I'm going to give you some of the top spots to meet guys, the places where you could cross paths with an available man are actually limitless. Wherever you are, there he could be. And isn't that the fun of it, really? As you go about this journey, it's not as important *where* you put yourself, as it is *how* you act while you're there.

When I was newly divorced, a married acquaintance said the most enlightening thing to me.

"I'm jealous," she told me.

"Why?" I asked, totally dumbfounded that someone would be envious of a single woman in her late thirties.

"When you're married, you pretty much know what every day is going to look like. But being single is exciting. Every day is a new adventure and a new possibility."

Girlfriend was right. And in that one conversation, my attitude about being single completely changed. Every errand I ran was an opportunity to find a new, great love. Every man I passed on the street had soul mate potential. (Or at least the cute ones did!) Who knew what – or who – was coming around the corner!

Listen, I totally get that if you're reading this book, it's probably because you're tired of being single and want to find a man. I understand. But I'd like to challenge you to rethink your attitude about being single. It's not necessarily a bad thing. It can actually be a lot of fun! And always remember being single is much, much better than being with someone who isn't right for you. I believe there is nothing lonelier than being in a bad relationship. Further, staying with the wrong guy will almost always prevent you from finding the right one. If you're currently in a relationship that makes you unhappy, you're not the only one. I'm sure many of us can relate to this question I received.

Location, location, location? It's not so much "where" as it is "how."

Dear Jenn,

Help! I've been with my boyfriend for over two years. He doesn't treat me very well, never takes me out, and would rather be with his friends than me. We fight a lot and I don't feel like I'm all that important to him. I know I need to break up with him but I can't seem to let him go. I guess I'm afraid I won't find anyone else and I'll be single for the rest of my life.

Can you tell me some magic words which will help give me the strength to leave?

Amelia

What women in Amelia's situation are dealing with is a fear of being alone. It stems from a lack of confidence that we can't make it without a man and a bad one is better than not having one at all. If that's your story, it's time for an attitude adjustment! A bad relationship will make you miserable 100% of the time. It will affect every aspect of your life – from your friendships to your work to your health. Sure, being single can make you feel lonely on occasion, but it is always better than being with a man who treats you poorly. Never let the fear of being alone prevent you from leaving a bad situation. Besides, now that you're reading this book and putting it into action, you probably won't be single for long!

DATING RULE #35:
A goddess knows that it's better to be single than in a bad relationship.

As you change your attitude about being single, something incredible starts to happen. You feel less desperate. You begin to make better choices when it comes to men. You're less likely to settle or to accept the unacceptable just so you won't be alone. With this shift also comes power. Now, your circumstances aren't controlling your life and subsequent decisions. You are. And it is exactly this goddess-like feeling of empowerment that puts you in the best place for a solid, healthy relationship.

So while you want to get out there and meet people, you also have to enjoy the process. You're not on a hunt and this isn't a life or death mission. You aren't trying to meet a guy to fill a void in your life. You are single and happy and want to live life to the fullest. When we truly believe this, that's when a great guy usually ends up finding us.

DATING RULE #36:
More than anything else, your attitude will determine how successful you are with meeting guys.

Let's take this a step further, shall we? Even if you are content with your own life and not totally miserable being single, the attitude you convey to the world will still factor heavily into whether or not you attract men. Can you relate to this reader's question?

Dear Jenn,
I'm having a hard time simply meeting guys. I'm not bad looking and have a good personality. Yet it seems like men don't approach me and plenty of women who aren't as much of a "catch" as I think I am have a lot more dates than I do. What's the deal? Is there something I'm doing wrong with guys? It's like I have a sign that says "Don't talk to me" on my forehead.
Nancy

The first thing women in Nancy's situation need to do is analyze what type of vibe they are giving off to men. Are you closed off? Do you appear to be unfriendly? Do you walk with your head down and refuse to make eye contact with the people you see in your day-to-day life? If so, it's time to turn your "available light" on.

Location, location, location? It's not so much "where" as it is "how."

Huh? Yep, that's what I call it. You see, I believe we all have an "available light," much like a taxi cab or an "open sign" on a store. When we are closed for business – i.e., not looking to meet anyone – we show that in the way in which we carry ourselves. Many of us have conflicting signage. We're single and we want to meet someone, yet we give off the vibe we are unavailable. How can we possibly expect a man to approach us or show us he's interested if we're giving him signals we wouldn't appreciate his initiative?

Here's an often used example. Imagine, for a moment, you are a guy. You're at a bar. Or a coffee house. Or anywhere, really. And you see a girl who is smiling and looks happy. She radiates warmth and friendliness. Right next to her is a woman (maybe even a "prettier" one) who seems closed off and bitchy. She looks annoyed with how long it's taking to get her cocktail or coffee. You're pretty sure if you tried striking up a conversation with her, she'd either look at you like you're crazy, give you major attitude, or would bite your head off. Which girl would you approach? Who's the goddess in this situation? Pretty much a no-brainer, right?

You might be the sweetest, most wonderful woman on earth, but if you aren't projecting that attitude to the men you meet, it really won't matter. So now is the time to cultivate a positive and friendly attitude. And to let it show by turning your "available light" *on*. I'm confident you'll be amazed by the results.

IS YOUR "AVAILABLE LIGHT" ON OR OFF?
Your light looks "OFF" if:
- You walk with your head down and don't make eye contact with anyone.
- You cover half of your face with a baseball cap as if to tell people to leave you the "F" alone.

- You refuse to engage in pleasant conversation with the people you encounter throughout your day. You speak only when absolutely necessary and when you do talk, you mumble.
- Your hair looks like it hasn't been brushed in weeks and you are wearing ratty old flannel pajamas and Ugg boots.

Your light looks "ON" if:
- You walk with your head up and make eye contact with people you pass on the street.
- You try to look good every time you leave the house. Even if you're rocking sweats and a ponytail, they are cute (and clean!) sweats. Always put on a little mascara, blush, and lip gloss. Always.
- You give off the air you are friendly, open, and happy. You easily chat with the grocery store clerk or the coffee barista.
- You smile. At everyone. Male, female, or canine. Your smile is the number one thing that will show a man you are available and approachable.

DATING RULE #37:
Your smile is critical when it comes to attracting a man.

Never underestimate the power of your smile. Not only does it make you seem happy and upbeat, it's also a signal to a man you would like him to make contact with you. It opens the door to conversation and perhaps more. Most men, even the very confident ones, are not inclined to approach a woman if she doesn't give them an indication she'd be receptive to their advances. Your smile is what gives him the courage to make the first move. So whatever you do and wherever you go, always bring along your smile.

Location, location, location? It's not so much "where" as it is "how."

Getting started

So you're feeling and looking your best. You know what you will and won't accept in a man. Both your smile and "available light" are shining brightly for all to see. In short, you've got your "goddess on." Now what? Where in the heck do you go when trying to meet men?

Dear Jenn,
I'm a 35 year-old single woman with a great career, good friends, and an awesome dog. The only thing I'm missing is a boyfriend and I'd like to know the best places to meet guys. Please don't say online dating...
Thanks,
Shelley

Like I said earlier, men are all around us. It's true. No matter how it may seem, *good men* are everywhere. They're in our office buildings and they buy their morning latte at the same coffee place where we buy ours. However, there are places where we are more likely to meet them – situations and gatherings which are more conducive to interacting with them. Back in my single days, I researched this and educated myself extensively. I now pass along all the lessons I learned to you, my dear reader...

HOT SPOT #1: THE GROCERY STORE
Basic Studies: Single guys tend to do their grocery shopping on Sunday evenings, thereby stocking up on eats for the week. Deli counters, freezer aisles, and any section where food is pre-packaged or pre-prepared is usually fertile ground.

Advanced Degree: You can even pre-screen men to some extent by choosing which store you visit. Whole Foods and other natural grocers for the outdoorsy, organic guys. Bristol Farms or "gourmet" markets for the more upscale, foodie gents. A "regular" grocery store will attract the vast majority of guys just looking for some sliced turkey and salad in a bag. Costco and other warehouse style stores are iffy at best. If he's buying in bulk, chances are good he's got a wife and two kids at home.

HOT SPOT #2: THE DOG PARK

Basic Studies: Don't have a dog? Borrow one. Dog parks are great places for meeting guys. Meeting a man who owns a dog usually shows he's capable of (a) loving something besides himself, (b) sharing his life with something besides himself, and (c) taking care of something besides himself. No, having a dog doesn't guarantee he's a quality guy, but it's not a bad place to start.

Advanced Degree: Don't be afraid to judge guys based on the type of dog they own. Personally, I like large mutts. It says "compassionate masculinity" to me. Men who have dogs known for their aggression are kinda like those who drive convertible Porsches (i.e., potential sexual inadequacies). On the flip side, be careful about investing too much time talking to a guy who has a "purse dog." He may share custody of it with a girlfriend. Or a boyfriend.

HOT SPOT #3: THE UPSCALE HAPPY HOUR

Basic Studies: Even if you are in your early twenties, I'm not a fan of meeting guys at nightclubs and trendy bars. But if you're in your thirties or forties, the upscale happy hour at a

Location, location, location? It's not so much "where" as it is "how."

nice restaurant is a virtual playground of eligible men. Look for an establishment that caters to the classy, professional set. Here's the scary part. Go alone. Bring a magazine if you need to. (Don't bring a book. That translates into "Don't talk to me, I'm busy.") Order food and make it your dinner. Have a glass of wine or a nice cocktail. Chat up the bartender. I did this myself many times. Not only did I meet a ton of men this way, I always had a fabulous evening.

Advanced Degree: You can tell a lot about a man by what (and how much) he drinks. More than two or three at a happy hour? Alcoholic alert! Liquor from the well? Cheapo! Also avoid: Men who use fruit juice mixers (wimpy), drink "chick drinks" (super wimpy), or imbibe cheap beer (perpetual frat guy). Men should drink like men. You need to watch what you drink, as well. Designer "fruit-inis" reek of high maintenance, "Sex and The City" wannabes. A glass with more fruit in it than a Brazilian conga dancer's headdress screams "immature palate." And never, ever have more than one of anything. Getting wasted at 6:30 on a Tuesday night while alone at a bar is a no-no. Drink classy, sister, drink classy.

HOT SPOT #4: THE SPORTS VENUE

Basic Studies: Most guys like sports. You'll find they tend to congregate anywhere there is a large television(s) and a sporting event going on. This includes both the sports bar and the live event itself. If you decide to watch it live, keep the following in mind: (a) Go with a girlfriend, not alone; (b) splurge on good seats and make sure you have access to the VIP areas (this will give you the best opportunity to engage in one-on-one conversations during intermissions); and (c) do not dress like a hoochie. If you show up at the basketball stadium wearing a skank dress and stilettos, guys will assume you're looking to get impregnated by a "baller" in order to ensure a lifetime of child support payments. Don't look – or act – like a jersey chaser.

Don't want to spend the cashola on the event itself? No problem. Sports happen year round on television. So hang at a nice sports bar on a Saturday or Sunday afternoon. Don't worry about guys paying more attention to the game than to you. That phenomenon happens only *after* you're in a relationship.

Advanced Degree: Guys like girls who genuinely like sports. I have a theory that the reason most girls don't like them is because they don't understand them. If that's the case, enlist the help of a male friend and have him explain the basics. Get into whatever game you're watching and cheer a bit. This will turn a potential suitor on more than you can imagine.

HOT SPOT #5: THE GROUP ACTIVITY

Basic Studies: What are *your* hobbies and interests? If you're into the outdoors, take a class at your nearest REI or L.L. Bean. If you're a runner, join a group training for a marathon. (Or sign up for a 5K if that's more your speed.) Into art? Go to gallery openings. Like live music? See bands. If you enjoy it or want to get involved with it, there's a group out there for you. Workshops, networking events, alumni groups, religious organizations, charity functions, and social clubs are all great places to meet new people and expand your social circles. Never be afraid to try new things.

Advanced Degree: Don't be worried if your dream guy isn't in that art or cooking class you signed up for. (Chances are great he won't be.) The whole point is to make new friends.

Location, location, location? It's not so much "where" as it is "how."

The cool chick you met may have a brother she's dying to set up. Or the married couple may have an amazing single buddy. The whole point is to get out there and have fun. When we do that, life has a way of bringing people to us.

HOT SPOT #6: THE OLD STANDBYS

Basic Studies: These methods for meeting guys may seem cliché, but that's because they're tested and true: (a) Friends of friends and friends of family members. Set ups aren't always a bad thing. Sometimes it's nice to have just one degree of separation. (b) The gym. I've never met anyone at the gym, but I know plenty of people who have. Maybe I've failed at this location because I never really went with any regularity and, when I did, I always looked horrible. If you're one of those lucky females who actually look sexy while sweating away on the elliptical machine… God bless you. (c) Starbucks or any other coffee house type of place. They're the singles' bar for the over thirty set. I've found evenings are the best bet for meeting available men. Guys who hang there on weekdays are usually unemployed. Just sayin'.

Advanced Degree: If you haven't dated in a while or are newly single, go out with everyone who doesn't have horrible breath or errant nose hairs. Date. And date a lot. By "trying on" all different types of men, we learn about ourselves and what we want. It also helps us brush up on our inter-personal communication skills, a.k.a. flirting. There's no law that says you have to buy. If, however, you've done the dating craze and know what you're looking for, it's okay to be a bit pickier. Don't waste your time on men you are certain aren't right for you.

DATING RULE#38:
Always be ready to meet someone. Anywhere you go, there "he" could be.

My thoughts on online dating

Have you done it? I have. I did Match.com, Plenty of Fish, and have Facebooked myself into oblivion. My results? Not so great. Here's what I have to say about the Match.coms and eHarmonys out there: They can provide a great distraction. If you've been single for a long time, getting a million winks and messages in your inbox is flattering. It keeps you in the dating game and gives you hope that maybe, just maybe, you really will find someone. Here's where it becomes a bummer: I believe 99% of the men who contact you through an online dating site range from disappointing to downright horrifying. Actually, I couldn't believe the awful quality of guys out there. Illiterate, sexually inappropriate, and socially awkward barely scratches the surface. Yeah, I've seen the commercials which say one in five relationships begin online. I would like to see the raw data on that stat and ask them their definition of a "relationship," 'cause I ain't buying it.

I think online dating is fine as an addition to actually getting out there and meeting people. It should never serve as your only source for introductions. Yes, I do know of a few women who met their husbands or boyfriends online. But if you're waiting for your dream man to suddenly appear in your Match.com email, my bet is you'll be waiting a long time. Of course I'm not going to leave you out to dry if you do decide to pursue the online dating route. I actually have a lot to say about the subject in the following chapter. For now, just keep the next dating rule in mind.

DATING RULE #39:
Online dating is a great addition to an already active social life, but it shouldn't be your entire social life.

Facebook is a different venue. It really has become a universe in and of itself, hasn't it? I'll talk more about Facebook and dating as we go along, but for now let me say this: As far as actually meeting a stranger through FB, I'd be as skeptical about it as I would any online dating site. Sure, it can happen. But much like other dating profiles, Facebook pages aren't necessarily an accurate representation of who a person truly is. However, Facebook absolutely helps us to reunite with people we've lost touch with and can create friends out of acquaintances. So if a man from your past finds you on Facebook, it's not always a bad thing. Just do yourself a favor and make sure he's really single (and sane) before getting emotionally involved.

The most important part

You know what it is, right? It's your attitude. It's your "available light." It's being open and receptive no matter where you are or what you're doing. It's being happy with your life and your circumstances. It's not acting desperate or like you'll die without a boyfriend. It's living free from bitterness and negativity. It's being a goddess. Get that part right and you'll find men are attracted to you in almost every situation, regardless of whether you met him at the market or online. It will cause them to move toward you and not away from you. Now wouldn't that be nice?

DATING RULE #40:
Where you meet men is not nearly as important as your attitude while you are there.

DO AS I SAY, NOT AS I DID
(My Own Journey from Doormat to Goddess)

When I was in my twenties, I was what is known as an "L.A. Party Girl." I went to a different club every night of the week and rarely made it home before 3 a.m. I'm not going to lie, there were some fun times. However, a lot of heartbreak came along with it.

In addition to being a club kid, I was also a serial monogamist. (Or at least somewhat monogamous depending on how my current boyfriend was treating me.) I jumped from relationship to relationship, boyfriend to boyfriend without giving real "dating" a shot. And where did I meet my pool of potential soul mates? Yep. At clubs.

Nightclubs and trendy bars are not good places to look for your next great love. They're fine for hook-ups if that's what you're after. Want to have a one night stand? Then by all means, go to the club of the moment on any given Friday night. But in terms of meeting men with relationship potential? Not such a great idea.

If I could go back in time and do one thing differently when I was in my twenties, it would be to not find my boyfriends while out clubbing. Guys who get wasted five nights a week rarely make for good partners. And there's just something so desperate about meeting people like that, isn't there? I remember feeling, on those rare nights when I was between relationships, that if I didn't get hit on by a certain number of men, I must not be looking very good. If I didn't meet a potential guy, that night would go down as a "bad night." Living that kind of life and meeting the kind of people it attracts can absolutely wear on your self-esteem.

Even if you love the party life, the reality is very few romance stories start with house music and sweaty bodies jammed into a dark room. Lasting relationships don't usually begin while grinding on the dance floor. Most men you meet in places like that are thinking "casual" or "for tonight only." Just because he wants you to come home with him, doesn't mean he wants to see you in the morning.

Location, location, location? It's not so much "where" as it is "how."

"J" was one of those guys I met at a club. Even though we had some friends in common, it doesn't change the fact our relationship was probably doomed from the start due to the nature of our meeting. He, like me, was a party kid. And I soon learned that it's pretty hard to have an adult relationship when one or both of you is a child.

XX

Step 4

The laws of attraction.

In dating, attraction is critical. Just like you have to be attracted to a man in order to see him in a romantic way, he also has to be attracted to you. Furthermore, attraction is usually a fairly instantaneous thing. Think about how it works for you. When you see a guy, he doesn't have to be the best looking man in the world, but there has to be something about him that makes you take notice. Maybe you like what he's wearing or you think the way he carries himself is sexy. Whatever they are for you, there are certain things about a man which will attract you to him almost immediately. It works the same way for guys. Maybe even more so...

As soon as a man meets you, he will put you in one of two categories. Are you ready for them? Because here they are. You are either:

- A woman he would sleep with

or

- A woman he wouldn't sleep with

That's pretty much it.

Again, I'm not about political correctness. Instead, I'm all about telling you the truth, even if it makes you wince. Why? Because unless we know the truth, we can't really figure out how to deal with it, can we? And what's written above is the honest truth.

Here's where I think a lot of women make a big mistake. We become very attracted to a man who is not attracted to us. And we think by becoming his "friend," he will be amazed by all of the wonderful qualities about us. Or we think if we pursue him, eventually he'll change his mind. If he's an a-hole, he might very well play along for a bit. He may even sleep with you a couple times (especially if there's alcohol involved), but mark my words: If a man is not attracted to you, he will never see you with long-term potential.

DATING RULE #41:
If he isn't attracted to you romantically, he will never see you with long-term potential.

Dear Jenn,

I'm "friends" with a guy I've known for several years. I put the word friend in quotes because the truth is I think I'm in love with him. Unfortunately he doesn't feel the same way about me and has basically told me this (in a nice way) on several occasions. I was hoping after his last long-term relationship ended, I might have a shot. As it turns out, I didn't.

He told me yesterday he's started seeing this new girl and that he's super into her. I am completely devastated. I don't want to come in between him and his new girlfriend, but I am just so depressed and I can't understand why he doesn't have romantic feelings for me. Is there anything I can do to get him to like me?

Becky

How to Be a Goddess

The harsh reality is not every guy we like is going to like us in return. If I could give women just one piece of advice when it comes to men it would be to stop obsessing over and going after guys who aren't into you. We waste time, lower our self-worth, and suffer unbelievable heartbreak by doing this. So stop it. From now on, you are only interested in guys who are interested in you, alright?

DATING RULE #42:
A goddess is only interested in men who are attracted to her. When you don't know him

Figuring out whether he's attracted to you or not often depends on the situation and circumstances. If he's a stranger, it's usually fairly easy to tell. Imagine you are at Starbucks, an alumni event, or a party and a man approaches you and initiates a conversation. That's a good sign. In fact, anytime a man places himself near you or makes an effort to engage with you is often an indicator of his interest. Sure, some men may just be friendlier than others, but if a guy you don't know wants to get to know you, you can pretty much be assured he's attracted to you.

This is why I think it's so important for women not to approach men. However, giving them signs that you're receptive to them is crucial; eye contact and a smile are often necessary. Conversely, going up to them and initiating a conversation out of the blue makes it much more difficult to determine their level of interest. Whenever a woman acts as the aggressor, she is immediately in a place of disadvantage. Not only is she less sure of the man's feelings, but he will also perceive her as wanting something from him. *And he will then be the one with the power to determine whether or not he will give it to her.*

DATING RULE #43:
If you approach men, they have the power, not you.

This reminds me of a conversation I recently had with a male friend of mine.

The laws of attraction.

"What's up with women being all aggressive with guys these days?" he asked me.

When I asked him to explain what he meant, he gave some examples of the ladies he'd dealt with in the previous couple of weeks. "This one woman I had a casual friendship with kept asking me out. I told her I just wanted to be friends, but she wouldn't let it go. So I took her out to dinner one night and then she got upset and cussed me out over the phone because I didn't ask her for a second date."

"Another one texted me non-stop starting the day after I was introduced to her at a party. I even told her I was going out of town that weekend! Listen, we like it when a woman is interested in us, but it works best when we show her our interest first. Otherwise it just seems desperate."

I know that plenty of guys say they wish women would be more aggressive. They say they get tired of being the ones to initiate contact. Maybe that's what they *think* they want, but at the end of the day, any guy worth anything wants to be the hunter. He wants to be the one to see you through the cross hairs of his rifle and take aim. He doesn't want to feel like *he's* the prey.

"But what if he's shy?" I hear you saying.

Ummm, yeah… No. Very few men are that "shy." Even "shy" guys go after girls they are attracted to. That's the kind of thing we tell ourselves in order to justify making the first move. Let me share a story to illustrate my point. It's one of my fondest memories and involves a guy who would be classified as "shy" by anyone who met him.

During the summer between my senior year in high school and freshman year in college, I was invited to participate in an intensive, two-week writing course at USC. It was supposed to give us a taste of what college classes would entail and although there was no "grade" per se, it did count for college credit and was considered quite the honor. My fellow classmates were selected from high schools all over Southern California and even though I was one of the few who would actually be enrolling at USC in the fall, we were all excited to have a preview into college life.

A few days into the course, I returned from a lunch break to find a note on my desk. It was a hand-written poem – a love note, really – and the author decided not to sign his name. It was the single sweetest thing a man had done for me up to that point in my life. Every couple of days, I would return from lunch to find another poem left on my desk. I remember frequently scanning the classroom, wondering which one of the male students was my secret admirer.

By the last day of class, I had given up hope of ever finding out. I figured he didn't want to be known and would never reveal himself. As I walked to my car that afternoon, I was stopped by Ben, one of the guys in my class. We made some chit-chat and said our goodbyes. Right before he walked away, he said, "Since I'm not going to see you again, I wanted to give you this." And he reached into his backpack and pulled out a note. My final note... I immediately hugged him and thanked him for the sweet poems.

As soon as I got into my car, I ripped open the envelope. This time it wasn't a poem, but a short letter letting me know how much he enjoyed meeting me over the summer and how he wished me the best of luck with college. That was it. Ben was off to a university on the East Coast and I was staying in L.A.

Even though that was the last time I ever saw him, I still have Ben's letters. For many years, I wondered if things would have continued if we'd gone to college in the same city. I think they might have. Obviously, Ben wasn't "the one" or things would have turned out differently, but every time a girl tells me she needs to make the first move with a man because she thinks he's "shy," I think of him. "Shy" guys may not come out and hit on you directly. Maybe they'll take a more subtle approach like Ben did, but they will absolutely make their interest known.

But what if he's socially awkward? Lazy? Used to women chasing after him? I'm still not going to let you off the hook. If you think about it, don't you want a man who is the type of guy who sees what he wants and then works hard to get it? As far as I'm concerned, if he doesn't have the balls to approach me and take a shot, he won't have the balls to go after other things in life, such as a successful career. And if he's used to getting his women without having to work for them, how invested is he going to be in me and working at the relationship?

DATING RULE #44:
Just because women can approach men, doesn't mean we should.

Instead, hang back and see who comes to you. If your "available light" is on and you're giving off the vibe you are available and receptive, it shouldn't be too long before a man takes notice. When you catch his eye (and if you like what you see), you should absolutely give him a warm smile. But let him be the one to make the walk over to where you are standing. That way, there will be no question in your mind about his level of attraction.

When you know him

What if you are friends with a guy and aren't sure how he feels? Or what if he's a casual acquaintance? Or if you work in the same business or run in the same social circles? This is where it can be a bit trickier. Some guys might be hesitant when it comes to crossing the line between "platonic" and "romantic." They aren't sure of the boundaries and don't want to burn a bridge. If they know you, it can also be harder for them to put themselves in a position of getting rejected.

So how do you know if a guy is into you and sees you as more than just a friend? I receive countless questions from female readers asking this exact question. They aren't sure if a man really likes them and want the clues to figure it out. Here is one example.

How to Be a Goddess

Dear Jenn,

I go to college with a guy who I think is really cute. He talks to me and is always very friendly but I'm not sure if he likes me in that way. He'll flirt and put his arm around me, but I think he might be like this with all the girls. I keep waiting for him to ask me out, but he hasn't yet.

How do I know if he's really interested in me?

Rachelle

It can be tricky to determine, can't it? So let me give you some of the tell-tale signs.

HE PROBABLY LIKES YOU IF…

- He finds a way to talk to you, include you in conversations, or get your attention. He often seems to be right where you are.
- He tries to impress you with stories of his accomplishments or successes.
- He's playful with you or teases you in a good-hearted way.
- He notices things about you. What you're wearing or the kind of music you like will not escape his attention.
- He initiates calls, texts, or Facebook posts. He wants to be in contact with you.
- He doesn't act like this with other women. This will show whether he's truly interested in you specifically or just a big flirt.
- Your gut tells you he likes you.

I think this last point is the most important one. More often than not, we just *know* when a guy is attracted to us and would be interested in taking things to another level. If you're constantly asking yourself if he likes you or not; if he's not giving clear indications that he's into you, then chances are great he's not. Men are actually pretty easy to read. They don't normally play "hard to get" or any of the games women employ. If a guy thinks you're hot, you'll usually know it. So check in with your gut and be sure to listen to it. It will rarely steer you wrong.

DATING RULE #45:
If you're constantly wondering if he likes you romantically, he probably doesn't.

So what do you do if all signs point to him being attracted and interested? How do you let a male friend or colleague know he's got a green light to pursue? Should you ask him out? Tell him you like him? Ask him how he feels about you? Just start making out with him one night?

No way. Not even close. Don't even think about it, girlfriend! The same rules above apply to this situation as well. Even if you've known him for twenty years, you still have to let him come to you. You still have to let him take the initiative. I understand you might feel quite a bit of frustration with this. He's not moving fast enough for your tastes (or maybe not moving at all) or you are confused as to how he feels. So you want to take the reins and make things happen. We've all been there. But you need to keep in mind the best, most fulfilling relationships start with the man being the pursuer, initiator, and aggressor. Those are the types of relationships where a woman feels secure and cherished. And that's the kind of relationship you want, isn't it? So I say hold your horses.

Instead of going after him directly (and as a result setting yourself up for possible rejection), what you want to do is let him know you are interested without actually letting him know you are interested. You want to be subtle and use your feminine charms to encourage and inspire him into action. You need to flirt with him a little and show him you think he's kinda cute, too. But the goal is to always come at him sideways instead of head on.

DATING RULE #46:

A goddess never makes it obvious she's into a guy. Instead, she flirts a bit and waits for him to make it obvious he's into her.

SIDEWAYS VS. HEAD ON

- Sideways – Mentioning something you both enjoy and opening the door for him to make a plan with you. Say, "I hear there's a really great art exhibit at XYZ gallery" or "Band X is playing on Saturday night at Club Y." Then see if he bites.
- Head on – Buying two tickets to the event and asking him to go with you.
- Sideways – Asking him to help you with something you know he's good at and that you don't know how to do. "Can you show me how to get to the next level on 'Angry Birds?' I'm stuck and you're so good at it." This compliments him and also lets him know you're paying attention to him.
- Head on – Saying something like, "You look so hot in those jeans and I bet you'd look even hotter out of them." This is the *wrong* way to compliment a man you're not in a relationship with, by the way.
- Sideways – Wanting his opinion on something he knows a lot about. "I'm deciding between getting a Samsung and the new iPhone. Which one do you think is better?"
- Head on – Inviting him to go with you to pick out a new phone and offering to buy him lunch in exchange for the favor.

- Sideways – Asking him about that trail he always hikes, where he likes to mountain bike, or any other activity he might be into. "I'm thinking about doing a half marathon. Where do you like to run that's close by?" Then see if he offers to show you in person.
- Head on – Showing up at a place you know he frequents and "accidentally" running into him. Stalker alert!

In addition to what you actually say and do with this guy, you've also got to give non-verbal cues you like him. In fact, the way in which you communicate non-verbally will often tell him more than anything that comes out of your mouth. So learn to flirt with your body! I think many women are clueless how to flirt and be sexy without being totally slutty. It's truly an art form. The following tips should help you to flirt the way a goddess does. These are my patented, trademarked, copyrighted, and super hush-hush secrets to flirting success.

HOW TO FLIRT LIKE A GODDESS

- If you know you'll be seeing him, look your best. Put on some makeup, do your hair, and wear a cute outfit. Not only will he be more likely to notice you, but you'll also feel more confident.
- Always appear happy when he comes your way. Give him a big "Hey!" and light up your face with a bright smile.
- Never stand with your arms crossed or talk to him over your shoulder. Face him, put one hand on your hip (thereby drawing his attention to your curves), and cock your head to the side playfully.

- Even if you're shy, maintain eye contact when speaking to him. Let that glimmer in your eye shine.
- If it's appropriate given your relationship, put your hand on his upper arm when talking to him. But touch him sparingly and for just a moment, however. It seems natural if you do this when you're emphasizing something you're saying. "You've *got* to check out the new Coldplay song," for example. And please, don't let your touches land anywhere but his arm.
- When sitting across from him, rest your chin on your hand and move your index finger back and forth across your lower lip for a few seconds. This draws his eyes to a sexual part of your body. But keep that finger above your neck, ladies! No touching of any other sexual organs allowed!
- Let him know you're interested in what he's saying. Raise your eyebrows when he gets to the good part of his story, laugh at his jokes, and lean in a bit closer to show him you're paying attention.
- Don't forget "the twirl." Twirl your hair, a pen, or your necklace when talking to him. Why this says "flirt" to a guy, I have no idea. But it does.

When flirting, it's important to always seem natural. You don't want it to come off looking forced, like you are playing a part, or over-the-top sexual. A little flirting goes a long way. It may be difficult at first, but the more you use your flirtation skills, the better at them you will become. I'd even suggest you practice in front of your mirror. Imagine you're talking to your crush and get your moves down. Don't worry – no one's looking and I promise I won't tell a soul.

The laws of attraction.

DATING RULE #47:
A goddess flirts in a way that is both natural and classy.

When you met him online

Even though I'm not a huge fan of online dating, I know it is a popular way to meet people these days. A good portion of the questions I receive are from women who've met a guy on an online dating site. Many of you are also curious about the etiquette of meeting men online and whether or not you should act differently than you would in the "real world."

> Dear Jenn,
> I recently started this whole online dating thing. I've heard a lot of success stories and I figured I'd give it a shot. So here's my question: How do I do it?? Do I just filter through the guys who contact me? Can I make the first move if I like someone's profile? Are the "rules" the same when it comes to online dating?
> Deena

If you decide to venture into Internet dating, the first thing you need to remember is men are men no matter where you meet them. Just like you shouldn't walk up to a strange man and tell him you think he's hot, you shouldn't send a "Match Message" to a guy letting him know you think he's got a great profile. It is – in effect – the exact same thing.

This very subject came up on a date I had with Dan, a guy I met on Match.com. Dan was very good looking and successful so he was used to getting a lot of attention on the website. Over a glass of wine, Dan told me he did not like it when a woman "made the first move" by sending him a "wink" or an email.

"It makes me think less of her," he told me. "I want to be the one to contact her first."

Other men I met during my foray into online dating reiterated Dan's sentiments. For example, when I first joined Match.com I told a nice man who sent me a message through the site that I was a "newbie" and he generously gave me some pointers.

"It's just like any other type of dating situation – let the guys come to you," he wrote in an email.

Although I knew he was right, I must admit I tested his theory on a couple of occasions. One man looked so great in his profile that I just *had* to contact him. We'd gone to the same college so I used that connection as a method (excuse) to introduce myself in an email. Although he responded and we wrote back and forth a bit, he never did "close the deal" and ask me out. Hmmmm.

Time and time again, I found the men who initiated contact were the ones who didn't disappear after a couple of emails. The guys who showed their interest first would usually end up asking me on an official date. None of them ended up being my "soul mate," but my dealings with them were much smoother than with the guys who I "winked" at first. Of course this makes perfect sense. The men who contacted me were interested in me. If they saw my profile and kept going, they weren't. Attempting to spark up a conversation with a guy who isn't attracted or interested will work as well as walking up to a guy in a bar who has barely looked at you does. Sure he may be polite and chat with you for a while, but he'll be moving right along the moment another woman catches his eye.

DATING RULE #48:
Online dating is still dating!

FINDING YOUR INTERNET MATCH
Online dating comes with its own confusion and pitfalls and since it's a relatively new phenomenon, most aren't sure how to tackle it. So use the following to help you navigate the tough terrain.

- Keep in mind anyone can make themselves look amazing online. Reserve judgment and don't get too excited until you've actually met him in person. I had a date with a guy who looked like a Hottie McHotterson in his pics. Reality was much, much different. Oh, and he was also a complete racist.

- Be safe! Always meet him in a public place and never get into a car with someone you don't know. Let a friend know all the vitals before the date: His name, his phone number, and the date/time/place you'll be meeting. When you're out with him, take your phone with you into the bathroom and text her an update. Be sure to call her and let her know when you've arrived home.

- Once *he's* initiated contact online, respond appropriately. If he sends you a "wink" and you like what you see, just "wink" him back and watch for his next move. There's no need to escalate things with an email. Let him be the one to move the flirting along. If he doesn't invest the time to send a short email, he's probably not going to invest in a relationship.

- Stay offline and don't use "chat" features. "Chats" and "IMs" are great ways for con-artists and predators to establish false intimacy with unsuspecting women. There are actually a lot of scams perpetrated through online dating sites. If – after a few chats – he tells you he lost his passport, is stuck in a foreign country, and needs you to wire him money, you're dealing with a swindler.

- Don't go back and forth via email with no end in sight. If he hasn't asked you out after four email exchanges, he's probably not going to. Cut your losses and shift your attention on someone else. Some guys use online dating as a way of interacting with women in cyberspace and have no intention of actually *dating* them.

- Watch out for the guy who doesn't have pictures posted and writes things on his profile such as, "I'm extremely private." Translation? He's married. Also be wary of guys who send the "form email." They are usually serial daters who lack creativity. One guy who contacted me through Match. com actually sent the exact same email to me — *three times*.

- Trust your gut. If he seems creepy, it's probably because he *is* creepy. After scheduling a lunch and exchanging numbers, one gent started waking me up every morning with a text that said, "Good morning, beautiful!" And this was *before* we went out. When I used my common sense and decided to flake on the date, he became enraged and verbally unleashed on me. Can you say "psycho?"

- I'm sure you know many men use online dating as a way to get relatively easy sex. I know of one guy who invites women to his place "for a glass of wine" the same night he sends them an email. "If I'm horny, I'll send a message to about ten women asking them to come over. I always get at least one who says 'yes,'" he explains. If he wants a last-minute "date," he's not really looking for a relationship. No matter what it says on his profile.

- Your profile counts, too! Make sure your pictures are recent and you don't deceive anyone when it comes to who you really are or what you actually look like. Almost every man I met through Match.com told me they'd been on dates with women who looked drastically heavier, older, etc, than they did on their profiles. In addition, your profile should be short and sweet. No need to disclose every highlight (and lowlight) of the past twenty years. Make him want to get to know you instead of feeling like he already does.

- In the same manner, don't share all your intimate secrets over email. Don't ramble on and disclose the details of your last break-up or how you're so desperate to meet a nice guy that you've just spent $130 on a six-month membership to the site.
- If you see a guy you really like and you're sure he hasn't already viewed your profile, here's a secret tip that works like a charm: "Favorite" him. Marking a man's profile as one of your "favorites" is like smiling at a man in the grocery store. It lets him know you think he's cute and offers him the opportunity to step up and make a move. If he likes your profile, he'll introduce himself. If you don't receive an email from him, forget it and move on.

I know how difficult it can be during the initial stages of attraction not to get ahead of the process. Waiting for a man to make his move can be frustrating whether he's a cute guy you see in your yoga class or your workplace crush. Either way, it is absolutely imperative you let him be the one to pursue you. Think about it. If you chase him until you are able to get a first date with him, how likely will he be to properly court you? How willing will he be to woo you in the way a woman needs to be wooed? You will always be the one trying to move the relationship along, which is a very unsatisfying and unsettling place for a girl to be. So whatever you do, DON'T do the following:

ATTRACTION STAGE DON'TS

- Don't try to get his attention by being overtly sexual or indicating you'd be good to go with him.
- Don't initiate calls, texts, emails, or IMs. Let him be the first to contact you.
- Don't walk up to him and offer to buy him a drink.
- Don't post on his Facebook page except in response to something he's posted on yours. (A quick "Happy Birthday" wish is the one exception.)
- Don't tell him you think he's hot, handsome, or sexy. "I like that tie" or "That's a cool shirt" is as far as you should go.
- Don't hang around him too long or start all conversations with him. He needs to be the one to come to you.
- Don't bake him cupcakes or cook him a meal in an attempt to make him fall in love with you because of your culinary skills.
- Don't ask him out.

A goddess won't pursue a man, thereby forcing him to either acquiesce or reject her. She would never chase after a guy hoping he'll notice her. Instead, she has the strength to stand still and wait for a man who is truly interested to come toward her. She knows how to distinguish the guys who are attracted to her from the ones who aren't. And she would never lower herself by working overtime to get a guy to like her. If a man isn't interested in her romantically, she moves on and has the confidence to know that another one will be.

DATING RULE #49:
A goddess knows there is great reward in letting a man come to her and be the one to ask her out.

DO AS I SAY, NOT AS I DID
(My Own Journey from Doormat to Goddess)

I am so hesitant to share this story. It is truly an embarrassing tale, which is why I think it's probably imperative I do tell it. It dates back to my law school years and concerns a guy I'll refer to as "M."

"M" was what I like to call "law school cute." Let me explain. Law school was, in many ways, the exact opposite of my college experience. While USC was filled with good looking people, the law school I attended…ummm, not so much. But you know how it is when you're with the same people hour after hour? When your whole universe consists of the same people day after day? Even the not so cute guys can become kinda cute, right? That was "M." In any other situation, I probably wouldn't have looked at him twice. But compared to most of the other guys, I thought he was a hottie.

Back to my story. I heard a rumor "M" thought I was cute. (I hoped not "law school cute!") But it was just a rumor and there was no overt evidence to confirm it. He was friendly and nice but I never really got the sense that he was "into me," you know? At this time, "J" and I were on one of our infamous breaks and I was on a serious man hunt. I thought, "Hmmm. Maybe 'M' could be a fun distraction." So I decided to throw caution to the wind, take this rumor as fact, and ask him out. On his voicemail. To a concert that was happening that weekend.

When I didn't hear back from "M," I surmised phone stalking him was the way to go. Yes, your "Jenn X" dialed that poor boy about fifty times between Friday morning and Saturday afternoon. I remember thinking to myself, "I hope he doesn't have caller ID." (This was back in the mid-nineties before caller ID was the norm.) But even the threat of getting caught didn't stop me from calling him every half-hour. Or maybe it was every fifteen minutes?

"M" never did call me back. I saw him at school the following Monday and he said, "I got your message. I was out of town."

I tried to play it cool, but from the smirk on his face I was pretty sure he did indeed have caller ID. In fact, he was probably home the entire time watching my phone number appear multiple times only to be followed by a series of hang ups.

That was pretty much the last time "M" ever talked to me and I always tried to avoid him in the halls, which made for a somewhat uncomfortable three years. However, this was one of my more important law school lessons. To this day, I've never asked another guy out.

XX

Step #5

In the beginning...
God created the goddess.

So you've met a guy. He's cute, funny, and has a decent job. And he's just asked you out. Congrats! Now the real fun begins...

If the initial few dates are key in determining the potential course of a relationship, the first date itself is critical. But here's what women often forget: Just as he uses the first date to determine if he wants to go out with us again, *so should we*. Think about it in terms of a job interview. As an applicant, it's not all about getting the job just for the sake of getting the job. We should also be using the interview process to screen the company and see if it's a place where we want to work. The same goes for dating. When we use this perspective to look at the early stages of a relationship, our attitude shifts. Suddenly, it's not about some guy deciding if we are "worthy" of a second date; we have to determine whether he's "worthy" of our time and emotions as well!

DATING RULE #50:
A goddess has the mindset she is a "selector," not merely a "selectee."

In order to contrast this perspective, let's take a peek at a question which is typical of many I receive.

Dear Jenn,

I met this guy online last week and I really, really like him! He's EXACTLY what I've been waiting for!! He's super cute and totally funny. We've been skyping a bunch and we're supposed to go out in a few days. I'm so excited!!! Can you give me some pointers for how to handle the first date??? I don't want to mess this one up!!!

Thanks!

Alicia

Although I appreciate Alicia's enthusiasm, being this spun over a guy you barely know is not a good place to be. It prevents us from being rational and objective in analyzing a man's character. Being certain you've met your soul mate before you've learned his middle name places the woman at a great disadvantage. She's convinced herself he's "the one" without knowing much about him. Her subsequent happiness now depends on earning his "approval."

Have you ever felt like Alicia? Have you ever met a man and felt such an instant attraction that before he even picks you up for your first date, you're already picturing the wedding invitations and imagining your monogrammed towels? Have you ever begun to spiral so quickly that the guy could turn out to be a complete Neanderthal and you'd think it was cute, overlook his behavior, or make excuses for it? I think we all have. And it usually causes us to waste weeks, months, or even years with guys who aren't right for us. So the first thing you want to do after that cute prospect asks you out for the first time is…relax. Take a chill pill. Don't obsess about what you're going to wear, spend $200 on a new hairstyle, or begin to envision your destination wedding. He hasn't proven himself worthy of an emotional (or financial) investment. Not yet. Instead, I'd like for you to make the following vow to yourself. Please repeat after me.

I, (insert your name here), being of semi-sound mind and sorta-rational emotions, do solemnly promise myself that I will not engage in any of the following behaviors before, during, or after my first date with (insert his name here):

- *I will not imagine us walking down the aisle together.*
- *I will not doodle what my married name would be.*
- *I will buy no new clothes for said date. In fact, I will not spend any money at all on said date, either directly or indirectly.*
- *I will not come up with a list of twenty five witty things to say or stories to tell in preparation for said date.*
- *I will not get ahead of the process and think about asking him to my cousin's wedding or to that concert I really want to go to next month.*
- *I will not worry about whether he asks me out on a second date. Nor will I do things I think might make him ask me out on a second date.*
- *I will not obsess, spiral, or spin in any way, shape, or form.*
  Signed,
  (Insert your name here)

Why did I have you sign your name – hopefully in blood – to this? Because now is the time when it is mandatory you go slowly. Maintaining the position of "selector" means you must maintain your perspective. Do not invest your emotions in someone until you are sure they are worthy of that investment. And if you haven't even had one date, how can you determine that?

DATING RULE #51:
A goddess does not make an emotional or financial investment in a man she does not know. No matter how hot he is.

All of this being said, it is still important to be aware of the way you conduct yourself on a first date. There are absolutely things you want to do in order to put your best self forward. And, in my opinion, they can be broken down into four categories.

THE FOUR THINGS A GODDESS SHOULD DO ON A FIRST DATE

- She should look good.
- She should be classy and interesting.
- She should be warm and open to getting to know him.
- She should not seem overly eager or desperate.

She should look good

I'm serious about not buying a new outfit, getting hair extensions, or having a makeover before a first date. And there's a simple reason behind it. The more we invest in something, the more we'll do anything to hang onto it. Take, for example, those shoes we bought at Target. We'd loan them to a girlfriend without batting an eye, right? But if we're ever lucky enough to own a pair of Blahniks, Louboutins, or Choos, I doubt we'd be as generous. The same goes for dating.

DATING RULE #52:
The more we invest in something, the more invested we become in its outcome.

My friend Sandra knows all about investing a lot for a man she barely knew. She met Cody at a business meeting and felt an instant attraction. He was handsome, seemed smart, and led the meeting with great confidence. So of course she was thrilled when he called later that day to ask her out for the following weekend. The dreamboat even suggested a fancy restaurant she'd always wanted to try. In preparation for the big date, Sandra splurged on a new little black dress ($200). Even though it wasn't necessary, she also had her hair cut and colored ($150). As she left the salon, she saw a bracelet in the window of the store that she thought would accent her new LBD perfectly ($40).

"What's wrong with wanting to look my absolute best for my potential future soul mate?" she thought.

Not long after Cody picked Sandra up at her house, she began to have a sinking feeling. The confident demeanor she saw during the meeting had transformed into out-and-out arrogance and rudeness. He didn't hold the car door open for her (let alone the door to the restaurant), he told her what she should order, and he did not stop talking about himself. To top it off, when the check came he asked her to pay for her portion. (That was another $60 – including tip.)

After Cody dropped her off at home and she tallied the damage, Sandra realized she was out $450. (Hey – at least her roots were covered for the next month.) When Cody called to ask her out again, she politely declined.

Why not learn a lesson from Sandra and wait until you've had a few dates before spending half a paycheck on that sexy dress you saw at your favorite store. Keeping your wallet securely in your purse will help you to keep some perspective on your new beau.

Nevertheless, you still want to look your best on a first date. I know a girl who insists on always wearing sweats when she goes out with a new guy. She says she's comfortable and thinks men should like her as she is. Wrong! Dressing shabbily tells him you don't think he's that important. I actually think it's disrespectful and insulting. If a man is taking you out and paying for dinner, one of the ways you show your appreciation is by looking nice for him. So always, always do the following:

How to Be a Goddess

- Do shower and have clean hair. Smelling good is important. Let's even go a step further. I'm not a big fan of heavy, flowery perfumes and I don't think most men are either. The guys I ask tell me the following scents are a major turn-on: vanilla (or anything that reminds them of a dessert baking), citrus, and smells that are crisp and clean. Always go light and sweet over heavy and musky.

- Do make sure your hands (and feet if they're visible) are manicured. No chipped polish, bitten cuticles, or nails of uneven length.

- Do put on some makeup. If you're having dinner at a candlelit restaurant, you can go for something a bit more dramatic. (Emphasis on "a bit.") If it's a more casual place, opt for a natural looking palette. Either way, forget the crazy fashion colors. Not many guys think electric blue eye shadow is hot.

- Do dress appropriately for the date. I'm a big fan of erring on the side of *slightly* dressier than the occasion. And I'm also of the opinion that a first date should be dinner. I know many guys (especially those met online) might want to do the whole drink thing or plan a daytime outing. I always view these men with skepticism. I think men who are seriously interested in getting to know a particular woman want to take her out and share a meal with her – even if all he can afford is a pizza and soda. So what you *wear* depends on *where* he takes you – to *dinner*!

WHAT TO WEAR – TO DINNER!

- If his budget only allows for the most casual burger joint, you still want to look feminine. If you must (and I mean must) wear jeans, be sure to pair them with a cute top. But how about trading the denim for leggings and an oversized sweater?

In the beginning…God created the goddess.

- Gina Hendrix, one of L.A.'s most exclusive matchmakers, has a "no pants on the first date" rule for the ladies she sets up with her bachelors. I think that's a great idea. Wear a dress or a skirt. Put on some heels. Men like women who look like women.
- Don't wear anything super tight, super short, or super revealing. Make sure you can sit in your skirt without showing your hoo-ha. No thongs sticking out either. You want to give him a glimpse of your body, not an eyeful.
- Shoot for a classically contemporary look. Mixing trends, over accessorizing, or looking like a fashion disaster are not appealing. Think Audrey Hepburn, not Lady Gaga.

DATING RULE #53:
Always keep the restaurant he's taking you to in mind when choosing your first date outfit. And dress slightly dressier.

Here's the deal on non-dinner first dates. Men who want to meet you at the dog park, go mountain biking, or take you to some sort of "guy thing" may not be "bad guys." But I'd wager they are not particularly romantic. So if he asks you out and has two tickets for a baseball game, go if you want. But don't blame me if your entire relationship consists of hot dogs and beer. If you are both big basketball fans and he gets amazing seats to a playoff game, that is a great first date. But he should still take you to dinner beforehand. Just sayin'.

I know some guys want to get all creative and do something "different." To them I say, "Don't bother." Short of a black tie affair (and how often does that happen?), dinner is the best first date money can buy. The first clue he will give you about your potential courtship is where he takes you on your first date. Pay attention and decide if you are cool with it.

How to Be a Goddess

She should be classy and interesting

Looking your best, although critical, is only part of the battle. What we say and how we communicate it are also vitally important. I think very pretty women often fall short in this. They rely too heavily on their looks to get them what they want without realizing that what men really want is the complete package. If you're hot, but can't carry on a conversation, a quality man will not be interested in having anything with you besides sex. If you don't seem fun and outgoing, he won't be likely to ask you out again. (Unless he's just trying to get sex.) If you don't have manners and conduct yourself appropriately, he's not going to be enthusiastic about bringing you home to meet mom. (After he tries to have sex with you.)

Let's discuss "class." What is it exactly? In my dictionary, it goes back to being feminine and tasteful. It is good etiquette and knowing how to act properly in any situation. No, you can't buy class, but you most certainly can learn it.

When I was young, my father would say to me, "Now sit at the table and eat your dinner like a little lady of distinction." This may sound antiquated and elitist to some of you, but the lessons my parents taught me have served me well. Manners and decorum are good things and I'm sad to see them cast aside by this ultra-casual, act-however-you-want world in which we now live. Just like men who act like gentlemen are a rare and treasured find today, so are ladies who act like ladies. Don't think he's not paying attention to these "minor" details, especially if he's of a certain class himself. A well-bred man I dated told me he could never be serious about a woman with bad manners. "If she doesn't hold her fork correctly, I know it's not going anywhere," he said. This may sound extreme, but it shows that people really do notice! Learning proper etiquette not only helps you in dating, but in all areas of life. It elevates your status and everyone from potential boyfriends to potential employers will see you as a bit more "special."

In the beginning…God created the goddess.

DATING RULE #54:
A goddess is a classy woman. As a result, men see her as high status.

HOW TO BE CLASSY

- Don't cuss around him. Even men who continually drop F-bombs don't like it when women do.
- Learn proper table manners and how to use silverware correctly. If you are unsure, Google it. Amy Vanderbilt or Miss Manners can help.
- Don't engage in overtly sexual conversations in the early stages of dating. If he starts to do it, change the subject.
- Don't get drunk. In fact, in the beginning never have more than two drinks on a date.
- Anything which could be construed as racist, offensive, or derogatory should never be uttered.
- Don't talk badly about people, especially other women. Gossiping, back stabbing, or snarky comments turn men off. You're the one who will come off as tacky.

Let's take a look at the story of "Liquored-up Lisa" as an example of how to *not* be classy.

Chris met Lisa the way many people meet these days – online. They arranged to meet for the first time at a bar and by the time Chris arrived on the appointed night, Lisa was already belly up and throwing back a shot. Within moments of the introductory handshake and seating himself next to Lisa at the bar, Chris could tell she was rip-roarin', stinkin' drunk. As it turns out, Lisa had been at the bar for an hour before Chris arrived and was already four shots of Jack Daniels deep.

How to Be a Goddess

While I believe most men respect it when a woman doesn't feel the need to pretty up a cocktail with a fruity mixer and a paper umbrella, very few will respect a sloppy drunk. And Lisa was as sloppy as it gets. It started with the too-loud laughing. Then she slipped off her bar stool a couple of times. Then she called him by the wrong name. When he corrected her, Lisa said, "Oooops. That was the guy I was out with last night."

As I'm sure you can imagine, that was the last time Chris saw Lisa.

While you don't want to come off like an out of control party girl, you don't want to act stuffy or cold either. Maintain your dignity while being fun, relaxed, and natural. There's no law against having a good time.

Let's talk about what makes a woman "interesting." There are two components: Being fulfilled while still being mysterious. He wants to know you've got a full life. He just doesn't want to hear every detail of it before the appetizers arrive. Having something to say is good; telling him everything about yourself isn't.

The object of a first date isn't to share your entire life story. It's to give him a little taste of who you are. *When a man wants to keep getting to know you, that's when he thinks you are interesting. When a man thinks he already knows everything about you, that's when he gets bored.*

Not having anything to say is just as bad as talking too much. If you are mute, respond to questions with one word answers, or often say, "Ummm, I dunno, whatever," he will not find you interesting.

In the beginning…God created the goddess.

DATING RULE #55:
If you want to be interesting, you have to give him something while leaving him to wonder about the rest.

KEEPING HIM INTERESTED VS. BORING HIM TO TEARS

- If you stay on lighthearted and positive topics of conversation, you will keep him interested. If you talk about depressing subjects – what you're working to overcome in therapy, that you had seven make-believe friends when you were little because no one liked you, or how you have "daddy issues" – you will bore him to tears. (Okay, he might be somewhat interested in what you're saying. But he won't be interested in you as a girlfriend.)

- If you discuss your work a bit and tell him how much you enjoy what you do, you will keep him interested. If you talk non-stop about your career and how successful (or unsuccessful) you are, you will bore him to tears.

- If you talk about an amazing book you read, movie you saw, or song you heard, you will keep him interested. If you tell him about everything you bought on your last shopping trip and everything you want to buy on the next one, you will bore him to tears. Don't come off like a materialistic airhead.

- If you don't discuss past relationships except when giving pertinent information (e.g., "I have been divorced for two years"), you will keep him interested. If you tell him every miserable thing your miserable ex did to make your life miserable, you will bore him to tears.

How to Be a Goddess

> - If you mention a hobby or activity you are passionate about, you will keep him interested. ("I am so excited to start training for the New York Marathon" is cool.) If all you do is talk about that hobby or activity, you'll seem obsessive and one-dimensional. Which will totally bore him to tears.
> - If the conversation flows and you both talk, you will keep him interested. If you monopolize the conversation or, alternatively, say very little, you will bore him to tears.

She should be warm and open to getting to know him

Remember that smile you had when you first met him? It's going to come in mighty handy on your first date as well. Don't forget to use it! In fact, all of the flirting tips discussed in the previous chapter are applicable here. Being warm and acting happy to be with him are vital.

What self-respecting person wants to be around someone who seems like they don't want to be around them? Yet women – especially as they get older – often go into dates with a big ol' chip on their shoulder. They give off the vibe they are closed for business unless and until he proves himself. I like to call this "Cold Bitch Disorder." It's a total turn-off and I'm convinced one of the huge reasons why so many women cannot seem to find a boyfriend. So let me tell you one of the secret keys to relationship success. Are you ready? Because this is a biggie:

DATING RULE #56:
A goddess starts every man off with a clean slate. She does not hold a new man accountable for the sins of an old one.

I don't care if your ex cheated on you with your sister, mother, and best friend – all at the very same time – and then videotaped it and put it on YouTube. I don't care if he stole every penny in your bank account and took out fraudulent credit cards in your name. I don't care if he used and abused you in every way possible. If you aren't ready to give another man a shot without thinking he's going to do the same (or worse), you are not ready to date. That's the bottom line, my friend. Save both yourself and the guy some heartache and start "dating" a therapist instead. Get over those issues before you get under a new guy, okay?

Even if you aren't bitter or angry outright, you still don't want to act as though he's got to apply and be interviewed for the position of "boyfriend." He doesn't have to pass through a series of tests and questions. It's dinner, not a business transaction. I understand that in today's world of successful, career-minded women it can be hard to switch from job mode to romance. But it's important you do. Treat him like a colleague and he'll see you like a colleague, not as a potential girlfriend.

Just like interrogating him with a series of questions will make you seemed closed off, so will not asking him anything about himself. I recently did a radio show with a beautiful, young actress. She confessed she was not always good at allowing her dates the opportunity to talk about themselves. Instead, she said she often went on and on about herself. Talk about radical honesty! But what a great insight, isn't it? Here's the deal with this kind of behavior. First, you come off as self-absorbed even if you aren't. Second, it doesn't really offer you the ability to get to know him and see if he's someone you'd be interested in continuing to date. I never think it's a bad thing if men talk more than women on a date. Usually, the guy loves it and (more importantly) it gives you the chance to get to know him without having to give too much away yourself. Sometimes it really is better to listen.

So relax, allow the conversation to flow, and be happy to be with him. That's what will help you to radiate warmth and openness. But in case there's any confusion, here are tips to help you avoid behavior that will appear cold (i.e., closed off to a relationship).

BRRRRR!! GET THAT MAN A SKI CAP!

You will seem cold if you:

- Roll your eyes, tell him his joke was stupid, or appear annoyed by his behavior. If you don't like him, don't go out with him again. But while you are with him, be courteous.
- Ask prying questions which seem like you're suspicious of him. "Why did you break up with your last girlfriend?" or "Are you seriously looking for a relationship or just to hook up?" are no-no's.
- Want to know where he "sees himself in five years," what his life goals are, or any other sort of job interview type of question.
- Say things like, "All men suck" or "I have trust issues."
- Talk non-stop about how important your job is and how you won't ever put a man before your career.
- Come across as high-maintenance, snobby, or hard to please. Don't complain about the food, the service, or anything really. He's taking you out. Be appreciative.
- Act pessimistic or negative. No one wants to hang around a "Debbie Downer."

DATING RULE #57:

A woman who radiates warmth and friendliness is a woman men want to be around.

She should not seem overly eager or desperate

I love my dogs. And, like every other canine owner in America, I am convinced I have the best dogs that have ever walked the face of the earth. My boy, Dudley, was my "first born." Even though he's nine years old and nearly 75 pounds, he still looks and acts like a puppy. Especially when he's begging for food. He gets these big eyes, will start to drool, and acts like he hasn't eaten in weeks and is desperate for a bite – just a bite – of whatever it is I am eating. And he will take anything I give him. It doesn't matter if it's a bit of lettuce or a bread crumb, Dudley will gobble it up like it's the tastiest treat he's ever had.

"Begging Puppy Disease" is the opposite of "Cold Bitch Disorder." While the latter primarily afflicts the older woman who's been through a few bad guys, the former seems to affect younger women. Those who feel they are at a place in life where they are ready to settle down, get married, and pump out a few kids are especially susceptible. Like Dudley, they'll act like they've never had a man pay any attention to them and will settle for whatever scrap a guy throws their way. They'll sit, beg, and roll over all to get a guy to like them – to choose them. And men can sense this from the very first date.

What happens to "Begging Puppies?" The man will either run, much like I do when I retreat to another room to get away from Dudley's whimpering, or he'll throw them a bone for a little while (both literally and figuratively). He will never give them a substantial portion. Acting overly eager to please a man at any cost is a big time turn-off. Desperation is never attractive.

My good friend Eric recently dealt with a woman named Claire who acted like a "Begging Puppy." Claire's first mistake was that she asked him on a date. Although Eric wasn't particularly attracted to her, he felt bad about turning her down and agreed to go out with her.

"She made all the plans," he told me. "I felt like I didn't have a say in what we did. But she was so excited that I decided to go along with it."

For the better part of an entire day, Claire dragged Eric from a farmer's market to a Victorian tea house for lunch and then to a bar afterward.

"It was *so* obvious she didn't want the date to end," Eric recalled. "I barely said a word the whole day. I can't believe she couldn't tell that I wasn't feeling it."

Even though Claire was oblivious to Eric's lack of interest, that didn't prevent her from expressing *her* feelings.

"She kept telling me how good looking I was and how excited she was to go out with me. I mean, it's nice to be complimented, but it came off as desperate."

Finally Eric couldn't take anymore. "I thought it would never end, so after a couple of drinks at the bar I told her I had to be getting home."

As Eric pulled up to Claire's house, she tried to keep things going even longer and invited him to come inside.

"When I told her 'no,' she looked like she was going to cry. She said to me, 'I'm not going to hear from you again am I?' I didn't know what to say."

Surprise, surprise – Eric never did call Claire, let alone go out with her again.

ARE YOU A "BEGGING PUPPY?"

- Do you laugh too hard, come off as nervous, or act like you are way too concerned with saying the right thing?
- Do you overlook bad behavior? Do you think a bad guy is better than no guy?
- Do you use sex to get him? Dress provocatively? Often go too far too fast? Drop hints that you'll keep him "satisfied?" Engage in sex talk on the first few dates?
- Do you tell dates how badly you want to get married and have kids?
- Do you let men push your boundaries or treat you with disrespect hoping they'll eventually approve of you?
- Do you accept last minute dates and show up whenever and wherever he asks you to? Even if it means canceling other plans?
- Do you feel desperate to the point you'd be willing to settle?

- Do you offer to split the check or even to pay for an entire first date?
- Do you try to extend dates by asking if he'd like to move on to a different location or come back to your place?
- Do you give him a lot of compliments much too early on? "You're so handsome." "Smart." "Funny." Do you stare at him with goo-goo eyes?
- Do you end first dates by saying, "I'd love to see you again" or something to that effect?

If you can relate to these questions, you might very well be a "Begging Puppy." Now is the time to stop that behavior. From this point forward, you are no man's pet. You are a strong, confident woman who doesn't need a guy to "complete her" or make her feel whole. You aren't willing to do whatever he wants in the hopes he will like you as a result. You won't allow a man to throw you crumbs and call them an entrée.

On a first date, keep in mind he is not the be-all, end-all of your existence. He isn't perfect. And he's not your dream man – yet. You want to be friendly, respectful, and polite. You don't want to be fawning and obsequious.

DATING RULE #58:
A goddess never acts like a "Begging Puppy."

Additional first date guidelines

Now that you've got the big picture on what you want to do (and not do) on your first date, let me help you out with some extra tips. Consider this bonus advice...

P.S. MISCELLANEOUS FIRST DATE DOS & DON'TS

- DON'T let him ask you out for the first time via text. If he tries to, text him back with something like, "I'd love to but don't know my schedule. Will you call me tonight after I've looked at my calendar?" That usually lets him know he's got to pick up the phone.

- DO let him plan the date. If he asks what food you like, tell him. If he asks where you want to go say, "Why don't you surprise me? I love surprises." This lets him step up and be a man, will show you the type of places he likes, makes you seem spontaneous, and indicates you will have confidence in his decisions. That's a win-win-win-win.

- DON'T spend twelve hours straight with him. End the date at an appropriate end point. Don't go to three different bars afterward or go back to his place for a drink. Leave him wanting more instead of feeling like he's had too much.

- DO say thank you right after dinner and when he's dropping you off at the end of the date. Tell him how much fun you had. However, no post-date texts reiterating it, okay?

- DON'T make out with him. I think an appropriate ending to a great first date is a hug and maybe a kiss on the cheek. (Side note: A handshake is way too formal and business-like. Only shake his hand if you have no plans to see him again.) Give him something to work toward. And most certainly never, ever sleep with him at this early stage.

- DON'T be the first to make contact after the date. Let him call or text you to tell you how much fun he had and that he'd like to see you again. If you never hear from him? Oh well! Send him off to potential boyfriend heaven and move on!

In the beginning…God created the goddess.

First Date "DON'T" Numero Uno

I was recently a guest on a radio show where the host and I discussed first date protocol.

"What's the one thing a woman should never do on a first date?" the host asked me.

I immediately responded in no uncertain terms, "Sleep with him."

Although we both started laughing after I said it, I was completely serious. And as if to prove my point, seconds later a caller rang through asking what she should do about a guy she slept with on their first date.

"I've texted him a couple times, but he hasn't initiated any contact," she explained.

Uh-oh.

This particular caller certainly isn't the first woman to have made this mistake. Nor was she the first to ask me about it. Just take a look at the following samples of the many questions I receive on this topic:

I totally messed up and had sex with him the first time we went out. I haven't heard from him since…

I met this guy at a bar and went home with him. We hooked up. Is there any chance I can turn it into something more?

We had sex on the first date. (Bad, I know!) Now the problem is he only texts me when he wants me to come over late-night. I really like him! Help!

Not having sex on a first date isn't about being old-fashioned or prudish. It's about being *smart*. It's about protecting yourself – emotionally and physically. Chances are great at the end of a first date – no matter how amazing it was – you will still be relatively uncertain about:

- Whether or not he's truly serious about getting to know you.
- Whether or not he has a sexually transmitted disease. (Sorry, but if condoms aren't 100% effective against pregnancy, they simply cannot be 100% effective against the transmission of disease.)
- Whether or not you will see him again.
- Whether or not he is your future boyfriend.

How to Be a Goddess

Is it worth the risk? I think not. When sex happens on the first date, the chances of having a relationship decrease significantly. More often than not, the man loses attraction and the inclination to pursue. It's "game over" and before he's changed his sheets, he's thinking, "Next!" Contrast this to what happens in a woman's mind. Unless she was completely inebriated and wound up in bed with a guy she would never want to see without wearing a thick pair of beer goggles, chances are she's going to start obsessing the moment her clothes are back on.

"Will I hear from him again?"

"Does he think I'm a slut?"

"Can this go anywhere now?"

"Will he respect me?"

"The condom didn't break, did it?"

"Oh God, he was cute. I think I might like him."

And on and on and on…

If the woman does hear from him again, it's usually in the form of a drunken text asking her to make a late-night pit stop. And if she likes the guy, she'll invariably make the mistake of immediately hopping in her car and high-tailing it to his place like she's Danica Patrick. "Maybe this is a sign he's really interested in me?" she hopes to herself as she speeds along. However, when things never progress past an occasional booty-call beckoning, she'll be forced into a head-on collision with the reality he's only interested in a "hit and run" every now and again. Ouch.

I'm often asked what a woman can do in order to prevent first date "crash-and-burn" sex. It's simple really.

HOW TO STAY UNDER THE SPEED LIMIT ON A FIRST DATE

- Watch your fuel consumption. If you remember the two drink limit, you'll be much less likely to make a mistake because you weren't thinking clearly.

In the beginning…God created the goddess.

- Don't maintain the track. Shaving and personal grooming shouldn't extend to certain – ahem – areas. If you save the slick track for your legs only, you'll be a lot more hesitant to show him the keys to your ignition.
- Pass on "pole position." In race car driving, "pole position" is highly coveted. On a first date, however, it's best to keep yourself away from touching anything remotely close to his stick shift. Heavy make-out sessions or even grinding on a dance floor can lead to a fatal accident.

Always remember it's a relationship you're gunning for, not the Indy 500. Using good judgment – by going slow and steady and keeping one foot hovering above the brake pedal – is what wins *this* race.

DATING RULE #59:
When sex happens at an accelerated speed, the chance of a real relationship hits the skids.

What about Him?

Okay. Now that you're all set, the rest is up to him and how he behaves himself. Guess what? You're going to want to pay attention to that. Close, close attention.

Dear Jenn,
I'm so tired of meeting guys and having a bunch of great first dates only to figure out they're a-holes later on. I don't think I'm noticing their behavior in the beginning. Do you have any suggestions for how I can size them up more quickly?
    Aileen

Indeed I do, Aileen.

DATING RULE #60:
If you pay attention, a man will tell you almost everything you need to decide if he's got boyfriend potential on the first couple of dates.

GOOD SIGNS ON A FIRST DATE

Here's a check list to use to evaluate your date's actions. How does he measure up?

- He asks you out in advance and via a phone call or in person. This shows he is respectful of your schedule, wants to book you ahead of time, and sees it as a formal opportunity to get to know you.
- He plans the date and makes any necessary reservations. If he tries to be creative and do something "different," that's okay if you're okay with it. But take note of what it is. If it's something which has your likes in mind as well as his, that's great. If he chooses an activity that's all about him and what he enjoys, that might not be so great.
- He makes sure he looks nice. He's not wearing a stained t-shirt and his hair is brushed.
- He is polite to hosts, servers, and anyone he comes in contact with. He does not treat others rudely or with disrespect.
- He has good manners. He holds open all doors, lets you walk to the table in front of him, and waits for you to order first. If he sees your water needs refilling, he asks someone to get you more.
- He watches what he says. He doesn't use a lot of profanity or talk about his sexual conquests. He tries to impress you by being a gentleman.

In the beginning...God created the goddess.

- He appears to like his work. He is enthusiastic about his job.
- He talks about his family and friends in a positive way. In fact, he has a positive outlook on life in general.
- He asks about you and your life. He seems genuinely interested in getting to know you.
- He appears to be well-adjusted and mentally balanced.
- He doesn't try to get overly personal or intimate. Although he wants in your pants (he's a man, after all), he shows restraint and respect. He's happy to walk you to your door and leave it at that.

On the converse, there are certain things a man might do that should be considered warning signs. Again, watch his behavior and pay attention not just to what he says, but how he acts.

FIRST DATE RED FLAGS

If he does any of the following, I'd suggest never seeing him again.

- He asks you to "hang out" one night. Usually at the last minute and without having to make much of a pre-arranged plan. What do you do? Say no. Showing him you're willing to accept something casual now means you'll never be more than anything casual.
- He takes you somewhere completely unromantic. If you want romance and he doesn't exhibit it in the beginning, he's certainly not going to show it later on.

- He is rude or disrespectful in any way, either to you or to anyone else. If he's not on good behavior now, he will never get any better.
- He checks out, comments lewdly on, or flirts with other women when he's with you. Just imagine what he'll do when you're not around.
- He seems unhappy, dissatisfied, or angry at life. You won't be the one to bring sunshine into his world.
- He is braggy, self-centered, or conceited. Unless you're interested in a selfish guy who only thinks of himself, steer clear of these men.
- He appears unintelligent, uninteresting, or boring. In the words of a famous comedian, "You can't fix stupid." No matter how hot he is.
- He expects you to pay your share of the bill or groans at the tab. Cheap is gross.
- He boasts about sexual conquests, how many girls want him, or how the last girl he banged is now stalking him. That's the stuff super insecure, wanna-be player types say thinking you'll see them as desirable.
- He doesn't ask about your life and doesn't seem interested in getting to know you. He monopolizes the conversation. Either he's not into you or is completely self-absorbed. Both are "deal breakers."
- He pushes you sexually either in word or in action. If he only seems to have sex on his mind, he's only interested in you for sex.

In the beginning…God created the goddess.

DATING RULE #61:
Analyze his behavior to see if he's worth more of your time and emotions. If he's not, cut your losses and run.

So how did he check out? Is he a dream guy or a dud? Wait! It's only the first date! He's still not your dream guy, okay? He's – at best – a good candidate for dream guy status. This is the mentality you want to have. *Even after an amazing first date.*

So take a breath and relax. Call your girlfriends and book plans for the next couple of days to take the edge off. Keep on going out and meeting guys. Don't sit around waiting for your phone to ring or buzz with a text alert. Don't contact him first. Don't start planning the wedding.

DATING RULE #62:
Even if it was the best first date you've ever had, he still isn't necessarily your soul mate.

But mark my words: If you handled the date right and he's a quality guy – not just a hit and run artist – you should receive a text within forty eight hours saying something like, "I had a great time with you." And aren't those some sweet words to read?

DO AS I SAY, NOT AS I DID
(My Own Journey from Doormat to Goddess)

Most of my first dates have been pretty good. Sure, I've met men I didn't feel chemistry with or who weren't for me. But a disaster due to both of us? Just one. With a man named "C."

I met "C" at a trendy bar on Melrose. He was insanely hot. Like crazy gorgeous. Naturally, "C" was an actor. Although he wasn't famous, if you'd watched TV at all back then, you'd know his face. He was in a ton of commercials and was the spokesman for a major soft drink. In addition, I learned through friends "C" was an heir to a beer empire. Hot *and* super rich? Surely the dating gods must be playing tricks on me.

I don't have space to detail the wild night we met, but I will say that it involved an after-hours club, Cher's boyfriend at the time (who brought along the Playgirl magazine he was featured in to show everyone), and a female porn star. (I told you I was a party girl, didn't I?) Actually, it wasn't really that bad and no, I didn't have sex with "C." In fact, I didn't even kiss him. (Or Cher's boyfriend. Or the porn star.) But it did last until dawn when I finally peeled myself away from the motley crew and got a cab home.

I was a bit surprised when I heard from "C" a couple of days later. I figured he was out of my league and our night together was a onetime deal. But he asked me out. Sort of. He said, "Since the last time we were together was so crazy, I thought maybe we could just chill and watch a movie or something." Because he was so hot (did I already mention that?), I agreed to drive from my place in Westwood to his in Pasadena the following evening. Not a short drive for those of you non-Los Angelenos out there.

When I arrived the next night, "C" had a surprise in store for me. Not only had I just spent an hour in my car, I also got to drive him to pick up the pizza he'd ordered. Not quite dinner reservations, but what did I expect considering his uninspired "date" plans? Back at his place, I was treated to a double feature. A Cameron Diaz movie and his demo reel featuring highlights of his commercials and television roles. He talked nonstop about himself, his acting career, and how he'd just broken Tori Spelling's heart. He'd only dated her for the connections, he said. But I bet he took Tori out to dinner.

In the beginning…God created the goddess.

Did he ask about me? Nope. Did he really seem interested in me? Nope. What did I do? I kissed the hot guy for a few minutes (wouldn't you?) and left.

"C" called about three weeks later. He said he'd just gotten back from a film shoot (riiiiight, buddy) and was wondering if I wanted to hang with him that night. I told him I was dating someone and never heard from him again.

XX

Step #6

Of noblemen and ladies. The courtship period.

I'm not going to lie and tell you that even if you followed the preceding chapter to a "T," every first date you have is going to be incredible. In actuality, odds are very few will be amazing. It may take some time – and maybe even a bunch of first dates – to have one where you both connect in that "special" way. You know what I'm talking about. The conversation flows, you both laugh and have fun, you both feel chemistry, and you both want to see each other again. It's like you are "in the zone" and things just happen naturally and easily. But it does – and will eventually – happen.

So what do you do then? *You do the exact same thing.* In fact, the next couple of dates should be a carbon copy of the first one. (Think of it like washing your hair. "Lather, rinse, repeat. Lather, rinse, repeat.") He should still be the one to ask you out. He should still plan what you are going to do. You should still be open and warm. You should still allow him to get to know you (and you should definitely be getting to know him) without revealing every dirty little secret. You should still be going over the check lists of good signs and red flags. You should still be keeping things out of the bedroom and allowing the physicality to progress slowly from a hug, to holding hands, to a kiss…

I love the word "courtship." And I love the idea of a woman being "properly courted" by a man. The origin of the word actually dates back to the 1500s and comes from a time when a nobleman would woo a lady in the royal court in the hopes she would accept a marriage proposal. He would romance her, write her poetry, and bring her tokens of his affection. He worked diligently to show her he prized her above all others and she alone was the object of his desire. Ahhhh! Now *that* is romantic!

While we shouldn't expect modern men to write sonnets describing our beauty, we should expect them to treat us well. And we most definitely must allow them the opportunity to do so. Yet here's what often happens in today's dating process. We meet a guy and have a great first date. We might play it cool and wait for him to contact us for the next one, but we want to totally bypass the "courtship" stage. So after a couple of dates, *we* become the ones to move things along. We start to call him regularly and initiate most of the contact. We begin to book up his time by inviting him to different activities. We begin to act like we are his girlfriend. And when we feel his interest lessening, we sleep with him hoping he will get back that initial fire. That may keep him coming around for a bit, but eventually he will be gone. He'll either disappear into thin air or he'll give the whole "I'm not ready for anything serious" speech. Sound familiar?

DATING RULE #63:
Do not deprive yourself of a proper courtship!

I think most women want what is commonly referred to as a "hunter male." We want an alpha-dog who steps up to the plate and goes to bat for us; one who we see as a "real man." In short, we want to be pursued. Why? Because when a man does this, we feel a sense of security. We have less anxiety over how he feels about us. When a woman takes on the "hunter" role, she often does so because she finds herself incredibly attracted to a man and is worried if she doesn't, he will be unwilling or incapable to do it himself.

When a man meets and begins to date a woman he really likes, he needs to be the hunter. He needs to have the ability to pursue her, to woo her, to *court* her. He needs to feel like he is the one leading the dance and setting the pace. He wants the opportunity to show you how great he is and to win your affection. If you don't allow him this time and instead begin to court him, you are depriving both of you. Here's what happened to Vanessa when she made this mistake.

Dear Jenn,

I've been dating this guy for a couple of months and I thought things were going really well. I'd go over to his place or hang out with him a few times a week and everything seemed good – I even introduced him to my friends! But as soon as I told him how much I was into him, he began to grow distant. He was quiet and didn't talk much the last few times we were together so I thought maybe if I did something nice for him, he'd be happier to be with me. I ended up buying this shirt I thought would look good on him. He seemed to like it, but it still didn't change his attitude. Things have just been...weird. I get the feeling if I wasn't texting him, I would never hear from him. He doesn't seem to want to see me anymore. What do you think is going on? What should I do?

Vanessa

Poor Vanessa. Like many women before her, she made the classic mistake of courting a man instead of letting him court her. She went over to his place (instead of having him pick her up for a proper date). She confessed her feelings (before he'd done the same). She bought him a gift (instead of being the one to receive the flowers). She was initiating contact (rather than waiting for him to get in touch with her). Who was moving things along? Vanessa. What happened as a result? Her man bailed.

Can you identify with Vanessa? Have you ever made one or more of the following "courting" mistakes?

HOW WOMEN "COURT" MEN

- We pursue them. After a couple of dates, we begin to initiate calls and texts.
- We romance them. We'll buy him little gifts, bake him cookies, or send him a sweet email telling him we were "thinking about him."
- We take over their duties. We ask him out and pay for dates. In short, we try to be the man in the relationship.
- We woo them. After two dates, we tell him how much we like him and how special he is to us.
- We "convince" them. We go out of our way to dazzle him, show him how great we are, and to impress him. Thereby attempting to prove that we are girlfriend material.

In every relationship, there are "roles" each person plays. By courting a man, you are taking over his "role" of being the man. You are usurping his duties. You may think you are being honest and forthright; doing and saying what you actually feel. But in reality, you are being selfish. You are doing what you want to do, when you want to do it, without giving him the opportunity to move things along. And moving things along is his task. Not yours.

If it is his responsibility to be the initiator, what should you be doing? You should be "responding." The ideal courtship is like a waltz or any other ballroom dance. The man initiates by asking you to dance. You say, "Yes." He takes your hand in his and walks you to the floor. He gets himself into position and you follow suit. He takes the first step and then leads you in the dance. I'm not much of a dancer, but I've heard it said that if a man is a good leader, his female partner does not even have to know the steps. He is able to guide her into the proper moves. That is how courtship should be. It isn't our job to plan the steps, but we do need to respond to his lead.

THE PROPER WAY TO RESPOND TO A MAN

In order to keep him coming around, you need to show him that you are interested and receptive to his advances. But the advances themselves must be his.

- Do not ask him out. But when he asks you out say, "I would love to!"
- Do not call him or text him first in the beginning. But when he does contact you, always seem happy to hear from him.
- Do not tell him where you want him to take you to dinner (unless he asks) or demand things from him. But always say thank you and tell him that you had a great time after a date.
- Do not offer him every inch of your heart immediately and on a silver platter. But, as he earns your trust, always be willing to share another small piece of yourself over time.

"But I don't want a man controlling me or deciding things for me!" you might be screaming. If you are, you're not alone. In fact, here's one example of a reader who thought the same.

Of noblemen and ladies. The courtship period.

Dear Jenn,

I don't understand why you think it's up to the guy to lead the relationship. Why can't I make the effort to see him when I want to? Why can't I take control? Women take charge in everything these days! We run businesses and households. Why can't we run the show in our dating lives? It just seems so old-fashioned to expect a guy to lead.

Carrie

It's not about being old-fashioned or adopting a 1950s mindset. You might think you are letting the man control you, but in actuality you are not. You are exerting control over yourself – the only person you actually have control over in the first place. You are also in control over if and how the relationship progresses. The only thing you aren't controlling is him. (And you shouldn't want to control a man anyway.)

Here's how it all works. It is completely up to you whether you want to dance with him in the first place. And you certainly don't have to accept a second dance. You can walk off the floor at any time. When you allow a man the opportunity to "show you his moves," you are actually able to see who he is and what he's made of. You get insight into the type of boyfriend he would make. You will have the information necessary to analyze whether he's someone you want to partner with on a regular basis.

Think about it. What's the best way to find out whether or not he's serious about you? Should you ask him straight out? Nope. (Believe it or not he might lie!) Should you try to pressure him into being your boyfriend either blatantly or subtly? Nope. Or should you kick back and watch how he treats you and what he's willing to invest in you? Ding, ding, ding!

When we try to lead the courtship, not only do we steal his job from him, but we also put ourselves at a great disadvantage. When we decide where we will go, what we will do, and how quickly we will get there, how do we determine how serious he is about us? How do we really get to know who he is and what his intentions are? Guys will easily tell you that they are looking for a relationship because it's what they think women want to hear. But only by letting him step up and show you what he's willing to *do* will you ever really know the truth. If you overtake him in the beginning, you will be left with one of two things: A weakling for a partner or the view of his back as he walks away. Neither of which should be very appealing.

DATING RULE #64:
The more you let him show you what he's capable of and willing to do, the more you will know how he feels about you.

In addition to responding, there are several things a woman should be doing during the courtship phase of a relationship.

WHAT A WOMAN SHOULD DO DURING COURTSHIP
- She should watch his behavior and analyze his character.
- She should challenge him.
- She should keep a level head.
- She should take it slowly when it comes to sex.

She should watch his behavior and analyze his character
Remember all those wonderful qualities we wanted in our soul mate? Our list of "must-haves" from Step #2? Courtship is the time when you need to break out that list and evaluate how he compares. Listen, no man will ever be perfect. But he needs to be sane. And have morals. And not have any major personality defects.

After each of the first several dates, you need to check in with yourself. Do you like the way he treats you and others? Does he seem solid?

Of noblemen and ladies. The courtship period.

Is he respectful? Does he make you feel good? If there are a bunch of things about him you can't stand or you think will end up hurting you, now is the time to end it before it goes any further and you get in any deeper. Never overlook behavior that will be a "deal breaker" for you. Never say, "But he's so cute. It's not that big of a deal." Or, "He's the best of my options. It isn't worse than being alone." It will be. Trust me – and your gut – on this.

So use the courtship phase to gather as much information about him as you can. Really look at who he shows you he is. And don't allow yourself to be dazzled by the exterior things. Just because he drives a nice car or is nice looking doesn't mean he is a nice guy. We can avoid unnecessary heartbreak and disappointments 90% of the time simply by walking away before we get in too deep with an unacceptable man. It's when we ignore the warning signs that we get ourselves into trouble.

My good friend Mel accomplished this perfectly with her boyfriend. After several years of being single and wasting time on "unacceptable" men, she'd had enough and decided to get her goddess on. When she met Greg, she made a conscious decision to do things differently. So she took her time getting to know him. She watched how he treated his friends and family. She made sure his words and actions matched. She looked for red flags and warning signs. Only after she was sure he was worth her heart and emotions did she give them to him. Even though Greg wasn't necessary her type physically – she normally likes men with darker complexions and Greg is a blue-eyed blonde – she looked past the exterior and focused on who he was on the *inside*. She now texts me about once a week to tell me how deliriously happy she is and how she's never been treated so well by a man.

How to Be a Goddess

DATING RULE #65:
If a man is the hunter, the woman is the gatherer. So gather all the necessary information, analyze his character, and act accordingly.

She should challenge him

Guess what types of guys want women quickly, easily, and without much investment? Players, Playboys, and Peter Pans. Guess what kind of men want women who are not super easy to get? Quality ones. Guess how you tell which type he is? By challenging him.

The notion of "challenging" men often gets a bad rap.

Dear Jenn,
Is "challenging" a guy the same as playing games? It seems like it might be manipulative. Isn't it better just to be upfront and honest with men?
  Piper

Let me be clear: Challenging a man is *not* about playing games or being manipulative. Quite the contrary, actually. It's about being honest with both him and yourself when it comes to what you will and won't accept. It's about maintaining a life and a spirit of independence which you won't give up merely because some guy gives you a little bit of attention. It's about having high standards which you refuse compromise. Is that game playing? Not even close. Playing games is leaving a bracelet at some guy's house after you sleep with him so you'll have an excuse to call him the next day. Playing games is calling to say thank you (for the fifth time) for dinner, hoping it will inspire him to ask you out again. A goddess doesn't play games. Why? *Because she doesn't have to.* When you actually are "hard to get," that's when there's no need to "play hard to get."

Instead, challenging a man is a two-fold process. It shows him you won't accept bad behavior and it also demonstrates you are not won over easily. Challenging a man means you give him an opportunity to show you how great he is. To him, it translates that you are a high quality, in demand woman who won't settle for the first guy who happens to take her to dinner. It shows him you deserve a man who has high standards and treats you with respect. Challenging a man is "Cherise's Rubber Duck Theory" in action.

DATING RULE #66:
When you challenge a quality man who truly likes you, he will want to rise to the occasion.

Doormats and "Begging Puppies" are all too eager to accept whatever a man – any man – tosses their way. As a result, he's not likely to give them much of anything. But not so the goddess. Because she is confident and strong, a man knows she won't put up with bad behavior. He knows he has to work a bit to secure her affection and attention. Therefore, he too wants to be his best self.

From the very beginning, you show a man how you expect him to act around you and the type of woman you are. On the first date, he starts to learn what behavior is okay and what isn't; what he can get away with and what he can't. So now is the time to show him. Yes, *right now*. You may think giving in a little bit will eventually get you want you want. It won't. In fact, what you will end up with won't have even a vague resemblance to what it is you truly want.

DATING RULE #67:
It's a lot easier to negotiate the terms of how you want to be treated upfront, rather than attempting to fight for them later.

Being a "bitch" isn't how you should challenge a man. Most men don't respond well to the in-your-face, take-it-or-leave-it type of woman. Especially not the hunter male/alpha dogs. Challenging a man is not the same as demanding things from him. The former works. The latter doesn't.

HOW TO CHALLENGE A MAN WITHOUT PLAYING GAMES OR BEING A TOTAL BITCH

- If you are busy when he calls, do not stop what you are doing just to talk to him. Instead, call him back when you are free and *never* feel obliged to explain "I'm so sorry I couldn't talk, but I was on the line with an associate in London."

- Do not accept last minute dates. If he calls you at 10 p.m. and wants to hang out at 10:15, you are unavailable. End of story.

- For the first month, you only have time to see him once a week. You have work, Pilates class, family obligations, your friends… Those don't take a back seat. If you aren't busy, get busy. During the second month, you can bump it up to twice a week. But not two days in a row.

- If he asks you a question you think is inappropriate or wants to discuss something you don't want to discuss, don't feel pressured to respond or get upset. Instead, be flirtatious, lean in, and quietly say "I'm flattered you think you know me well enough to ask that." Smile mischievously and change the subject. (Outcome: He is *challenged* to want to get to know you better while seeing you have boundaries.)

- Don't tell him how hot he is or how you've never seen someone so good looking. When he compliments you, the correct response is to warmly and genuinely say "Thank you." That's it. "Thank you." Don't say "I look fat" or feel like you have to reciprocate.

- If he asks you out but you already have other plans, never ever break them. "Bummer! I'd love to but I'm busy that night!" is what you should say.

Of noblemen and ladies. The courtship period.

- If he asks when he can see you next, don't tell him you are free any and all nights of the week. After all, you aren't, right? Say, "I am free on Friday."
- Don't stay up all night talking to him on the phone while sharing your most intimate thoughts, hopes, and dreams. Keep calls brief and lighthearted.
- Never ask "How soon would you like to get married?" or "How many kids do you want?" Marriage and kids shouldn't even be on your radar until you know him better.
- Don't freak if he goes out without you. Give him plenty of space to do his thing. If you think he's out partying and picking up on girls, you probably shouldn't be investing in him anyway.
- Don't get upset if you don't hear from him for a couple of days. When he calls, act like no time has passed.

She should keep a level head

If you've ever had too much to drink, you can probably relate to lying in bed and thinking the room is spinning around you. You feel like you're on an amusement park ride and sleep is nearly impossible. Sucks, doesn't it?

Much like a night of heavy drinking, having a couple of great dates with a guy who seems great as well can cause us to lose rational thinking, feel like we're "head over heels," and develop a case of "the spins." We begin to mentally plan our first vacation together, imagine our wedding, and wonder if our kids will have "his eyes." And this usually gets us into major trouble.

Karen recently dealt with this big time. After only a couple of dates with William she became certain he was "the one." She began to think about him non-stop and started to plan her life around him. She'd flake on friends at the last minute if William wanted to see her. She began to text him several times throughout the day just to check in on him and she'd flip out if she didn't hear right back. The closer Karen tried to get to William, the more he would pull away. The more he would pull away, the more frantic she would become. Eventually, William pulled away completely and stopped returning her calls.

Can you relate to Karen's story? I think most of us have gone "crazy" over a guy at some point in our lives. If that's what you are feeling now, I've concocted the following test. It will help you to analyze just how "love drunk" you might be. Consider this your relationship breathalyzer…

QUIZ: DO YOU HAVE A CASE OF "THE SPINS?"

- Do you find yourself thinking about him constantly, dreaming about him nightly, and/or wondering what he's doing nearly every minute of the day?
- Are you so distracted by thoughts of him that you have trouble concentrating at work or at school?
- Are you always checking your phone to see if he's called and/or texted?
- Do you plan your next date (what you'll do, what you'll wear, etc) in your head before he's even asked to see you again?
- Do you get freaked out and start hyperventilating if twenty-four hours pass without hearing from him?
- Are you ignoring your friends, family, hobbies, and interests to make time for him?
- Are you convinced he could be "The One?"
- Do you spend more than one night a week with him?
- Do you obsess over how he feels about you?
- Do you regularly imagine your wedding day and picture him as the groom?

So how "drunk" are you? Do you need to sober up? Is it time for a love intervention?

During the courtship process, it's very important to slow down and take some deep breaths. Do not let your emotions run faster than your rational and logical thinking. Falling too hard, too fast is a great path to heartbreak. It causes us to have unrealistic expectations both of the man and the future of the relationship. And this often sets us up for disappointment, doesn't it? This is why it is so important to be looking at his character, not spending too much time with him, and taking things slowly.

DATING RULE #68:
Keeping a level head will protect your heart.

I know there's a lot of relationship advice which says one of the easiest ways to not start spinning over a particular man is to date several guys at once. After my divorce, I employed this technique and I do think it can work to some degree. But here's my problem with "dating in multiples." Even if we date five guys at once, there's always going to be *that one guy* who far outshines the rest. And the others will be nothing more than a small distraction. In fact, sometimes the disparity between *that one guy* and the others will cause us to obsess about him even more. If you happen to meet a couple guys you like, feel free to date and get to know both of them. But I don't think a woman should ever go out of her way to meet and (essentially) use a couple guys just so she can try to keep a level head with the one she's crazy about. In my opinion, it won't work and it seems unfair to string the other guys along.

Instead of thinking dating more than one man will be the cure for "the spins," be sure to follow this next piece of advice. It is the most important thing you can do to prevent them from starting in the first place.

How to Be a Goddess

She should take it slowly when it comes to sex

Can women have sex without an emotional attachment? Yes. I think under the right circumstances, and if they are so inclined, women can – and do – have sex with men without wanting anything more. I think there are a lot of ladies who can go to a bar, get drunk, and hook up with a guy without wanting to spend another second with him. (I do wonder if some of that is due to a tad bit of shame?)

But can a woman have sex with a man she really likes without getting emotionally attached? No way in hell.

Dear Jenn,

I am so upset and I don't know what to do. I've been on four dates with this guy and I think he is totally great. He seems to be everything I've been looking for.

Two nights ago, we went out and I ended up having sex with him. I feel like it was too fast and I can't stop thinking about him. I haven't heard from him since then and I'm worried I never will again. He usually calls or texts every day and it's been nearly forty-eight hours with nada – no communication whatsoever.

What should I do, Jenn? Do I contact him? I am totally making myself sick about this.

Lauren

If you are attracted to a man (when sober), enjoy spending time in his company (when sober), and are excited to hear from him (when sober), you absolutely positively *will not* be able to have sex with him without deeper feelings getting involved. That's just not the way we work. I've heard it said that sex is the glue that bonds two people together. At its ideal, I believe it's the culmination of all the feelings you have for each other expressed in a physical way. And it is next to impossible for a woman – who is already starting to have deep feelings for a man – to turn those off once she sleeps with him.

Of noblemen and ladies. The courtship period.

DATING RULE #69:

No matter what your friends, MTV, or the magazines say, you absolutely cannot have sex with a man you like without becoming even more emotionally attached.

Women mess this up all the time and it is the cause of so much heartbreak. But it is the most important thing you can do during this phase of the relationship process. In fact, I am so adamant about it that if a woman said she was only going to follow one piece of my advice during courtship, I would tell her it should be to not sleep with him. Why? There are so many reasons...

WHY YOU SHOULDN'T SLEEP WITH HIM DURING COURTSHIP

Having sex too soon is often the kiss of death for a relationship. Sure, there are those urban dating legends where two people have a one night stand which turns into a marriage with two kids, but that is the vast exception. It's a gamble you should not be willing to take. Especially if you think you might really, really like him. Here's what can happen if you sleep with him too quickly:

- He might lose interest. Especially if that's all he wanted in the first place. It's less hurtful to find out his intentions by not sleeping with him. If he disappears because of that, isn't it better than him vanishing *after* you have sex?

- He might think you are promiscuous. Especially if you have sex with him on the first couple of dates. Very few men want a "promiscuous" woman as a girlfriend.

- He might stop "courting" (i.e., wooing, pursuing) you. One authority on relationships actually believes the "courtship" period ends when you have sex. I don't necessarily agree it has to, but many men do tend to ease up on the

romance after sex happens. They don't feel they have to
try as hard.

■ We get blinded by the "sex haze" and aren't able to see who
he is as clearly. Our judgment becomes impaired and we are
less objective about his character.

■ We attach even more. We go from having fun dating him
to wanting a relationship. We start to think long-term and
that what we have is serious. He might still be thinking it's
casual.

■ We might become possessive, obsessive, and maybe a bit
crazy. Now that he's "had" us, he is connected to us. We
want to mark our territory and brand him as "ours." Not
a good thing to do when there is no commitment involved.
And if you act like this, I guarantee no commitment will be
coming anytime soon. In fact, he will be running from you as
soon as he sees you.

I think one of the reasons why the early stages of dating ("courtship")
can be so frustrating and confusing to us is that women and men very
often go into it with completely different objectives. Women want a
boyfriend and men want sex. I call this "The Great Divide." The irony
is that, when executed correctly, these seemingly divergent objectives
work together perfectly. This may sound crazy but it's absolutely true!

Here's the reality: Most men don't start dating a woman thinking
marriage and babies. They just aren't wired that way. They're thinking,
"Man, I would love to see her naked." As women, we need to accept
this and be cool with it. He's a guy. That's just how he thinks.

We're different, aren't we? Sure, we probably fantasize about him naked
as well, but when we're dating a new man our thoughts are more like:

- "I wonder what kind of boyfriend/husband/father he would make?"
- "I wonder how long until he wants a commitment."
- "Is he dating anyone else?"
- "Does he really like me?"

That's the stuff that keeps us up at night.

Instead of trying to change our thinking, I say we embrace it. You want a relationship? Fine. He wants sex? Fine. How do we make both of our dreams come true? By having a proper courtship. That's the key.

DATING RULE #70:
You want a relationship and he wants sex. The way for both of you to get what you want is through a proper courtship.

When a quality man is courting you (i.e., trying to get you into bed), he will pull out all the stops. He'll work to win you over. That's the reason for the dinners and the flowers. That's why he keeps calling and coming around. He's hunting. And you, my dear, are the prey. But he's also learning how to treat you the way a woman needs to be treated in order for her to feel adored. *He's learning how to be your boyfriend.* And in the process he is becoming emotionally attached to you, even if he didn't think he was looking for a serious relationship, per se. Because he's investing in you, he is now becoming invested in the relationship. This is exactly what you want to happen in the first couple of months of dating.

DATING RULE #71:
If he's properly courting you, he will act like a boyfriend without being your boyfriend. Which will make him want to be your boyfriend.

I bet you're wondering two things. You want to know how far you can go sexually without having sex and you want to know when you can actually have sex. So let's address those issues.

How to Be a Goddess

Dear Jenn,

OK, OK! I get it! Don't have sex with a guy right away! Wait awhile!

I've made this mistake over and over again and the outcome is always the same – they lose interest pretty quickly afterward and I get hurt.

I've heard you say this many times and I'm finally ready to listen. So now what? What do I do going forward?

Dawn

HOW FAR SHOULD YOU GO SEXUALLY DURING COURTSHIP?

I say not that far. And I think it's good to have some clear cut boundaries with yourself.

- Kissing, hand holding, and playful "non-sexual touches" are all cool. Putting your hand on his leg at the movies is good. Affectionately touching his hair is great.
- Making out on his couch is okay. Just don't have hour-long sessions. When I first started dating my boyfriend I tried to limit the kissing to a few minutes at a time. It actually got to the point where he said one night, "I don't want to kiss you because every time I kiss you, you leave." This totally warmed my heart. If you feel things about to go to a place of no return, politely tell him you had an amazing evening, but you need to be getting home.
- Don't be a tease. By limiting the making out, you are actually doing both of you a favor. Don't get him all excited and then shut things off. That's just not right.
- Don't get naked. In fact, all clothes should stay on during courtship.
- Dry humping, grinding, and crotch groping are no-no's.
- Don't spend the night at his place until you are ready to seal the deal. "Just cuddling" rarely happens.
- Oral sex still counts. Don't even go there.

Don't let things go any further than you want them to. Stay sober, be rational. Protect yourself from making a mistake because you "got caught up in the moment." Keep your head straight and remember your goals.

DATING RULE #72:
If your goal is to have a lot of sex with a lot of different guys, sleep with men quickly. If your goal is to have a relationship, don't sleep with them for a while.

When should you sleep with him? Ahhh, there are so many theories on this, aren't there? I think the reason no one can really agree on it is because there's no one-size-fits-all rule here. But let me give you some guidelines.

WHEN SHOULD YOU SLEEP WITH HIM?

- As previously discussed, don't sleep with him on the first date. It's the kiss of death.
- Forget the "three date rule." That's way too soon. I believe that "rule" was concocted by a group of men who wanted us to think it was okay to have sex quickly.
- It should be more than a month for sure. If you are dating him once a week for the first month, four dates is still too fast.
- You should never sleep with him until you have thoroughly checked out his character and like what you see. If there are "deal breakers," having sex won't fix them. You'll just attach to an a-hole. Awesome.
- There needs to be a certain amount of trust and security. He may not have said the word "commitment," but you should be confident he's totally crazy about you and is dating you alone. If you have insecurities about it, sex will only bring them out.

- Don't sleep with him unless he is treating you well. If he disappears for a week at a time, acts hot and cold, or seems ambivalent about you, having sex won't turn him into a model boyfriend.
- Ideally, you should not have sex until *he's* initiated "the talk." (Find out how to get there in the next chapter.)
- Unless you have religious or moral beliefs which preclude premarital sex, or are both in agreement to wait longer, don't push it more than a few months. That's usually right around his pain threshold.

My vote? Again, this isn't a hard-and-fast (pun intended) rule. I say three months. Ninety days. If you are dating once a week for the first month, and twice a week thereafter, that puts you right around twenty dates. Can you handle that? I bet you can. Twenty dates to check out his character and see how he conducts himself in day-to-day life. Twenty dates to give him the opportunity to show you the kind of man he is and for you to show him the kind of woman you are. Twenty dates to get to know him.

Despite how it may seem, the courtship period is actually one of the best times in a relationship. Just think how cute he looks when he picks you up – hair combed and smelling nice. You'll both be excited and feeling good. One of the sweetest things I ever saw my boyfriend do was after our third date. He walked me to my car and I swear I saw him *skip* as he walked away. Yes. A forty one year-old man with salt and pepper hair actually *skipped*. That made my heart skip, let me tell you. Enjoy those moments. Enjoy this time. Don't be in such a hurry to rush it.

DO AS I SAY, NOT AS I DID
(My Own Journey from Doormat to Goddess)

I hate to write this. Not because what I did was so awful, but because I am now friends with this person and there's a chance he'll read it. Sorry, "B." But you were there and know firsthand the things that I did wrong. And I think they are worth repeating.

I met "B" when I was in my late twenties, but the background details really aren't the point of this story. The important part is that I was a grown woman who was completely responsible for her decisions and actions. And I hold myself accountable.

I knew fairly quickly that "B" and I probably weren't meant to be, but instead of keeping it brief, I attached. This isn't something I normally did right away. (A couple months in was when the "crazy" would begin.)

But something about "B" made me "crazy" from the start. Looking back, I think it was because he was very good at getting me to confess my feelings for him without reciprocating. I often felt I was standing out on a tall tree limb by myself. He'd ask me to go there and when I turned around I felt like he was back on the ground waving up at me. When I asked him about this he said, "It's not my fault if I'm better at getting you to tell me how you feel than you are with me."

It's hard to argue with that line of thinking.

There was no courtship with "B." Mostly because I sabotaged any chance of that. Some days he was attentive and wonderful. Some of the things he said were some of the nicest things a man had ever said to me. But in the "in between" times, I allowed my head to spin out of control. I couldn't sleep. I was consumed with mass amounts of insecurity and uncertainty and I literally had no idea how he felt about me. If anything *I* was courting *him*. *He* was challenging *me*.

Instead of having confidence and realizing it just wasn't meant to be, I kept pushing it. It was my best friend at the time who eventually said the words which opened my eyes: "I don't like you when 'B' is in the picture. And I bet you don't like yourself."

She was right. I didn't. I do, however, like that my experience with "B" helped me to see many things I was doing wrong. It taught me the importance of keeping a level head. And it made me realize that a relationship which makes you feel insecure, unsettled, or filled with confusion is not a relationship worth having. But the thing I like best about my time with "B" is that he is a huge reason why I do what I do; why "Jenn X" was first created. And for that, my dear "B," I'll always be grateful you came into my life.

XX

Step #7

From courtship to commitment.

I know how frustrating the dating process can be. I know how hard it is to find someone who you are crazy about and who is crazy about you in return. I know what it's like to over think, over analyze, and over critique every step of the way. And there's not much that is more difficult than waiting for a man to be ready to commit to you.

I've often read it takes most men three to six months to get to a place where they want a commitment. How different is it for us women? We'd usually like a relationship in three to six minutes! All it takes is a couple great dates and we're already thinking "boyfriend." So letting a man get there on his own takes patience and self-control.

If you employ the techniques in the preceding chapter, it actually makes things a bit easier. Using courtship as an opportunity to reserve judgment, get to know him, and to let him step up to the plate can actually help you to relax. And the better you conduct yourself during that period, the faster he will want to be with you exclusively.

DATING RULE #73:
The amount of time it takes for him to get to "commitment" is directly proportionate to how proper your courtship period is.

It all goes back to "investment." If he's properly courting you (and you are allowing him to do so), he's investing a lot in you. He's taking you out and beginning to attach emotionally. You are becoming a part of his life. And as he's investing, he's becoming protective of that investment. He's starting to see you as "his girl." He's not going to like the idea of another man coming in and stealing what he's worked so hard to earn.

So here we are, facing the age old question, "How do we get a guy to want to commit to us?" The short answer is: "We don't." At least not in a way which makes it obvious or puts pressure on him. Instead, what you need to do is show him you are the type of woman he should want to commit to. And if you've been paying attention to this book so far, you are already doing exactly that.

DATING RULE #74:
A goddess never puts pressure on a man to commit. But because she is so desirable, a quality man will want a commitment on his very own.

From the very beginning, a man analyzes whether you have long-term or short-term potential. He's figuring out whether you are someone he just wants to hang with for a bit (or hit and run) or whether you've got what it takes to keep his attention. Laying the right foundation in the first few months is critical to whether or not you're the girl who will inspire him to turn off his "available light" and turn on the "no vacancy" sign.

However, it's important to note you should never want a commitment with a man just for the sake of getting a commitment. That's not necessarily the goal. You should only ever entertain the notion of exclusivity if you are sure he's someone worth committing to. *The point of courtship is to determine if he is boyfriend material.*

From courtship to commitment.

When it comes to monogamy, here's what you have to know. The number one thing men prize and are afraid to lose is their freedom. Just the thought of words like "commitment," "girlfriend," and "relationship" – especially when uttered too soon – will send many men into a full-fledged panic attack. He begins to envision his Sundays – once filled with football, beers, and his boys – now spent with you at Bed, Bath, and Beyond shopping for throw pillows. He believes every Friday night will consist of dinner and a chick flick. Not to mention all the other women he wonders if he will miss out on... It's a miracle any of us make it to girlfriend-land, isn't it?

I'm sure we can all relate to this reader's question.

Dear Jenn,

I've been dating a guy for about three months and he is awesome! I'm following your advice and watching his character. I've been going slowly and doing everything you say.

One problem, though: I really want a commitment and he hasn't mentioned it yet! I'm starting to get a little impatient. Is he ever going to bring it up? Should I ask him his thoughts on making things exclusive? I'd rather he initiates that conversation, but I don't want to keep dating without a commitment for all eternity. How do I get him to seal the deal?

Hailey

Alright, all you "Haileys" out there. I'm here to tell you exactly how to get a man to commit to you. And not only to commit, but to commit happily all on his very own and without any regrets later on. Sound good? I bet it sounds fantastic. So if you've decided you'd like to have a relationship with the man you've been dating, let's get started.

**THE FIVE LITTLE "c'S" TO GET TO THE ONE BIG "C"
– COMMITMENT**

- Pick "c"arefully.
- Be "c"ool.
- Practice "c"hastity.
- Be "c"onfident.
- Keep your mouth "c"losed.

Pick "c"arefully

No matter how hard you try, some guys are just not fit for a real commitment. You could be the smartest, most beautiful woman on earth. You might be a goddess in every possible way. But if he's not boyfriend material, you should never attempt to make him your boyfriend. And that's the bottom line.

Yet women do this all the time, don't we? We try to convert playboys into priests, a-holes into angels. We think if we wear down the edges just enough, that square peg will fit into a round hole. We suffer untold heartbreak in an attempt to make it so. I say it's time to stop. If you want a relationship with a man, you have to make sure he's relationship material.

DATING RULE #75:
You can only have a healthy relationship with a man who is relationship material.

If you're doing your homework and following this guidebook, you've been doing this from the first moment you met him. You've been looking at his character objectively and taking notice of his behavior. You have passed on the "deal breakers" and the "Mr. Wrongs." You have only attached yourself to a quality guy and you have let the unacceptable ones go. If – and only if – everything checks out, should you want to move on to a commitment.

From courtship to commitment.

In addition to being of good character, a man also has to be open to a relationship. Many women want to ignore the warning signs that the man they are casually dating isn't interested in a commitment. Here's a typical question I receive about this.

Dear Jenn,
I've been seeing this guy a lot recently. He keeps asking me out and we just slept together for the first time. The big problem is he told me from the start he doesn't want a relationship or a girlfriend. I really like him and I don't want to become a booty call. Do I keep seeing him and hope he changes his mind about the girlfriend thing?
Misty

Listen up, ladies. One of the fastest paths to heartbreak is to get involved (especially physically) with a man who has told you straight-up he doesn't want to be in a relationship. These men rarely change their minds. You won't be able to woo him with great sex or by being as close to perfect as a woman can get. If you attach to a man who has been honest about his intentions with you, you only have yourself to blame when you are unable to secure a commitment.

On the flip side, I've had many a confused man ask me why women do this. "I've told her I don't want a relationship, why does she think I'll change my mind?" they ask me. My answer to them is always the same. "First off, if you've told her point blank you don't want a relationship, it's not your fault if she keeps moving forward with you and ends up hurt. Secondly, many women have the delusional belief they can get a guy through sex. They think once he's gotten a taste of her he'll be unable to let go."

We goddesses know it doesn't work that way. We know it is how we conduct ourselves – not our sexuality – which makes a man want to be with us. If we want a relationship and the man doesn't, we move on.

How to Be a Goddess

Being "open" doesn't mean that he's specifically looking for monogamy. Most men aren't, actually. At least not in the beginning. Being "open" just means he's not totally opposed to the idea. So how do you determine that?

IS HE "OPEN" TO A RELATIONSHIP IN THE FIRST PLACE?

Listen to what he says, but always pay more attention to what he does. If there's ever a discrepancy between the two, it's how he acts that counts. "Actions speak louder than words" is a cliché because it's true.

■ Check out his friends. Who does he spend his time with? Are the vast majority of them single, "player" types? If he's loving "the scene," he might not be ready to settle down with just one woman. Further, if his friends tease him about being a player in front of you, it's probably because he is one.

■ What about his career? Does he work so much that he doesn't have time for a relationship? If he's consumed with his job, he won't have much energy left for you.

■ Is he recently single? Has he just gotten out of a serious relationship or gone through a divorce? Unless he's a serial monogamist who just wants a woman for the sake of having a woman (and you don't want one of those, by the way), most men need some "single time" after a relationship. If it was long or especially traumatic, he'll be good for no one for at least a year afterward.

■ If he lets you know from the beginning he isn't interested in "anything serious," believe him. If that's what you want — especially if that's what you want with him in particular — run. Waiting around or trying to convince him to change his

---

146

mind is heartbreak waiting to happen. Better he sees you as the girl who got away than the girl who tried to pressure him into a relationship.

- If he tells you things like, "I don't ever want to get married (again)" or "I never want kids," take him at his word. If it's important to you to keep those options open, don't waste months or years of your life with a man who doesn't share your goals.

- By far the biggest clue is how he treats you during the courtship. If he acts like a boyfriend, he's open to being your boyfriend. If he doesn't, he's not. Never, ever ignore this.

DATING RULE #76:
A goddess watches to see whether he's truly open to a relationship. If he's not, she moves on and doesn't try to convince him otherwise.

I'd like to also point out I think women make a mistake when it comes to classifying guys who don't want to be "a boyfriend." Just because he's not interested in a commitment doesn't mean he's an a-hole. A guy can be a "good guy" and still not be ready for exclusivity. In fact, a quality guy who doesn't want a girlfriend will be honest about it. An a-hole will lie to you, become your boyfriend, and then cheat on you with a skank in a tube dress. Which one would you rather deal with? So if he tells you he's not interested in getting serious, thank him for being direct and then find someone who is.

Be "c"ool
Let me tell you a great way to get him to *not* want to commit: Start treating him like he's your boyfriend before he's actually your boyfriend.

Yes, you want *him* to act like he's a boyfriend during courtship. But how *you* behave is completely different.

DATING RULE #77:
Don't act like a girlfriend before you're his girlfriend!

HOW TO ACT LIKE YOU'RE HIS GIRLFRIEND*
(*And Scare Him Away As a Result)
- Start calling him daily and for no reason in particular.
- Send him sweet and loving texts and/or emails in the first couple of months and before he's done the same. Wake him up with texts which say, "Good morning, handsome!"
- Write him a love letter telling him you've "never felt this way before."
- Bake cupcakes and show up at his work unannounced to deliver them. Or show up unannounced anywhere you know he'll be. With or without the cupcakes.
- Tell him, "I love you" before he's even said, "I like you."
- Ask him to accompany you to all of your family and work functions. Automatically assume he's your "plus one" and begin booking up his schedule.
- Keep tabs on him. Question his comings and goings. Request he "checks in" when he gets home at night.
- Send his friends and family members Facebook friend requests.
- Make it super obvious you have no intention of dating anyone else. Ever again.

I've been told by a few people that my references to a woman baking cupcakes for a man are unrealistic. "Women don't really do that, do they?" they ask me. I can assure you they absolutely do. Just ask my friend Brian. After his first date with Tina, she had a batch of home-made cupcakes delivered to his office.

"Don't get me wrong, they tasted good. But I thought it was a little strange. Creepy, actually. I mean, it's one thing if a girl you're dating cooks dinner every once in a while. This was very different." he told me.

Even though he quickly told Tina he didn't see a future with her, she continued to act like Julia Childs and kept the baked good coming.

"The next week she showed up at my house with chocolate chip cookies."

"What did you do?" I asked him.

"I invited her in and we had sex."

Who's the big loser in this situation? Tina, of course. She's out a few bucks in baking ingredients and the several hours she spent in her kitchen cooking for a man who wasn't serious about her. The big winner? Brian. Both his libido and his stomach were satisfied thanks to her culinary efforts.

I've also had several friends who engaged in "girlfriend behavior" well before they were actually girlfriends. One brought lunch for a man's entire work group – after only a couple of dates. Another invited a guy to a friend's wedding even though she'd only known him for a week. And yet another made a mix CD for a man who'd taken her out twice. "To say thank you for dinner," she explained.

What women who engage in this type of behavior fail to under-stand is that up until the time of commitment, acting as if there's a commitment is *his job and his alone.* When you take on the role of "girlfriend" before there is an actual commitment, he feels pressure. This pressure always works against you because no man wants to feel pressured into being your boyfriend! Likewise, the reverse is also true. The less he feels pressured to be your boyfriend, the more he will work to become your boyfriend. So stay cool and let him do his thing. As long as you act interested in him and responsive to him, he'll keep coming toward you.

Practice "c" hastity

Hopefully I scared you so much in the previous chapters you'll be keeping those pants on for a long time. So I'm not going to beat a dead horse here. But I do think it bears reiterating that one of the biggest factors in determining if and when he commits is how quickly you sleep with him.

A quality man doesn't want to be committed to a woman he thinks gives it up indiscriminately. And unless your reputation precedes you, the number one way he determines this is by how quickly you sleep with him. Jump straight into bed and he'll be flattered at first. He'll think you were so overcome with his studliness you just couldn't help yourself. But very quickly, he'll start to wonder how many men you've found equally studly.

Never forget that once you have sex, the biggest part of his mission has been accomplished. All too often that's when the "courtship" ends and he feels less of an inclination to pursue you. So I say it's best to wait until there's a commitment.

Dear Jenn,

I think I made a big mistake. Here's what happened:

Last week, I had sex with the guy I've been dating for a couple of months. We aren't officially boyfriend/girlfriend yet but we've both made it clear we aren't seeing anyone else. So far, it seems like every-thing is still going okay – he's still the same great guy – but I'm nervous it will make him less likely to make things "official" with me. Can you give me any advice?

Caroline

Wouldn't it be great if relationships always went according to plan? Sometimes they don't and we have to make adjustments. Maybe you are in Caroline's situation. Maybe you have slept with a guy you're dating seriously but before there's an expressed commitment. If that's the case, it's very important you don't slip into "beck-and-call-girl" status. You aren't his booty call. He doesn't get to come over late at night just for sex. He can't go out with his friends, get drunk, and "hook up with you later." If he takes you out on a *real date* and you have a sleepover afterward – okay. Anything less and you'll find yourself moving further away from girlfriend status, not closer to it. Always remember that you aren't his girlfriend just because you've slept with him.

DATING RULE #78:
Sex does not equal a commitment, at least not in his mind.
Be "c"onfident
Men rarely commit to a woman who is needy. Revolving your world around him and making him the center of your universe is not the trick to securing a relationship. In fact, that's the stuff which makes him much less likely to commit.

Keeping busy with your life, having interests besides him, and doing your own thing are actually what draw him toward you. Women are often tempted to think that if we make a man our be-all, end-all, that's what will seal the deal. Why? *Because we expect them to think like us.* We think that just because we want a man to make us his world, that's what they want as well. They don't. So let's stop acting like they do.

Early on in my "Jenn X" career, I received an email from a woman that illustrated this point perfectly.

Dear Jenn,
I've been with my boyfriend for two years and initially things were great. But lately it's been awful...

> We are both in medical school and we moved in together right when we started dating. I've lost most of my friends because of our relationship and my whole world revolves around him. I've been neglecting my studies to spend time with him and I have exams coming up. I feel like everything in my life is falling apart.
>
> He recently decided to move out and he's completely pushed me aside. He acts busy and irritated when I call and he often doesn't call me back. I told him to end it if he's so unhappy but he says he doesn't want to. I'm not sure I can survive without him.
>
> What should I do? Please help!
>
> Anna

So often, women revolve their lives around a man like he is their sun. Everything else becomes secondary – her work, her friendships, her hobbies, even her family. This doesn't create for healthy relationships. Anna is proof that even smart women with stellar education levels can make stupid decisions when it comes to men.

Men commit to a woman who is confident and in charge of her own life. They want a woman who knows how to pay her bills and can handle her business. A quality man doesn't want to rescue a damsel in distress. He doesn't want someone he has to "fix." A solid and complete man will never want a woman who acts like she would be unstable or incomplete if he's not in the picture. Keep in mind that if he's the type of guy who wants a woman like that, he's got some serious issues.

DATING RULE #79:
A quality man commits to a woman who can confidently handle her life whether or not he's a part of it.

Keep your mouth "c"losed
Men hate the dreaded "talk." You know what I mean, right? It's the discussion where we bring up questions like:

- "Where is this going?"
- "Do you see things becoming long-term with me?"
- "How do you feel about having a relationship/making things exclusive/being my boyfriend?"

Do not do this. Ever.

I'm of the belief you should never bring up the whole commitment talk. I think the best relationships are those where the man gets to that place on his own. I'd much prefer being with a man I am certain wants to be with me and me alone, than a guy I had to subtly (or not so subtly) pressure into a relationship. How about you? If you've followed my advice so far, you've conducted yourself in a way which lets him know you're not the type of girl he could date casually for all eternity. You'll have differentiated yourself from the pack. You'll have held yourself out as a prize and he's going to want to keep that prize all for himself. I know it can be tough to wait, but remember that patience is a virtue and delayed gratification is a sign of maturity. Stay calm and let him come to you. If he's the man you think he is, he will. Usually right around the three to four month mark.

DATING RULE #80:
A goddess never initiates "the talk." In fact, words like "commitment" and "exclusivity" are not uttered during courtship.

But what happens if you've been dating for months upon months and no commitment cometh? What then?

Dear Jenn,

When the hell is he going to ask me to be his girlfriend?? I've been trying to be patient but it's been 7 MONTHS!!!

It's getting VERY DIFFICULT to not say anything!! I know he's not seeing other girls so why won't he just ask me to be his girlfriend already?? Help!!!

"Freaking Out"

How to Be a Goddess

The first thing "Freaking Out" and all women in her position should do is look back over his words and actions. Did he attempt to tell you he didn't want a relationship but you decided to ignore that conversation? Does he show you by the way he treats you that he thinks of you as a potential girlfriend? Are you confident he is not dating other women? Have you refrained from giving him the nookie? Is everything else moving along smoothly – no big fights or blow ups – and all systems seem good to go? Is the lack of an articulated commitment the only sign anything is amiss?

If it's been six months or longer and he's made no mention of it – and everything else is A-OK – it might be time to assess his procrastination. Keep in mind this isn't "the talk." You are merely trying to ascertain where he stands without putting pressure on him. The bigger you make this, the more likely he is to back away. So wait for the right time (specifically when you are both happy and in a good mood, not after a fight) and do this once. And I mean *once*…

When it's time to assess his interest in a commitment

- Never start with the words "We need to talk." This will scare him away faster than you can say "wedding reception." It sets a bad tone and makes him feel like he's done something wrong. He's instantly put on the defensive and won't be receptive to what you have to say. Instead try this: "You're such a great guy! I've really been enjoying our time together." Warm fuzzies, right? And now you've made him feel good and open to what you have to say next.
- Make it a statement, not a question. Say something like, "I've been thinking it through…" This shows you are logical and rational and not acting like every other emotionally needy woman who wants a boyfriend just so she can be in a relationship.
- Follow it up with "…and I'd be open to dating you and you only." I think this statement is brilliant, if I do say so myself. Look at what you've done. You've (a) let him know you think you'd like to see him exclusively without putting direct pressure on him because,

well, you aren't 100% certain, (b) it plants the seed in his brain that if he doesn't snatch you up, some other guy will, and (c) you haven't mentioned any "scary" words like monogamy, commitment, or girlfriend. In fact, you've let him know that nothing will change. You're still the cool, classy girl he's been dating. The only difference? Going forward, you'd be dating only him.

- Now what? Now you shut your mouth and listen to what he says. Seriously. Shut it. Make sure he is the next to speak.
- Be prepared to walk if you don't get the response you want. Here are the only acceptable things he can say back:

"I've been thinking the same."

"I'd like that, too."

Or some variation of either.

If he hesitates and changes the subject? If he says he's not ready, is unsure, or wants to keep things "as is?" If he seems reluctant? Drop it. You've gotten your answer. Keep dating him if you like, but be sure to make yourself less available. Get busy with your friends and start accepting dates from other guys. Don't act like he's your boyfriend if he doesn't want to be your boyfriend.

If you don't like what you hear and you don't want to see him anymore, that's fine, too. In either scenario, maybe he will eventually come around and maybe he won't. Only time will tell. But whatever you do, don't try to talk him into it. Even if he agrees, you'll eventually end up driving him away.

To sum it all up

Moving from courtship to commitment without pushing him may not be quick. It may not be especially easy. But it is totally achievable. I once asked a male friend when my boyfriend was going to bring up the subject of exclusivity. He said, "Probably two weeks after you think you can't stand it anymore." He was exactly right.

How to Be a Goddess

My hope for you during this time is that you are patient. That you keep doing your "goddess-like" thing and don't obsess over his time-frame. I hope that he is so taken with you that he cannot resist making sure you are his and his alone. I hope he wants that commitment not just to apply to you, but that he really, really desires to be faithful to you in return. And I hope you'll allow him the opportunity to make it official.

Let's face it. There's not much better than the man you're crazy about asking you to be his girlfriend and then feeling like the luckiest guy on earth when you say, "Yes."

DO AS I SAY, NOT AS I DID
(My Own Journey from Doormat to Goddess)

I'm not a particularly patient person. My parents may have done a lot of stuff right, but one thing they failed to instill in me was the joy of delayed gratification. To top it all off, I'm also a pretty ambitious, type-A personality. I'm one of those people who will push the button for the elevator until it arrives and the "walk" sign until it changes. I have the delusional belief that if I want something to be, I will make it so, goshdarnit.

For most of my dating career, I had the same attitude about relationships. Here's how mine played out: I'd meet a guy. I'd like him. I'd want to "win." And so after a few weeks of dating, re-gardless of how things were going, I'd make him my boyfriend.

It's true. I pushed for commitment and initiated "the talk." I wanted control and to know exactly where things were going. I was not content to let things happen naturally and when the man in question was truly ready to be with me and me alone. Invariably, they acquiesced to my wishes. Although I might have "won," my behavior didn't result in successful relationships.

My dating history might look decent on paper. My college boyfriend and I were together for two and a half years. Next was my post-college beau who I spent two years with as well. "J" and I were a couple for the better part of four years. And my marriage lasted for over eight. There were a few short-term guys in between and many first dates. But as I told you, I have been a serial monogamist.

How many of those men ended up cheating on me? I'm not sure, but with the exception of my ex-husband, I am fairly confident all of them did. My tactics might have gotten me a "boyfriend," but my relationships were more nightmares than the stuff of dreams.

It wasn't until after my divorce and other dating disasters that I began to really think about what it means to be courted and to have a man come to me instead of the other way around. Although I always knew how it *should* work, it wasn't until then that I actually *let it* work that way. So I decided to take my hands off the wheel and stopped trying to control both the man and the situation.

What an amazing sense of relief! What an incredible feeling it is to practice patience. What an awesome thing it is to be with someone you are sure wants to be with you for who you are and not because you've pushed him into it.

Relationships are tough enough. One thing I've learned is that being with a man who really, really wants to be right where he is makes everything else that much easier.

Step #8

How to love your boyfriend. Goddess-style.

So you've got yourself a boyfriend, huh? Awesome! I'm excited for you! When you've got a good guy by your side, there's a lot of joy that comes with being his girlfriend, isn't there? And yet, there's also a lot of work that needs to go into maintaining and cultivating a healthy relationship. Just because you now have a commitment doesn't mean your job is complete. Not even close. Just like our man has to keep working at the relationship, so do we. There are things we can do that not only will make him happy, but will encourage him to treat us the way we want to be treated.

Dear Jenn,

I've been following your advice for some time now and I have to tell you – it worked! The guy I've been dating just told me he wants to make things exclusive and he is now officially my boyfriend! Yay!

So here's my question: What do I do now? How can I keep being a goddess now that I'm in a relationship? I haven't always been the best girlfriend in the past and I really want to do things differently with this guy. He's awesome!

How do I make sure my goddess-behavior continues?

Lisa

What is it exactly that both men and women need to feel content and fulfilled in a relationship? Here's the short answer: We both need to feel loved. This may sound simple enough, but it is actually quite complex. Why? *Because what translates as "love" to each gender is really very different.* In a man's mind, he feels loved when he is respected. To a woman, love means that she is adored.

DATING RULE #81:
Women feel loved when they are adored. Men, however, feel loved when they are respected.

The things which make men feel loved are not always the same as those which make us feel loved. Women often make the mistake of loving a man in the way in which they themselves want to be loved. So the first thing we've got do when it comes to loving a man properly is to stop loving him the way *we* need to be loved and start loving him how *he* needs to be loved. Guess what happens when we do this? He loves us the way we need to be loved in return. Pretty cool, right?

Maybe some couples are able to do this naturally. But for most of us, especially if we didn't have good examples growing up, this is something we need to learn how to do. And we have to keep working at it throughout the lifespan of our relationship. It's most definitely an ongoing process. So let's take it piece by piece and break it down. But before I start, I have to include this caveat: Learning how to really love a man should only be attempted with one who is truly worthy of your love. If you are with someone who is not deserving of your respect, don't even bother. Only a quality man should ever be lucky enough to have a hold on your heart.

DATING RULE #82:
You should only respect a man who is worthy of your respect. And you should only love a man who is worthy of your love.

What makes a man feel respected?

In a man's mind, there are two components to respect.

A MAN FEELS RESPECTED BY A WOMAN WHEN SHE MAKES HIM FEEL...

Admired and Trusted

From his perspective, one of the reasons why it is so important for him to take the lead during courtship is because a man needs to feel like his opinions and decisions count. He needs to feel like he has a say in the course of the relationship and where it's going. Very few men want a domineering woman who tries to control him in order to get what she wants. When a woman tries to control a man, he does not feel respected.

Doug dealt with this with his ex-girlfriend Tracey. She often vetoed his suggestions on everything from restaurant choices to where they should vacation.

"It was her way or the highway," he recalled. "I often felt like I didn't have a say in the decisions. It's one thing to be strong. It's another thing entirely to be a dictator."

My friend John also dated a woman who didn't show him respect.

"As soon as we moved in together it was like I couldn't do anything right. She'd roll her eyes at me and would apologize to people on my behalf if she thought I said something silly. I started feeling like a total loser. Eventually I told her that if I was so terrible, she should find someone she liked better. So I moved out. And the whole time she was begging me not to leave. Go figure."

Something interesting has been going on in television commercials recently and it illustrates Doug and John's points perfectly. Maybe you've noticed it yourself, and if not, I'll bet you'll start to. In almost every ad that has some sort of male/female dynamic (like a married couple, for example), the man is portrayed as somewhat of a bumbling buffoon who can't seem to do anything right or figure anything out on his own. And his wife? She's the one who has to explain it to him or put him in his place. I like to call this the "emasculation of the modern male." Personally, I think it's awful. I'm not sure how it is in other countries, but here in America, it's practically an epidemic.

How did we get to the place where women want to lead men around by their noses? Do women really think weak and passive men are sexy? I sure don't. Any man who would let me emasculate him is not a man I would respect. And I think "the emasculation of the modern male" has become an enormous problem in many, many relationships. If I were writing a book to men, one of the things I'd tell them they need to do is get their balls back and stop letting a woman dictate their lives. Just as we should never accept a man who tries to dominate or control us, we should not want to dominate or control a man. Bust a guy's balls and you'll eventually end up with a guy with busted balls. And there is nothing attractive about that.

Men resent it, too. At first they may acquiesce and adopt the whole "happy wife, happy life" mentality. But it's not too long before they rebel. Some check out of the relationship, some escape into alcohol or fantasy football, and some even cheat. In fact, I have a lot of attached guy friends who are unfaithful to their wives and girlfriends. When I've asked them why they do it, more often than not they tell me it's because the other woman doesn't give them a rough time. She accepts them, makes them feel good about themselves, and doesn't try to boss them around. Take Mike for example. He's a (mostly) faithful husband who has been married for nearly twenty years.

"With my wife, everything is just so damn difficult. She either ignores me or she manages to find fault with almost everything I do. I'm not a good enough father. I didn't take the trash out. I don't dress well. Sometimes it's all too much. Most days I feel like I am her fifth priority – after our three kids and the dog. Yep, the dog outranks me when it comes to gaining her approval."

Listen, there's no excuse for cheating and I'm not trying to say that there is. But most men have egos which need to be treated carefully. They need to feel respected (trusted and admired) by the woman they are with. If they aren't, it's not too long before the relationship sours. And if he's a quality guy, busting his balls will eventually drive him away completely.

DATING RULE #83:
If you emasculate him, not only will you lose respect for him, but he will lose respect for himself. And it won't be long before he finds something or someone who builds him back up.

HOW TO EMASCULATE A MAN IN TEN EASY STEPS

- Tell him where you want to go and what you want to do each and every time you're together. Pick out every restaurant and movie you go to together.
- If he says something silly or makes a joke that isn't funny, roll your eyes and scornfully tell him he's lame. Especially do this when in public or while out with friends.
- Say things like, "You always mess this up," "You never do it right," or "Why do you think it's so difficult?"
- Grab whatever he's about to fix out of his hand and say, "Never mind, let me do it."
- Tell him he's doing something incorrectly and offer unsolicited advice on how to do it better.
- Offer unsolicited advice. Period.
- Become annoyed, irritated, or angry over the little things you think he does wrong.
- Try to change him. Tell him you don't like his friends or how he spends his free time. Insist he adopts your love of antiquing on Saturdays.
- Criticize him every chance that you get.
- Be adamant that things must be done on your terms and yours alone.

Women often take on the ball-busting role when they are in a relationship with a man they do not respect. They don't trust him. They don't admire him. Maybe it doesn't start out that way, but after a few mistakes on his part they begin to adopt the mentality their guy is just a "dumb guy" who can't do anything right. And so they have to do it themselves unless they want it done wrong or not at all.

> *Dear Jenn,*
>
> *I am at the end of my rope. I am constantly fighting with my boyfriend and it is completely draining me emotionally, mentally, and physically. He's always messing things up and it's like he doesn't even care about me or the relationship. Just last week, he completely forgot to pay our rent and when I got home tonight there was an eviction notice on the door! The madder I get about his mistakes, the more he checks out. I feel like I'm stuck carrying all the weight.*
>
> *I know I'm acting more like his mother than his girlfriend these days but I have no idea how to change things.*
>
> *Michelle*

Relationships like Michelle's are not healthy. Listen, if a man is not meeting your needs, you should not be with him. End of story. If he isn't a quality guy with good character, you will never respect him and (quite frankly) he's not deserving of your respect. But even a good man is human; he's going to make mistakes. Pointing out his flaws, telling him all the ways in which he disappoints you, or trying to control him and his behavior will only end up hurting both of you. So if he's worthy of your respect, be sure to respect him. And how do you do that? By showing that you admire and trust him.

The first component of respect: Being admired
Every man needs his woman to admire him. He needs to know you think he's smart, sexy, capable, and good. He needs to feel he's allowed to make mistakes and that you aren't going to think he's less of a man because of them. In short, he needs to feel like he's your superhero.

IS IT A BIRD? IS IT A PLANE? NO! IT'S YOUR BOYFRIEND!

Want to make your man feel like a "superman?" The trick is to make him feel admired without being clingy, needy, or fawning. Here's how:

- Compliment him on a job well done. "I'm so happy you picked that restaurant. Great choice and the food was amazing!"
- Praise him and his accomplishments. "You're so good at your job. I'm proud of you."
- Acknowledge his strengths. "I'm impressed with how well you handle difficult people."
- Be appreciative of the little things he does for you. "Thank you for dinner..." "Hanging that picture for me..." "Filling my car with gas." Never act entitled or like you are owed the things he does for you. Appreciation is a big piece of admiration.
- Tell him he's a stud and that you desire him physically. "You're such a good kisser."
- Learn to overlook little mistakes. Don't beat him up over the dumb stuff.

It's not about putting him on a pedestal or making him your be-all, end-all. It's about appreciating him and taking the time to show him that appreciation. If he's done his job during courtship, he has properly won you over. He's proven himself to be a quality guy of good character and has earned the title of "boyfriend." Once you are in a *healthy* relationship, you need to make sure you acknowledge all of the great things about him.

Kylee does this perfectly with her boyfriend Joseph. Every time he does something nice for her – whether it's taking her out to dinner or buying her a small gift – she makes sure she shows her gratitude. She also lets him know that she appreciates his great personal attributes as well.

"I try to never miss an opportunity to express how awesome I think he is and how happy I am to have him in my life. It's wonderful to be able to tell someone you think they are handsome, smart, funny – whatever – and to really mean it. It's a good reminder for both of you how lucky you are to have each other. I totally believe in building a man up. It works much, much better than tearing him down! Being appreciative of Joe makes him feel good and it makes me feel good, too."

DATING RULE #84:
A man needs to feel admired by the woman he is with. It's what makes him feel like a man.

The second component of respect: Being trusted

Trust encompasses so much more than simply fidelity, although that's definitely part of the equation. A man needs to feel you trust him not just with commitment, but that you trust him to handle his own business, your heart, and the relationship as a whole. He needs to feel you believe in him.

Dear Jenn,

I know I have trust issues. Every guy I have ever been with has cheated on me. Now I have this amazing boyfriend who has never given me any reason to be suspicious. But I can't shake the feeling he's going to cheat, too, and it's making me crazy. I don't like it when he goes out without me and I've convinced myself he's going to hook up with every girl he talks to. We've started fighting about it more and more and I know I am the root of the problem.

He keeps telling me I need to trust him and he will never hurt me that way. I'm having such a hard time doing that! Why can't I just trust him?
Melanie

How to love your boyfriend. Goddess-style.

I know it can be difficult to fully trust a man. Especially if you've had a few bad guys in your past who proved themselves to be untrustworthy. But as I said earlier, it is imperative you put your trust issues aside. Don't judge your new man based on the actions of an old one.

My boyfriend once told me the best thing I ever said to him was "I trust you." We weren't even talking about cheating or anything like that. In fact, those words came out of my mouth while he was cooking. He had mixed a whole bunch of ingredients together that, on paper, would seem like they'd make a horrible combination. He looked at me as he stirred and asked, "Do you trust me?"

I thought about it for a second. Not because I didn't trust him, but because I realized the greater significance of his question. When you tell a man, "I trust you," you are not only saying you trust his fidelity, but that you trust him to make good decisions. You are telling him you trust he is the man who he says he is and that he is trustworthy when it comes to handling your heart. It's a very big deal.

"I trust you," I told him. "Completely." And by the way, the meal was delicious.

"IN MY BOYFRIEND I TRUST"

Placing your trust in a man should not be done lightly. Again, that's what courtship is all about – getting to know his character and determining if he's truly trustworthy. If he is and he becomes your boyfriend, be sure to show him you trust him.

- Don't try to tell him how he could do things better. Don't offer your two cents on everything he does. Let him make his own way.
- If he asks for your advice or opinion, give it. But always follow it up with a statement like, "I know you'll make the right decision."

- If you find out his best friend is cheating on his girlfriend, don't try to convince him to stop hanging out with him or suspiciously say, "You better never do that to me." Instead, tell him, "I'm so thankful you are a faithful guy and wouldn't hurt me like that."
- Don't micromanage him or watch over his shoulder as if waiting for him to mess up.
- Don't require that he give up boys' night or that he call you when he gets home. In his mind, giving him his freedom means you trust him.
- Don't accuse him of hitting on every girl he talks to.
- Never miss an opportunity to show him you believe and have faith in him. Always encourage him that he is capable of achieving his goals.

Never forget your trust is earned. You have the right to revoke it at any time should he betray that trust. But unless he gives you a reason not to trust him, show him that you do.

DATING RULE #85:
When you show a quality man you trust him, he will want to honor that trust.

When a woman admires and trusts her man, he feels respected. He feels esteemed. In his mind, this is exactly what he needs to feel loved by her.

Women are different, aren't we? The things which make a man feel loved are not necessarily what we need to feel loved. This is one of the reasons why relationships can be so tricky and confusing. Instead of loving the other person in the way he or she needs to be loved, we put our own expectations and desires on them. Women often try to love a man the way she wants to be loved. *Which doesn't make any sense to them.*

To figure out what it is we do wrong, let's first explore what makes a woman feel loved. In a woman's mind, she is loved when she feels adored. And, like respect, adoration has two components.

A WOMAN FEELS ADORED BY A MAN WHEN HE MAKES HER FEEL...

Cherished and Protected

DATING RULE #86:

When a man cherishes and protects a woman, she feels adored. In her mind, that translates into being loved.

The first component of adoration: Being cherished

What are the things which make you feel like your boyfriend cherishes you? When he surprises you with a gift or flowers? When he texts you something sweet randomly during the day? When he plans a romantic evening for the two of you? All of the above?

Like men, women need positive, verbal affirmations. But even more than that, we need concrete, tangible acts of love. We need time and attention. Most men are usually pretty good at instinctively knowing this. This is why a quality guy who really likes you is often very good at courtship. He knows what it takes to romance you – the dinners, the tokens of his affection, the sweetness. The slower you go during courtship and the longer you allow him to court you, the more this "cherishing" type of behavior will become a permanent part of your relationship. *To repeat: Do not sell yourself short during courtship!*

When I receive a question from a reader telling me her boyfriend doesn't exhibit actions that say, "I cherish you," I immediately wonder two things. First, did he treat her well during courtship? And secondly, how long did he court her before they became boyfriend and girl-friend? If you rush into a relationship with a man who didn't woo you, he won't start wooing you once he's your boyfriend. That's not the way it works.

Dear Jenn,

I've been having major problems with my boyfriend and I seriously need your help. I've been with him for a little over a year and a half. Although he says he loves me, I think his actions tell a different story.

The main problem is he really doesn't treat me like I'm his girlfriend. We have a good time if we're just hanging out, but as far as going on dates, being romantic, or anything else couples are supposed to do – that stuff is non-existent. I feel like he sees me as more of a "friend" than his girlfriend.

I've talked to him about it and we've even gotten into fights over it. He always says the same thing: He's just not a romantic guy and I should stop trying to change him. Truthfully, I didn't think he was very roman-tic when we first started dating and I had hoped it would change once we were in a relationship. Of course it hasn't.

Is there anything I can do? I'm tired of feeling like I'm not that special or important to him.

Jill

DATING RULE #87:
If he didn't act like a boyfriend during courtship, he will not act like one once he actually becomes your boyfriend.

Having a boyfriend for the sake of having a boyfriend shouldn't be your goal. Instead, your goal should be to have a healthy, loving relationship – a relationship where you feel cherished. Anything less and you will never be fully satisfied. So if that guy you call your boyfriend doesn't treat you like you are the woman he cherishes *because you never required it of him*, you have one choice and one choice only. You need to tell him.

HOW TO EXPLAIN TO HIM THAT YOU NEED TO BE CHERISHED*
(*If You Never Showed Him Before)

Although this book is designed as a step-by-step guide beginning before you meet "the guy," some of you reading may already be in relationships. If this applies to you and you're involved in a less than ideal situation, now is the time to attempt to remedy it. As I often say, it's a lot easier to negotiate how you want to be treated in the beginning rather than attempting to fight for it later. But sometimes things are what they are. So try this:

- Start out the conversation on a positive note. Just like any time you need to discuss something "heavy" with a man, you should never do it during an argument, when one or both of you is in a bad mood, or if he's distracted with other things. Find a time when you are both happy and start with a compliment. Tell him something you admire about him. For example, wait until he says something funny and say, "You're hysterical. I love how much you make me laugh." Then smile and change the subject by...

- Citing an example of when he made you feel cherished – even if you can only recall one occasion. If he's your boyfriend, he can't be all bad, right? Say, "Remember when you took me to that French bistro? It was so fun and you really made me feel special."

- Explain – without getting angry or putting him on the defensive – you'd love to do more of those things with him and how they make you feel like he really cares about you (or "loves you" if you're at the "I love you" stage of your relationship.) Keep it brief.

> ■ Try this a couple of times and then watch what he does.
> If he attempts to be more romantic, praise him and thank
> him. Show him you've noticed the changes he's making. If he
> doesn't, you need to decide if you're okay with that. If you
> want to feel cherished and he's not making an effort, will
> you ever really feel loved? If you won't (I know I wouldn't),
> that is a total deal breaker.

For those of us who have worked to be goddess-like from the very first time we met our now-boyfriend, this shouldn't be so much of a problem. Why? Because we have only attached ourselves and committed to a quality man who pursued us and showed us that he grew to cherish us during a nice, long courtship. (Right, ladies? Right!) And as a result, our boyfriend/ girl-friend relationship is not much different than when he was courting us.

Even so, there comes a time in most romances when the man eases up on the "cherishment." Maybe he gets a bit complacent. Maybe he's just not a super romantic guy. Maybe you're going through a bit of a "dry spell." Or maybe the "cherishment pull back" hasn't happened for you – yet – and you want to decrease the chances of it happening at all. (Or to at least decrease its severity.)

Dear Jenn,

I think my boyfriend and I are in a rocky patch. Don't get me wrong, he's great.

However, I've noticed he's not as spontaneous and romantic as he was in the beginning. He lets me make all the plans and I'm pretty sure if I didn't, we'd be sitting on the couch every Saturday night watching sports. I know we both have to keep working at "the spark." I'd appreciate some tips on how to do that!

Thanks!

Lindsay

Here's the mistake most women in Lindsay's situation make to keep a man in cherishment mode: We "cherish" them. That's correct, we employ the moves which should be theirs in an effort to get (or keep) the cherishment coming around to us.

HOW A WOMAN ATTEMPTS TO CHERISH A MAN HOPING HE'LL CHERISH HER IN RETURN

Much like how a woman will court a man, a girlfriend often tries to cherish her boyfriend in an attempt to make him cherish her more. She thinks that by being sweet, affectionate, and loving, he will do the same.

- She writes him love letters.
- She buys him gifts.
- She cooks and cleans for him. She thinks the way to his heart is through domestic bliss.
- She plans the dates and is willing to pay.
- She sends him thoughtful texts throughout the day or posts cute notes on his Facebook wall.
- She says, "I love you," ten times every twenty four hours.
- She says, "I miss you," when it's been one day since she's seen him.
- She starts to initiate all of the affection and non-sexual touching.
- She gives up her friends, hobbies, and interests hoping he will want to spend more time with her.
- In essence, she treats him the way she wants to be treated and loves him in the way she wants to be loved.

Am I saying that a woman should never be sweet or loving to a man? Of course not. My point is we cannot give cherishment in an effort to get it ourselves. If your guy is acting like he cherishes you easily and freely, you should absolutely give it back. If he texts you that he loves you, text him back that you love him, too. If he tells you how crazy he is about you, tell him you feel the same way. If he takes you out on a fabulous date, absolutely thank him profusely and tell him how wonderful he is. Just like in courtship, you always need to be responding. When he's putting himself out there, the best way to encourage his good behavior is to mirror him and to praise him.

DATING RULE #88:
When he is cherishing you, respond to it by letting him know you cherish him and appreciate him, too.

Once you pass the courtship period and are now in a committed relationship, you also need to be *reciprocating*. Reciprocating is actually different than responding. To understand this further, think of responding as a direct result to his actions.

- "Thank you for dinner."
- "I like you, too."
- "I'm looking forward to this evening. Thank you so much for planning it."

Those are examples of responding and you should start them from the beginning and never stop. Reciprocating, on the other hand, means that you start to take some initiative and begin to do things for him, too.

During courtship, I'm of the opinion that only very rarely should a woman ever open her wallet. It's okay to, on occasion and after several dates, buy him an ice cream cone or a glass of wine. But you should never buy him gifts or expensive dinners. That's his job.

Once you are living in girlfriend-land, you absolutely have to start reciprocating. Treat him to breakfast one morning. Cook him dinner one night. Again, the *vast majority* of the dates and the romance must be coming from him, but you need to do your part as well. No man wants to feel like he is being used for his bank account or for what he can provide. By reciprocating, you show him you are now investing in both him and in the relationship. And he absolutely needs to feel that.

Here's the rub: Men don't feel loved just because you reciprocate and begin to do "loving" things for them. The way to his heart is not through planning a candlelit dinner for two at a five-star restaurant. Yes, that's how *you* feel cherished. He may appreciate the gesture, but it doesn't translate as love (respect) to him. And it won't make him become more loving toward you.

DATING RULE #89:
You need to reciprocate in order to be fair, but not as a means to get more love.

When Yvette felt her boyfriend's cherishment going cold, she attempted to warm things up by doing loving things for him.

"I started inviting him to romantic dinners and I even planned a vacation to Hawaii. I thought if I was more romantic, he would be, too. Instead, I felt him slipping away even further. Men don't respond to those gestures the way we do."

So how do you do it? How do you get back that lovin' (cherishin') feeling? By appealing to him in a language he understands. Specifically, by respecting (admiring and trusting) him.

O ROMEO, ROMEO, WHEREFORE ART THOU ROMEO?

Has your man been lagging a bit in the romance arena? Is there more sputter than spark? Use these tips to kick start his engines.

- Don't complain, nag, or say things like, "You never take me out anymore."
- If he takes you out on a nice date tell him how much you appreciate it and how much fun you had. Tell him how wonderful it was to spend that time with him.

- Say, "You're the best" when he does something thoughtful and romantic and you will always make him feel like a hero.
- If he asks what you want to do, tell him straight up that what you want more than anything is for him to plan an evening for the two of you. Tell him how special that makes you feel and how much you love when he surprises you. Show him you trust him to plan an evening for you.
- Never tell him you don't like a gift. Unless it's a kitchen appliance. In that case you have my blessing to hurl the offending item at the wall. Of course I'm joking, but the reality of it is if a guy gives you a completely unromantic gift for a special occasion, he probably doesn't feel that romantic toward you. I know a guy who bought his girlfriend a toaster for her birthday. He claimed she loved it. I suspect they'll be breaking up soon. If it's anything other than a household electric, tell him his gift is incredibly thoughtful, sweet, and amazing. In fact, go into raptures over it. Seem ambivalent or blasé and you can forget about getting another gift anytime soon.
- If you want him to be more affectionate, tell him how much you love his touches, his kisses, and holding his hand.
- Remember positive reinforcement always works better than negative reinforcement. Praise much more than you criticize. Everything he does that you want him to keep doing, tell him how wonderful it is.
- If it's been weeks since he's planned anything more than sitting on the sofa, watching sports, and drinking beer (and therefore praise is not an option), follow the suggestions in "How to Explain to Him That You Need to Be Cherished." They'll work here, too.

Do you see what you're doing here? You are showing you respect him (by admiring and trusting him). You are communicating to him in a way he understands. You are loving him in the way he needs to be loved and as a result, he's much more likely to love you in the way you need to be loved as well. How great does that sound?

Yvette thought it sounded pretty great so she decided to give it a shot.

"Nothing else seemed to be working and my relationship was heading for disaster, so I figured what the hell. Instead of chasing after him, I pulled back and didn't put any pressure on him. I quit with the nagging and expressing my disappointment every chance I got. Almost immediately he started to warm up again. Whenever he would take me out or plan a special night for the two of us, I made him feel like a stud. The more I did that, the more he would romance me. Honestly, it worked like a charm and I'm happy to report that we are back on track."

DATING RULE #90:
As long as he's feeling respected (admired and trusted), a quality guy who is crazy about you will always strive to make you feel cherished.

The second component of adoration: Being protected

I'm not sure most men really understand how deep our need to be protected runs. For a woman to be vulnerable, soft, and open, she needs to feel she is in a safe space. She needs to feel the man she is with not only has her back, but her heart as well. As we feel protected, that is how we begin to trust. Protection (love to a woman) and trust (love to a man) are absolutely intertwined.

The best relationships are those which establish protection and trust slowly and over time. They are built bit by bit; right on top of the other. As we see that he protects us by being thoughtful, considerate, and gentlemanly, we begin to trust him. And that trust is the necessary foundation for a woman to truly feel secure and loved in the relationship.

Problems occur when courtships are rushed and the woman doesn't feel protected. The man hasn't earned her trust, but she's attached to him anyway. And so she often begins to test him to see if he really does protect her. It is this behavior that men will often call "psycho."

Dear Jenn,

Help! I've been with my boyfriend for about nine months and we've been living together for six of them. I've been very insecure about his feelings for me – almost from the beginning. I'm pretty sure he's still hung up on his ex and I'm not positive it is totally over between them.

He's been acting very suspiciously lately. He's on his phone a lot and never lets me see who or what he's texting. A few days ago I decided to check his email while he was at work. I didn't find anything from the ex, but he's been emailing with this other girl who he has always said was just a friend. The emails were flirtatious but I could tell that nothing has happened between them – yet.

When he got home I confronted him. He said they were just goofing around and there's nothing going on. He told me he couldn't believe I'd snooped through his email and that I was acting "crazy." I'm not crazy! But not trusting him is totally making me feel crazy. What should I do? Is there any hope for us?

Cheyenne

Cheyenne isn't alone. Just take a look at some of the common things women are capable of doing when they're in a relationship where trust and protection are don't exist.

HOW WE GO "PSYCHO" WHEN WE DON'T FEEL PROTECTED

- We make sure he knows about every other man who is interested in us. We think if we alert his competitive nature, he'll step it up. Show me a woman who tells her man, "OMG! That guy over there was totally hitting on me!" and I'll wager she doesn't think her boyfriend protects her and is willing to cause a bar fight just to prove herself wrong.

- We tell him about the office bitch we think is out to get us and become furious if he doesn't take our side.

- We check up on him, hack into his email and Facebook accounts, and snoop through his texts certain that he's up to no good. I actually knew a girl who went so far as to wear a wig, rent a car, and begin nightly surveillance on her boyfriend.

- We give up our friendships, hobbies, and other important aspects of our lives to make more time for him. And then we *demand* reciprocity. "I never go out with my friends. Why do you have to?"

- We ask how he feels about us, where we stand, or what he sees for us in the future. In fact, we obsess about such things because he hasn't shown us how he feels.

When a woman acts in these ways it is almost always because she has attached to a man who she does not feel protects her. She has given her heart to an unworthy guy and she is scared of what he's going to do with it. As a result, she's not giving him the trust he needs and the relationship is more than likely doomed from the start.

DATING RULE #91:
Unless he is a trustworthy man, you will never know what it is like to feel protected, and therefore truly loved.

When you are in a relationship with a man who protects you, not only will you not feel the need to search his drawers, you'll also be a lot less likely to micromanage and check up on him as well. Being "needy" or "clingy" is not even a thought in your head. You won't want to bust his balls to make him step up and be the man because *he* already is the man. And you'll be much more inclined to let the little things go. Who cares if he forgot to buy the milk when you've got a man who guards your heart?

On the converse, some women are conditioned to act as though they don't want a man to protect them. This is especially true as we move from our twenties into our thirties and don't want to feel like we have to rely on a man for anything. We can take care of ourselves just fine, thank you very much.

This is the attitude my friend Sabrina carries into her dealings with men.

"I'm a strong woman. Honestly, I don't need a man for anything. I make a great living, have fabulous friends, and my trusty vibrator is right by my bed if I'm feeling lonely."

Is it a surprise that Sabrina has been single for nearly a decade?

On one hand, Sabrina is right. We *can* take care of ourselves. But if you want a man in your life, you have to be willing to let him in. You have to be willing to let him protect you. It's what shows him that you trust him. And it doesn't make you needy to need a man.

NEEDING VS. NEEDY

Remember Dating Rule #4?... **Men want a woman who needs them, not a woman who is needy.** When you act "psycho" because you don't feel protected, you are being needy. Men don't like that. But men absolutely want to be needed by the woman they love.

- It's not politically incorrect of me to say that most men are just stronger than most women. It's biology! If you're carrying a heavy load, it doesn't make you a weak woman if he gives you a hand. *Needing* him is graciously saying thank you when he takes a bag from you. Being *needy* is expecting him to carry all of your stuff like he's your man-servant or getting upset when he doesn't hop to it and saying something like, "Are you going to carry this or what?"
- If there's something around your house or a work question you need help with, it doesn't mean you aren't capable if you ask for his aid. *Needing* him is showing you appreciate his skills and expertise. Being *needy* is demanding he drops whatever it is he's doing and immediately comes to your rescue.
- He needs his paycheck to be appreciated, not taken for granted. *Needing* him means he knows you appreciate how hard he works and that he shares the fruits of his labor with you. Being *needy* means you expect or demand he treat you like a princess and finance your way in life.

DATING RULE #92:
Needing a man doesn't make you needy. It demonstrates you trust him to protect you.

Men seem to understand this dichotomy better than women do. They easily see the difference between being needed and being with a woman who is needy. The former is imperative to their happiness in a relationship. No man wants to feel as though he is unwanted or unnecessary. Neediness, however, is a huge turn-off. One man I spoke with described it like this:

"I don't want to feel like she can't exist without me or that she expects me to take care of everything for her. That is neediness to me and it is very unattractive. The fact she wants a man to add to her life is not neediness. Appreciating what a man can bring to a relationship is crucial if you want a guy in your life. Having an air of 'I don't need a man' is just as unappealing as a woman who is so desperate that she'll cling to any guy who takes her to dinner."

Do you see how admiration and cherishment are linked? And likewise trust and protection? It's nearly impossible to have one without the other. As he acts in ways which show that he cherishes us, we begin to admire him for the man he is and for how he treats us. And as we learn that he is a man who will protect our hearts, we begin to trust him. This is how we love each other in the way in which we truly need to be loved. This is the way love works when it's at its ideal.

Those three little words

I can't very well write a chapter on love without discussing the actual declaration of love itself. Saying "I love you" may really be only three little words, but they are a very big deal.

Dear Jenn,
I have a debate going with my friends. We're arguing about who should say "I love you" first. They say it doesn't matter and whoever feels it

should just say it. Their opinion is if you say it and he doesn't say it back, at least you'll know. I think the guy should be the one to say "I love you" first. It seems like guys take a longer time to be able to identify their feelings for a girl as "love." And then they have to be comfortable enough to say it. I think if a woman says it too soon, it might scare him off.

What do you think?

Courtney

I completely agree with you, Courtney! In fact, I couldn't have said it better myself. I'm sure you've noticed I am a fan of letting the man set the milestones in the relationship. Saying "I love you" is no exception. Further, as Courtney astutely pointed out, men are often not as in touch with their feelings as women are. They may have a bunch of tender, warm, and even intense emotions for a woman, but they usually take awhile to recognize them as "love." If a woman says "I love you" before the man has time to process and identify his feelings, it can absolutely send him into a panic. It even has the potential to cause him to back off. He might think, "Whoa, she's moving too fast. I need to slow this train down."

I clearly remember the first time I realized I was in love with my boyfriend, "L." We were in Las Vegas at one of those cheesy dueling piano bars. We'd just had an incredible dinner at a steakhouse in The Wynn and seen a Cirque du Soleil show. (Yes, I felt especially cherished that night.) There he was, looking so handsome in his suit and tie, and there we were, laughing and people watching. I took a sip of my drink and looked over at him. In that one moment, it hit me.

"I am in love with this man."

At this point, "L" and I had been dating for exactly three months. Two weeks earlier, he'd asked me to be his girlfriend and took me to Vegas to mark the beginning of our new relationship.

Throughout our courtship, "L" was very direct about expressing his feelings to me.

How to Be a Goddess

"I like you," he'd tell me point blank. "A lot."

"I miss you," he'd say if I hadn't seen him in a few days.

He was consistent with texting and calling. He did what he said he was going to do. He made me feel cherished and protected. He courted me the way a woman needs to be courted and I allowed him the opportunity to do so. But had he said "I love you" to me? Not yet.

I knew a man like "L" – a man of good character – would not use those words lightly. He would say it when he really meant it and not just to get something he wanted or to placate me. He is the type of man who wouldn't say it back because he felt obligated. And I didn't want to mess it up by saying it too soon and before he felt the same.

Up until this point, my "I love you" stories had not been especially successful. Besides my father and close male friends, I had said those words to exactly four men. And I remember each and every time.

- I told "M," my college boyfriend, "I love you" first. Over the phone. He didn't really respond. Although he eventually told me "I love you" a couple of days later, it was on a card and he wrote "(gulp)" afterward.
- My post-college boyfriend, "R," actually said it to me first. We were standing out on his balcony overlooking the ocean. He had his arm around my shoulder and he squeezed me and said, "I love you." We'd only been dating for a few weeks and even though we'd been friends for years before that, I still felt like it was too soon. I think I mumbled back, "You, too."
- When I told "J" I loved him, he responded by giving me a blank stare. That was awesome. So my feelings got hurt, I got upset, and we got into a fight about it.
- My future ex-husband tried to tell me first. But I could see he was struggling to get the words out, so I thought I'd give him a hand.

"I know what you're trying to say. And I love you, too." A few days later he told me that I'd "stolen that moment" from him. Yeah, that pretty much made me feel like shit.

I didn't want to make the same mistakes with "L." Everything else about our relationship had been moving along so well. With him, things truly were "different." But I can't lie and say the wait was easy. It was actually torture and there were definitely moments when he'd do something incredibly cute or amazingly thoughtful and it was all I could do to not yell out, "I love you!"

But I didn't. I let him get there on his own. The wait felt like an eternity (actually it was only three weeks), but it was well worth it when he said, "I have to tell you something and I hope it doesn't scare you. But I am in love with you." What made it perfect was I knew he absolutely, positively meant it. And I was absolutely, positively certain when I said, "I'm in love with you, too."

DATING RULE #93:
A goddess waits for a man to say "I love you" first. That way, she knows he really, really means it. And she only says it back if he's a quality guy and she really, really means it, too.

So obviously, I get your struggle. You're in love with your boyfriend and dying to tell him so. Be patient. You've allowed him the opportunity to court you and to ask for a commitment; you should also let him tell you "I love you" first. That way, you'll know that he didn't say it back out of pressure or obligation and there will be no chance of receiving a blank stare.

I will, however, give you these tips for moving the process along and helping him feel confident enough to say those words.

WHEN "I LOVE YOU" IS RIGHT AROUND THE CORNER

- If he tells you how he feels about you, "I like you" for example, always say, "I like you, too." Don't ever let him think he's investing in you in vain. If he's putting himself out there, there's no need to be coy.
- In the beginning, use the "like" word in conversation. "I really liked that restaurant." "I like that shirt you're wearing." "I like spending time with you."
- As you move along, start to use the "love" word more and more. Make it a part of your vocabulary. "I really loved that restaurant." "I love that shirt you're wearing." "I love spending time with you."
- If he does something thoughtful, tell him you "loved" it. (Not *him*, mind you!) If he buys you a gift say, "Thank you! I love it!" and give him a kiss.
- See the signs he is getting close. They'll help you to relax. Right before "L" said "I love you," he put a note on my car that said, "I adore you, Jenn." This helped ease my worries that I would never hear those three little words from him.

The big picture

Do you remember the quote from the movie "Moulin Rouge" which says, "The greatest thing you'll ever learn is just to love and to be loved in return?" I've always thought that was beautiful. And I think it's completely true. At the heart of each of us – both male and female – is the desire to love and to be loved. It's what we search for throughout our lives. And if we don't get it, we long for it.

Loving a man the way in which he needs to be loved and being loved by a man who loves you the way in which you need to be loved is *truly love*. It's an amazing gift and one that is special and rare. Why? Because most people never think about it in that context.

So hopefully I've been able to shed some light on the subject. Hopefully you'll now look at love in a whole new way. It's not how someone else makes you feel. It's not all about what they can do for you. At the end of the day, the quality of love you receive is dependent on the quality of love that you give.

DO AS I SAY, NOT AS I DID
(My Own Journey from Doormat to Goddess)

I would like to share a small story about my marriage with you. I'm sure my ex wouldn't mind – I'm not revealing any big secrets here – and I think it does a good job of illustrating several points made in this chapter.

I should start out by explaining I have always been a safety conscious person. Yes, in my younger (and wilder) days, I threw caution to the wind from time to time. But as I've gotten older – and as a general rule throughout my life – I've always placed a high importance on personal safety. Maybe it was due to the fact I have a Sicilian mother. Maybe it's because I went to college in (essentially) South Central Los Angeles and often heard gunshots at night or stories of sorority girls being raped. It's probably a combination of a lot of things, but whatever the reason, it is who I am. I like locked doors and burglar alarms. I like seat belts and (at this point in my life) would never climb on the back of a motorcycle. I'm certainly not boring, but I absolutely know bad things can – and do – happen and I try my best to minimize those odds.

How to Be a Goddess

My ex was very different from me in this area. There were several times when he'd search for his keys in the morning only to discover he had left them hanging from the outside lock on the front door all night. He didn't grow up in a house where doors and windows were shut tight and he'd never had any sort of alarm system until we lived together. He'd open the door to anyone who rang and often forgot to bolt the door behind him.

How did this make me feel? Like I wasn't protected. Like my physical safety was not a priority. And how did I respond to that feeling? By not trusting him. By asking him if he locked the door and even when he said, "Yes," not believing him and getting up to check it myself. By becoming upset when he'd open the door and talk to anyone who was selling anything, no matter how shady I thought they looked.

Who was at fault? I think we both were. Protection in this area was never established and I never acted like I trusted him. I didn't feel adored. He didn't feel respected.

Obviously, this wasn't the reason why my marriage ended. But looking back, I can see its greater symbolism. It demonstrates that if we don't love each other in the *right way*, it often feels like there is no love at all.

XX

Step #9

Let's talk about sex.

Can I tell you how excited I am to write this chapter? I am *super* excited! Minus a couple of exceptions for one of my columns, I rarely ever talk about sex except to tell you to wait to have it. But here's my opportunity to get down and dirty and share a little nasty talk amongst girlfriends. Oh heeeeyyyyy!

I'd first like to start off by saying I know many of my readers have religious beliefs which include no sex outside of marriage. Personally, I think that's commendable and although I have never held myself out as a "religious writer" per se, I haven't been especially surprised my writing resonates with those ladies. As I've walked along this journey to relationship happiness, I've discovered many of the traditional – or sometimes labeled "old-fashioned" – rules are still applicable today. For example, the way to find fulfillment and contentment with men is not to be promiscuous, but instead to "save yourself" for someone who truly values you. I strive to include my own sense of morality, combined with the mistakes I've made and the resulting lessons I've learned, throughout everything I write.

So if you're one of my girls who will not be having sex until there's a ring on your finger and the wedding vows have been exchanged, I support you. But I do hope you'll read this chapter anyway. Just tuck it away when you're finished and be sure to break it out again when the time is right. Everything I'm going to say applies to you as well.

"The wedding night"

Just because the rest of us have decided not to wait until an actual wedding night to have sex, doesn't mean we shouldn't have a "wedding night." I once heard relationship expert Dr. Patricia Allen say something similar. She explained every relationship, whether or not it actually leads to a marriage, deserves a "wedding night." I loved that!

Dear Jenn,

My wonderful boyfriend and I have been dating for close to three months and I am finally ready to have sex with him! Since we've waited awhile, I think it needs to be an important occasion. I don't want it to happen after we've grabbed dinner at a fast food restaurant, if you know what I mean. Can you give me some tips for how to make it a great night without putting too much pressure on us?

Emily

A "wedding night" does not occur if you sleep with him on your second date after you've both had way too much to drink. A "wedding night" does not happen if it's not a special moment for both of you.

A "wedding night" is what you should wait for when consummating your relationship. It should be meaningful and it should represent what you two have built together emotionally during your relationship thus far. When a couple has a "wedding night" the woman is much more likely to feel cherished and protected. She's less likely to have morning-after regrets or begin to obsess about where she stands or the future of the relationship. Why? Because she already knows. Those details were established well before the "wedding night."

DATING RULE #94:
Your "wedding night" should be a physical culmination of everything that's been built throughout your relationship.

HOW TO HAVE A "WEDDING NIGHT"

- **Plan it.** It should occur on a night that is a bit more "special" than a regular date. Maybe it happens on your first trip together or after a big party or event. At the very least, it should take place after a romantic dinner.
- **Get it in your head it will be that night.** Yes, you can always back out or change your mind. But if you resolve to hold out until then, you'll be a lot more likely to wait until that particular evening.
- **He doesn't have to know about it.** If you *must* discuss it beforehand, then do. But men prefer to feel that sex is spontaneous. If you'd like, drop a hint. "Is it okay if I stay over after the New Year's Eve party?" Assuming you've followed my advice and haven't had a sleepover yet, that should be enough to get his mind racing. There's no need to exclaim, "Tonight's the night, lucky boy!"
- **Let him initiate.** Don't push him up against a wall or attack him. He needs to feel he has romanced you and won you over with his manly charms. This is another reason why he doesn't need to know your plan.
- **"Wear white."** Listen, he knows you're no virgin. But he doesn't have to be reminded you're no virgin. So save the dog collar and crotch-less panties for later on down the line.

How to Be a Goddess

A woman's struggle

I think one of the things that can make sex, and sexuality in general, difficult for women is we aren't really sure how we should view it. When we were young, we were often taught by parents and other traditional role models that sex was something we were not supposed to do. We learn "good girls don't" and "bad girls do." And then, as we grow up and hit the teenage years, we receive so many mixed messages. We see our friends starting to have sex. We're told by magazines a certain outfit or lip gloss or hairstyle will make us sexy. We see sixteen year-olds getting pregnant and raising babies on MTV. But yet, we still feel the pull that "good girls don't."

> *Dear Jenn,*
> *When I was young, I was told that sex was something that I wasn't supposed to do. Even though I was never "promiscuous," I still felt guilty when I had sex.*
>
> *I recently got married and I'm having a hard time thinking of sex as "good." I feel like there is something wrong with me and I'm not sure what to do. How do I alter my thinking and learn to enjoy sex with my husband now that it's something I'm supposed to do?*
> *Anastasia*

Anastasia isn't alone. Many women are in this predicament. We wonder how to transition our thinking that sex is "bad" to thinking that sex is "good" once we are in a healthy, committed relationship.

I discussed this topic during a recent talk show interview. The male host openly shared he had been involved with women whose "sex guilt" was apparent. He explained that men want to feel the woman they are intimate with enjoys being sexual. Of course they do! No one wants a partner who has sexual hang ups or acts like they'd rather be doing anything but *that*.

So instead of believing the lies that sex is "bad" or that we shouldn't enjoy sex, it's time we learn the truth. Here it is:

Let's talk about sex.

DATING RULE #95:
Good girls do. But they only do after a certain level of commitment and trust is established.

It can be very difficult to get out of the "good girls don't" mindset once you are in a committed relationship with a quality guy. It can be difficult to shift gears even after you are married. But it is essential that you do. How? *By giving your amazing man exactly what he needs from you sexually.* And what is it that he needs? Of course I'm going to tell you!

DATING RULE #96:
As the modern version of the famous saying goes, a man needs his woman to be a lady in the streets and a freak in the sheets.

Men don't want a slutty woman for a girlfriend or partner. He wants a girl he can bring home to mom. He just wants to know that girl's going to screw his brains out afterward.

Women usually make one of two mistakes. They either act like a "lady" all of the time or a "freak" 24/7. And neither one of those scenarios is appealing to a quality guy.

HOW A WOMAN ACTS LIKE A "FREAK" 24/7
- She wears extremely provocative clothing in public. Her boobs practically fall out of her top and her skirt is so short you can tell whether or not she's wearing underwear. Which she probably isn't.
- She talks about sex early on in the relationship. She goes into details and describes her sexual past with the men she dates. She shamelessly tells them every position, act, and location.
- She makes sexual jokes and innuendos starting on the first date. If he initiates such behavior, she doesn't politely put a stop to it. Instead, she joins in and seems to love every minute of it.

- She's made a sex tape with Ray J, Tommy Lee, Rick Soloman, or any D-List wanna-be. Her moment of glory came when it was the most popular search on Google.
- She has a stripper pole in her house.
- She talks to others about sex with her guy when he is present. "Last night, David did the *craziest* thing to me. He started by licking my…" Poor David won't be able to excuse himself fast enough.
- She sleeps with men quickly and without a commitment.

Danielle was one of those women who seemed to exude "Freak 24/7." She often slept with guys on the first couple of dates (or the first night she met them) and liked to boast about her conquests to males and females alike. Her Facebook profile pictures showed more skin than a Maxim spread and it was rare to see her in dresses larger than a postage stamp. The word "discretion" was definitely not a part of that girl's vocabulary. What were men's opinions of her? They considered her to be temporary, "good time only," and low-status. She allowed herself to be passed around from guy to guy and soon her reputation was mud.

Men want a woman who is a "freak," but they want her to be *their* "freak" and in the privacy of their bedroom. (Or living room. Or laundry room. Or hallway.) If you give the impression you sleep with men quickly and easily – usually by wearing your sexuality on your sleeve and by sleeping *with him* quickly and easily – he will think you are just a "freak." Period.

He also doesn't want a woman who acts like a "lady" all of the time. Seeming uptight, stuffy, or like you won't enjoy sex with him is a big time turn-off.

HOW A WOMAN ACTS LIKE A "LADY" ALL OF THE TIME

- She blushes, plugs her ears, or gets upset if he makes a sexual joke or comment early on. The correct response is to laugh a little, smile at him, and then change the subject.
- She downplays her physical attributes. She always dresses ultra-conservatively and keeps everything buttoned-up. Instead, you want to give *a hint* of sexuality. Expose your shoulders or just one part of your body at a time.
- She doesn't know how to flirt. She is not relaxed and seems rigid. Act rigid and he'll think you're frigid!
- She appears uncomfortable with touching. He places a hand on her knee and she stiffens. She gives him no signs she desires him physically.
- She becomes embarrassed or uncomfortable at the mere mention of the word "sex."

Veronica, a woman I knew, was extremely uptight about sex. In fact, whenever you brought up the subject of sex around her, she would go red in the face and attempt to change the conversation. If you wore a skirt that hit more than a few inches above your knees, she'd wither you with a disapproving look. I often wondered what kind of love life Veronica had with her husband. From my observations, they seemed to lack romance and passion and had a marriage which looked more like a business arrangement. And I know for a fact her husband had – at the very least – a wandering eye. Is it that surprising? If he's not getting it at home, it's not too long before he begins to seek it elsewhere.

So how do you balance the lady/freak dichotomy? If you've been reading this book and putting it into action, you'll be doing the things that make him see you as lady-like. You'll be feminine, charming, and dignified. You've shown him you're not promiscuous and you don't treat your body lightly. But you're also warm and fun. You know how to flirt and he sees you as a sexual being – he doesn't think of you as a family member or a platonic friend. Yes, he desires you sexually and thinks you'll be amazing in bed. Yet he also respects you and knows that you have high morals. That's what makes a goddess a goddess.

DATING RULE #97:
A goddess knows there is a time to be a "lady" and a time to be a "freak." And she has no trouble moving from one to the other.

This is how you reconcile the good girl vs. the bad girl mentality. You are not exclusively one or the other. You are both at the same time. But only with a quality man who is crazy about you.

How to blow his mind in bed
What do 99.9% of men want from their woman when it comes to sex? I think it can be broken down into five things. Here they are:

WHAT A MAN WANTS SEXUALLY

- He wants a woman who is comfortable with her body.
- He wants a woman who enjoys sex.
- He wants a woman who is open to experimentation.
- He wants a woman who is "dirty."
- He wants a woman who gets off.

He wants a woman who is comfortable with her body
I am well aware nearly every woman has some sort of body "issue." None of us feel like we're "perfect." Does it surprise you to know guys are much less critical of us than we are of ourselves? Yes, most guys

want a woman who is in good shape and looks like she takes care of herself. But very few will notice if your left boob is slightly bigger than your right or if you've got a dimple or two on the back of your thighs. (And if he does and disapprovingly points it out to you, he's not someone you want anyway.)

Guys find a woman who is confident in her own skin sexy. If you'll only have sex in pitch blackness or rush to cover yourself up afterward, it's going to turn him off much more than a slight pooch would. A man I know slept with a woman who instantly slid to the floor to grab her clothes while wrapping herself with a sheet after they were finished. He never had sex with her again. Likewise, if you're focusing more on how you look during sex than on the sex itself, he's not going to find the sex very exciting. Here's how one man I know described it.

"Guys don't really understand why women are so critical of their bodies. If we're involved with you, we think you are attractive. I don't know any guys who say, 'My girlfriend is great, but I wish her butt was smaller.' If we don't like your body type, we don't go for you in the first place. It's not very sexy to be with a girl who is constantly complaining about her looks. I don't want to have to reassure a woman that she's 'worthy' of being sexually attractive."

Being confident with yourself is also not freaking out after you have sex.

Dear Jenn,

I just had sex for the first time with my boyfriend. In the past, guys lost interest a little bit after we sleep together and it's making me nervous this will happen with him. It's not like they totally become uninterested, it's just that they don't feel like they have to try as hard. Is this true? What can I do to prevent this from happening with my boyfriend?

Brittany

Once you sleep with him, it's important to act like nothing has changed. You don't start calling him all the time. You don't pressure on him by asking, "Where is this going?" And you don't close in on him by leaving your tampons and hairdryer at his place. If you are still the same cool girl he's known up until this point, you will show him you are confident about sex. If you start to get clingy or needy, it will show him the opposite.

This is another reason why it's important to go slowly and be sure of your decisions. If you get caught up in the moment (i.e., drunk) and you sleep with him on the second date, you can't very well tell him, "I made a mistake. That's not like me to have sex so quickly. I'd like to slow things down." First off, he's going to doubt you aren't "that kind of girl." (You were with him!) Second, you don't come across as someone who is in control of herself (which will scare him). Third, there's no turning back to "kissing only." Once you sleep with him, you can't pull the plug. Attempting to do so shows you don't have a lot of confidence and, as a result, you make bad decisions.

DATING RULE #98:
A goddess is confident with her sexuality.

Let's talk about bedroom clothes for a moment, shall we? What do men find sexy? I think it depends on the man. Some guys love the whole garters and stockings thing. Some think it looks staged. So here's how to play it safe and still look sexy, while learning about what each other wants.

BEDROOM CLOTHES THAT ARE THE RIGHT AMOUNT OF "SEXY"

- Flannel PJs, baggy sweats, and old t-shirts are not particularly sexy. If he loves you, he'll think you are sexy no matter what you wear, but dressing like this doesn't set the right tone. You want to throw some fantasy into his reality. Even if you've been married for a decade, don't look like a slob at night.
- You don't have to be shocking and wear a nurse's outfit or dress up like Pocahontas. At least not until you discover you're both into that at a later date.
- All of the men I have asked say they like lingerie. Again, it shouldn't look like a costume. I'm going to give a plug here. There's a lingerie line called "b. tempt'd" and I think it is *exactly* what men find sexy. It's super hot without being outrageous. It's comfortable, but flattering. It's high quality but doesn't cost a fortune. You can buy it online or at most Macy's and Bloomingdales. It's almost all I wear and no, they aren't paying me to say this. Wearing sexy, but tasteful, lingerie will always make you feel sexier.
- When it comes to actual sleep time, I'm a big fan of boy shorts and a tank top. If your style is more silk nighty, that's cool as well. Again, you don't want it to be over the top. But it shouldn't be fuzzy slippers and a big bath robe either.

I'm going to push the envelope even further. Let's talk about…(I'm going to be delicate here for a moment)…hygiene. Here's the deal, ladies. You are supposed to have hair on your head (long hair, preferably). You are supposed to have eyebrows and eyelashes. But that is pretty much it.

How to Be a Goddess

Starting off slowly on this topic: If you have a moustache, wax it. Hair on your toes? Pluck them. Shave your legs and your armpits. In fact, if you have anything but light peach fuzz on your forearms, you should probably wax them, too. I've never understood women who can go days in between shaving. Personally, I can't stand the feel of stubble on my legs. Guess what? Men don't like it either. He's a man; he's supposed to have hair. You're a woman; you're not. Take care of it and never let him see you looking furry.

Getting down to brass tacks: The "bikini region." (Oh gosh, I'm really going here, aren't I?) Let me share a story to make my point. A few years back I was at a spa getting a pedicure. There were two suburban "soccer moms" checking out at the front desk. One of the women said to her friend, "Have you ever heard of a *Brazilian wax*? My masseuse told me about it. Can you even *imagine*? *How gross!*" Her friend seemed to know what she was talking about. The woman continued. "Wait until I tell my husband about this. He's going to be *shocked*!" The pretty, young girl working the register said exactly what I was thinking. She told Mrs. Soccer Mom, "He'd probably love it."

I'm going to be honest here. I totally judged this woman. In fact, I think my first thought was, "Lady, are you really that *stupid*?" I know for a fact the receptionist was right. He *would* love it. I'm even going to wager Mr. Soccer Mom is probably well aware of what a Brazilian wax is. My guess is he sees plenty of them when he sneaks off to the study to look at Internet porn once Mrs. Soccer Mom is asleep.

This, too, goes back to the "lady" vs. "freak" distinction. From the time they are young boys, men look through Playboy. They treasure their Sports Illustrated subscriptions for the month when the yearly swimsuit issue comes out. They sneak a peek at the Victoria's Secret posters when they're walking by the store. This is just how they are. And I think it's wrong to stifle how they are created. Do you want a guy who's obsessed with porn? A guy who cannot control his libido? Of course not. But let's face it; men get turned on by the "freak." I say the best way to keep them feeling satisfied and not thinking the grass might be greener (or trimmer) elsewhere is to give it to them yourself. That's the reason for the pretty bras and panties. That's why you get the Brazilian wax or the Playboy wax. (The latter is actually what most of the men I've polled about this subject tell me they prefer. If you don't know the difference, look it up.)

There is nothing wrong with keeping a man satisfied. Listen; if you require him to keep you satisfied with romance, love, and emotional support, don't you have to do your part? I think it's only fair. No, you don't want to get all corseted up and pluck all your body hair off for just any guy. But the man who treats you like a goddess? The man who worships you and thinks you're the greatest woman to have ever walked the face of the earth? I say, bring on the waxing strips...

DATING RULE #99:
Because he works to keep her satisfied, a goddess has no trouble wanting to keep her man satisfied in return.

He wants a woman who enjoys sex

It's not about acting like a porn star or screaming, "Give it to me, you big stud," at the top of your lungs. Men can tell when our enthusiasm is forced or unnatural. My good friend Dave told me about an exgirlfriend he dated who insisted on howling like a banshee when they had sex.

"It was like something out of a bad porn movie," he told me. "My neighbor in the apartment next to mine was always knocking on the wall and yelling for her to keep it down. It was embarrassing and I never felt like it was authentic. It seemed like it really didn't have that much to do with me or with what I was doing in bed."

Like Dave's ex-girlfriend, if you play the part of "freak," he'll quickly figure out it's an act and believe it's something you do with every guy you sleep with. A man wants a woman who authentically enjoys sex – *with him*. Not a woman who acts like she enjoys sex – *with everyone*.

How to Be a Goddess

This is one of the reasons why a woman makes a big mistake when she talks about her "sexploits" with a man. She may think she's showing him how much she likes sex, but he'll think she sounds slutty. He doesn't need to know "your number." Ever. When a man asks a woman how many guys she's been with, the "lady" will lie and say, "Three guys." Telling a man you've slept with three guys is like telling a police officer you had two beers before you got behind the wheel. It's such an obvious lie it's become a cliché. The "freak" will probably be honest. "Twenty seven men." Either way you lose. If he ever asks you that question you should make it into a joke. Say, "Hmmm. I hope I've been with more men than you have!" And then change the subject.

On the flip side, you don't want to appear disinterested or ambivalent about sex. He needs to know you find him sexually appealing and exciting. Just as he desires you, he needs to feel desired as well.

Colin was involved with a woman who made him feel like sex with him was her least favorite thing in the world.

"She hardly ever made a move toward me unless she'd had too much to drink. When I'd start kissing her, I'd often feel her tense up. During the act itself, it was like she was practically frozen. One time, I made it pretty obvious I was in the mood and she rolled her eyes like she was disgusted. It all made me feel terrible."

Never act like sex with him is a chore or an obligation. Show him you love being with him by telling him or initiating it sometimes. Be into the moment. Listen up: If you really don't like having sex with him, you shouldn't be having sex with him in the first place.

While you want to enjoy sex, you also don't want to be a complete horn dog. Your relationship is not 100% about sex. (And if it is, you need to start this book over from the beginning.) There has to be talking besides saying, "Oh yeah... right there... that's it." You need to engage in activities outside of the bedroom. If there's no emotional connection, the sex fades very quickly.

He wants a woman who is open to experimentation

It's probably not a huge shock men often get bored sexually much faster than women. They need to mix things up and enjoy variety. Most guys want to know their woman is comfortable with trying new and different things. (Again, *with him only*.) Of course he needs to respect you if there are lines you won't cross. If he doesn't, that's a serious problem. But there's nothing wrong with keeping the sex hot. In fact, you should. You just don't want to set him ablaze all at once.

> *Dear Jenn,*
> *I'm pretty wild when it comes to sex. There's not a lot I wouldn't try or haven't done. My boyfriend, however, seems pretty conservative. Is there anything wrong with showing him some of the things I'd like to do? I don't want him to think I'm slutty.*
> *Sydney*

Imagine if the first time you slept together, you wore a leather bustier and tied him to the bed. Not only will that scream "freak 24/7," but what will there be left to do a year or twenty down the road? Maybe you keep a stash of toys in your bedside table. Hand him your "magic bullet" to pleasure you with and he won't be fantasizing about the times you've used it by yourself. Instead, he'll be wondering how many other guys have used it on you.

DATING RULE #100:

Don't deal him your wildest card upfront. Instead, keep the fires going by starting off with a slow burn.

HOW TO KEEP IT HOT WITHOUT BURNING HIM TO A CRISP

- Don't always do the same three things over and over. Learn a new trick every once in a while. But don't use them all at once.
- Don't break out the sex swing and the handcuffs in the beginning. If you're into kinky, let it develop slowly over time.
- Don't recycle your toys! They should always be new and purchased for the particular relationship. I don't care how much you spent on that water-proof vibrator. The price you pay to buy a new one will be far less than the cost of how badly a "used" toy will mess with his head. How would you feel if the situation were reversed?
- Don't let him know how far you're willing to go (or not go) sexually from the beginning. If he's got to wonder what's coming around the corner, that will keep things spicy.

There's one sex act in particular a lot of women are willing to do upfront and (in my opinion) much too soon, but once the relationship is fully committed or a ring is on their finger, it ceases to be a part of the repertoire. And that is oral sex. I also know many religious girls who "save themselves" for marriage but are all too eager to indiscriminately offer blow jobs as some sort of consolation prize. I've never understood this. Oral sex is still sex and I can't imagine thinking your ticket into heaven is assured because you let his penis into your mouth and but not your vagina before you were married.

Worse still are the women who give blow jobs as a sort of "preview" and then cut off the action once he becomes her boyfriend or husband. And then the poor guy feels duped. "But I don't really like it," she'll whine. So why in the heck did she do it in the first place?

No guy wants to feel like you think a part of his body is gross. And especially not something as meaningful to him as his johnson. I don't think it's a coincidence the vast majority of times men employ a prostitute it's to get a BJ. I know one man in particular who cheats on his live-in girlfriend by getting oral sex. Guess what? It's something his girlfriend did in the beginning but once they began sharing a garage, she stopped. If you don't like it, don't do it. You can't start off with it in your bag of tricks and then cut him off.

I think many times women are unsure of what it is they're supposed to do when they take a trip to the land down under. I'm not going to go into details or technique. (This is a "goddess manual," not an "oral sex manual.") But I will make another plug. Right after my divorce, one of my girlfriends suggested a book. It's called "Tickle His Pickle" by Sadie Allison. Feeling more like a "lady" than a "freak," I was too embarrassed to purchase it myself. But I told one of my more "freaky" friends about it and she promptly bought me a copy. It is a racy and raunchy good read, let me tell you! Yes, there's some stuff in the book I personally found too risqué, but it explains the art of (as Sadie calls it) "penis pleasing" in fantastic detail. So if you're uncertain of your skills, I highly suggest it.

Speaking of girlfriends, I am fortunate to have a very diverse group. Some are more the "lady" type, some more of the "freak." And I love to get their thoughts on the subject of sex and what they are into and what they are not. I think I've come to the place in my life where I truly believe that whatever you are comfortable doing, you should do it. If you are in a loving and committed relationship or marriage with a man who adores you and one who you respect completely, whatever floats your boat is fine. It's totally your business and yours alone. But I do think there is one thing that should never be done in a relationship. (Okay, more than one. But I'm not talking about the obvious bestiality, incest, necrophilia, etc, etc.) *And that "one thing" is the threesome…*

Dear Jenn,

I've been with my boyfriend for several years now and he recently told me he is interested in having a threesome with me. He says he's never done it and has always wanted to try it. He asked if it would be something I'd be willing to do with him. I told him I didn't like the idea at all but that I would think about it. Since he first brought it up, he has continued to pressure me about it constantly. He's even gone so far as to drop hints that if we do it, he'll be ready to marry me since he'll have fulfilled all of his sexual fantasies.

I'm not sure how this is supposed to make me feel. On one hand, I appreciate his honesty. But I can't help but think it's a way for him to have sex with another woman with my permission.

Frankly, it hurts he even suggested it. Am I wrong to feel this way? I love him but I'm not sure I can be with someone who wants to try this when he knows I don't like the idea.

Monica

Monica is most definitely not wrong for being upset with her boyfriend's suggestion. In fact, it should be a total deal breaker for her.

WHY A THREESOME SHOULD BE OFF LIMITS

I know it's all sexy these days to have a threesome. We think the biggest fantasy a guy has is to be with two women at once. Bringing your girlfriend into the bedroom with your boyfriend is practically a rite of passage among many college-aged girls. But it shouldn't be. Here's why:

- Any man who wants to share you is not a man you should be with. Even if it's with another woman. If he truly loves you, the thought of you with *anyone* else will make him sick to his stomach. If he tries to give you a bunch of BS how it will make your relationship stronger, he's full of shit and you should dump him.

- Don't judge him if he's done it in his past. Whatever. He's no virgin. But it shouldn't be part of your present with him. And if he tries to persuade you into it by telling you his last girlfriend had a threesome with him, he's *not* a quality guy.

- No matter what you may think, if you really love him it will kill you to see him with another woman. And if you don't really love him, you shouldn't be sleeping with him in the first place.

- Just because he's doing it in front of you, doesn't mean it won't bring up major trust issues.

You should never feel forced, coerced, or manipulated into doing something you aren't comfortable doing. Any man who makes you feel like you aren't "good enough" in bed isn't a man you should be with. But never feel like you can't do something simply because it wouldn't be "proper." Show him that you're open to experimentation and improvisation and you'll keep him a very happy camper.

How to Be a Goddess

He wants a woman who is "dirty"

There are two types of "dirty." There is good "dirty" and there is bad "dirty." And most women have a tough time knowing where that line is. Like almost everything in this chapter, it goes back to the "lady/freak" dichotomy. Bad "dirty" is acting in ways which are over-the-top sexual as if you are looking to receive attention and validation from any man who will give it to you.

Good "dirty" is what you do to create sexual tension, intrigue, and excitement. That's the kind of "dirty" a man wants. And that's the kind of "dirty" a goddess gives him.

There is nothing sexier to a guy than a woman who can go to a fancy affair all dressed up to the nines – looking and acting every bit the "lady" – and then whisper in his ear at the end of the evening that she can't wait to get him home and rip him out of his tux. See how that works? In public (the streets) she is a "lady" and one he can proudly show off. But in private and for him only (the sheets) she is a "freak." Let's see how this plays out in a few other scenarios.

BAD "DIRTY" VS. GOOD "DIRTY"

- Bad "dirty" is sending a naked pic of yourself to a man you don't know very well hoping he'll like you as a result. Good "dirty" is sending your partner a text in the middle of the day telling him what you want to do to him when he gets home from work.
- Bad "dirty" is telling a guy who is courting you how much you want to bang him. Good "dirty" is telling your boyfriend how much he turns you on.
- Bad "dirty" is discussing what you like in bed on the second date. Good "dirty" is talking nasty to your husband in the bedroom.

- Bad "dirty" is discussing your sex life with anyone who will listen. Good "dirty" is doing whatever feels right but keeping those details between the two of you.
- Bad "dirty" is getting drunk, making out with him at a bar, and grabbing his package. Good "dirty" is giving him a quick kiss when in public and whispering, "Do you *really* think we can get through a movie after dinner?"
- Bad "dirty" will make him wonder if you might say or do something when he's out with you that would embarrass him. Good "dirty" will make him wonder what's going to happen when you get home.

My friend Darlene is a master at being "good dirty." By all outward appearances, she is the loveliest and classiest of ladies. None of her husband's business associates would have a clue that she occasionally slips a pair of her panties into his suitcase when he travels for work or that she often sends him a text while he's at the office letting him know she has a "surprise" for him when he gets home. Her husband is always proud to show her off at the various functions they attend and he is always very happy to come home to her as well.

DATING RULE #101:
A goddess is "dirty." In a totally good way.

He wants a woman who gets off

What's the best description of a man who's a good lover? His number one concern is satisfying his lady. If he's a quality guy, the thing he wants more than anything is to please you. And this absolutely applies to sex. The hotter you get, the hotter he gets. Anything less and you're dealing with a selfish guy.

How to Be a Goddess

Every man wants to feel like a stud. He wants to know that he is desired; that his woman craves him physically. Men feel amazing when they make a woman see stars. I think most of us realize this, which explains why faking orgasms is so widespread. Here's the deal: A good guy would much rather know what does it for you than for you to keep quiet and improvise a climax.

In fact, I don't think a goddess would ever fake an orgasm. Why? Because then she's not being true to herself. She's selling herself and her needs short. And she's not being honest with her man either. It's much better to show him what you want than to not say anything and have an unsatisfying sex life. So if you're in a situation where your guy isn't meeting your physical needs, it's time to be honest with him. You don't want to be critical or complain. Just say something like, "I really like it when you do_____." Or "I think_____would feel great. Wanna try it?" If he's a good guy, he'll be more than willing to accommodate you.

Let's get honest…

Now that we've looked at what a guy wants sexually out of a relationship, I think it's time we discuss *our* needs, don't you?

WHAT A WOMAN WANTS SEXUALLY

- We want a man who makes us feel beautiful.
- We want a man who makes our pleasure his priority.
- We want a man who makes us feel "safe."
- We want a man who connects with us before, during, and afterward.
- We want a man who takes charge.

Dear Jenn,

I don't really buy into the whole concept of waiting a while to have sex with guys. Isn't it better to know if he's good in bed before you get emotionally involved? What if you fall for a guy and then find out that he's a lousy lover? That would be a total bummer.

Ally

I've heard Ally's reasoning before and I've known plenty of women who feel the same way. It's a common excuse and women will say they want to make sure he satisfies her sexually before she gets too involved or wastes too much time. Ridiculous! Nine times out of ten, you'll find out pretty much everything you need to know about the kind of lover he will be just by taking your time and watching how he behaves *before* you sleep with him. So if this list is representative of what you want in terms of sex, compare it to how he acts while you are dating to find out if he'll satisfy you.

DATING RULE #102:
You don't necessarily have to have sex with him to figure out what kind of lover he will be.

We want a man who makes us feel beautiful

What woman doesn't want her guy to think she is the hottest woman in the world? Especially when she's buck naked and doing the dirty. Being with a man who makes you feel gorgeous on a day-to-day basis is imperative to feeling comfortable with him sexually.

When Casey started dating her fiancé, she decided to wait a couple of months before consummating the relationship. As someone who hadn't always exercised a lot of sexual restraint, it was a new concept for her. However, she really liked him and wanted to give the relationship the best shot at working out.

"I watched how he treated me *in the daytime*. Was he considerate and loving? Was making me feel attractive important to him? I figured if he worked at making me feel good about myself outside of the bedroom, he would do the same once our relationship moved inside of it. I was totally right."

Take a lesson from Casey and look at his behavior before you sleep together. Does he compliment you? Tell you how beautiful you are? Look at you with "that look?" If he doesn't do those things before you sleep with him, he's not going to start once he gets you into bed.

We want a man who makes our pleasure his priority

I've heard a lot of women describe their lovers as "selfish." What exactly does this mean? Usually it's that he and his enjoyment are the only things that count. He expects oral sex but won't reciprocate. He makes sure he gets off without paying attention to whether she does. Not cool! As discussed above, a quality man will be concerned with your pleasure because that's what gives him his.

> Dear Jenn,
> I'm just going to come out and say this: My boyfriend isn't good in bed! He doesn't act like he cares that much about my enjoyment or giving me pleasure. It's gotten to the point where I don't want to have sex with him and when we do I find myself faking orgasms to get it over with. The more I think about it, the more I realize he doesn't act very concerned with my feelings outside of the bedroom either. Do you think the two are related? I'm starting to think he thinks much more of himself than he does of me.
> Krista

Krista would have been much better off if she'd paid attention to the warning signs *before* becoming sexually involved with this guy. What are some of the common red flags? A guy who acts like he only thinks about himself. A man who is less concerned with making you happy than he is with making himself happy. A man who always puts himself first, even if it's at your detriment. If you see this behavior while you are dating him, things should never progress to sex. He's a selfish man and will be a selfish lover. Both are "deal breakers."

We want a man who makes us feel "safe"

Most women need to have a certain level of emotional connection to truly get to a place of being comfortable sexually. Even though women can (and do) engage in casual sex, generally speaking it's not our preferred method of connecting physically. When we are with someone we trust, we are much more open to experimentation and exploration. If we feel secure with a man outside of the bedroom, we're going to be much more secure inside it, as well.

I totally get that many women find "dangerous" men exciting. When I was younger, I certainly did. It's the whole "taming of the beast" mentality. But getting involved with guys like this doesn't make for a satisfying relationship. And once you have sex with them? Ugh. That's when the head and heart really start aching.

Marianne discovered this firsthand when she started dating Brad, a certifiable "bad boy."

"He was a total player, but he was incredibly good looking and a lot of fun. I thought, 'What the hell, I'll just hang out with him for a little while.' Of course I ended up falling in love with him and – at first – we had tons of good sex. But I was always so uncertain with how he felt for me. I was never sure if he really had feelings for me or was just playing games. I became more and more insecure, which didn't make me want to have sex with him. Once that fizzled, so did everything else."

A man who is crazy about you will want you to feel "safe" with him. He will be straight up with his feelings for you and won't play mind games. He won't disappear for a week at a time and there won't be a lot of guesswork involved with how he treats you. Boring? No way. Quit thinking like that! This "safety" is exactly what you need to feel like you can truly express yourself sexually.

DATING RULE #103:
Very often the "safer" you feel with a man, the hotter the sex will become.

We want a man who connects with us before, during, and afterward

Very few women are content with the "wham, bam, thank you, ma'am" feeling. When a man romances us, it warms us up and puts us in the mood. When we are in the middle of sex, we want a man who looks at us, talks to us, and kisses us. And afterward, we want a man who holds us and engages with us. Anything less and we feel used and expendable.

My boyfriend once told me he believes a man shows a woman exactly how he feels about her by how he treats her right after sex. I think that's true. If he can't get away from you fast enough, he's not in love with you. End of story. But why wait until that moment to figure it out? Isn't it better to determine that *before* you sleep with him?

How does he connect with you during courtship? Is he affectionate and loving? Does he treat you warmly and like he cherishes you? If he's cold, sex won't cause him to heat up.

We want a man who takes charge

I'm going to spend the most time on this one because it's the most controversial. It's the one we are the least likely to admit to ourselves. But let's get real. The vast majority of women are turned on by strong men. And this absolutely carries over to the bedroom. This is why we often feel more comfortable when they initiate sex. Regardless of who actually makes the first move, most women like to feel that the guy is in control. Here's what my dear friend Kristy recently wrote when we were emailing about the subject:

"Show me one woman who doesn't love it when a man pushes her up against a wall, grabs the back of her hair, and lays one on her. That guy is in like Flynn. Pin her hands? Bonus points. *That's* chemistry. *That's* biology. *That's* testosterone telling estrogen what to do."

One of the most common complaints women have about their sex lives is that their guy is not aggressive enough in bed. Truthfully, this doesn't surprise me at all. Why are bodice-ripping romance novels so popular with bored housewives? Because bored housewives fantasize about hot guys ripping off their bodices. Why do women think firemen, cops, and military guys are sexy even when they're not that cute? Because their uniform makes them seem powerful and masculine.

We like take-charge guys. We want the hunter male. Often, the stronger the woman, the more of a hunter she desires. Why? Two reasons. First, she feels like she has met her match. She knows this is a guy she can't bulldoze over or emasculate. Sometimes the sexiest thing a man can say is "No." Second, when a woman feels that a man has pursued her, romanced her, courted her, and wooed her to the point where she says, "Take me," there is no question in her mind how he feels about her. He has chased her because he knows what he wants and what he wants is her. There is nothing hotter than a man who goes after what he wants. That's why we like successful and influential men. To us, it says "virility."

So how do you determine if your guy is a take-charge guy? It's often very easy. Just look at how he acts *outside* of the bedroom.

IS HE A STUD OR A DUD?

- What type of affection does he give you? Is he needy, like a little boy wanting to cling to mama? Or does he grab your face and kiss you passionately?
- Does he ask for permission to kiss you? He may think he's being a gentleman, but it always comes off as wimpy.
- How does he handle his career? Does he work for what he wants? Does he keep going despite setbacks?
- Did he play team sports when he was younger? Athletic men are usually more driven and competitive.
- Does he let other men (or women) intimidate him? Does he walk and carry himself with confidence?

How to Be a Goddess

Embracing this part of our womanhood does not mean we aren't a feminist or are looking for a man to control us. In fact, Kristy is a major feminist, an attorney, and a powerful woman in every way. Nor does it mean we think spousal abuse and rape are good things. Abuse is never okay and is always a sign of weakness. A strong man will always treat you like you are something precious. He just knows there is a time for cuddling on the couch and a time for hot, passionate sex.

Here's the bottom line on sex: It's a big deal. You should never treat your sexuality carelessly. Your body and your heart are sacred. They aren't to be given to men indiscriminately or lightly. But sex isn't something that is "wrong," "bad," or "shameful." That's as big of a lie as the one that says women can sleep around without an emotional consequence.

I like to think of sex the same way I think of affection. At its best, it is the physical manifestation of how we feel about someone. It's bonding to another in a tangible way. It's special and magical. And when it is set in the context of a wonderful relationship with two people who are crazy about each other, it is absolutely amazing.

Dear Jenn,

I wanted send you a quick thank you! For most of my adult life, I felt like I was being used by men. I'd gotten myself into a couple of booty call arrangements and I'd date casually here and there, but I was unable to find a healthy, loving, and passionate relationship.

After discovering your blog and the advice you give to women, I started to think about how my actions were preventing me from what I truly wanted – a great relationship with a great guy. I decided to stop with the casual sex and hold out for a man who is crazy about me and treats me well.

About nine months ago, I met him! He's everything I've wanted and we are so great together. You are absolutely right when you say that sex is the best when there is a physical and an emotional bond. I've been waiting for years to be this happy with a man! Thank you!

Kat

Kat (and all the goddesses out there) have learned the following lesson when it comes to sex. It is one of the most valuable pieces of advice I can share with you…

DATING RULE #104:
A goddess only has a sexual relationship with a man who meets both her physical and emotional needs.

Ladies, I had so much fun writing this chapter and officially earning my title of "sex-pert." Hopefully it was as good for you as it was for me.

DO AS I SAY, NOT AS I DID
(My Own Journey from Doormat to Goddess)

With one notable exception, I've never had sex quickly with a man I was dating. In fact, I usually made them wait quite awhile. But looking back, I can't say I did it for the right reasons. I was always going after the bad boy, player types and I knew if I had sex within the first month, they would lose interest and move on. To me, it was a game. Make him wait and I'd make him fall for me.

It usually worked.

But because I didn't view the courtship period as a time to get to know him and to analyze how he treated me, what difference did it really make? He might have treated me better than he did his casual hook-ups, but these still weren't quality guys who were really in love with me. My game became a game for them as well. One of them told his friends, "I'm going to keep going out with her until she has sex with me. Even if it takes a year." As a result, I got the guy. But that didn't mean that my relationship was spectacular.

Eventually, their true colors would show and they'd end up being the same disrespectful, cheating bastard they always were. Did any of this make for a healthy sex life? Not even close. In the end, almost all of my relationships devolved into a platonic war. My emotional needs weren't being met. And neither were the physical ones. For either of us.

I, too, grew up with a lot of mixed messages about sex. It wasn't something that was talked about in my home and so I learned about it from my friends, Cosmo, and first-hand experience. It's taken me a long time to get to a place where I am comfortable with it.

It's a wonderful thing to actually be able to view sex how it is supposed to be viewed. It's not about being accepted or validated. Any woman who tries to validate herself through sex will only know heartbreak. It shouldn't be used to manipulate someone or to get what you want from them. Nor is it a chore, a duty, or an obligation. As I said in an earlier dating rule, great sex is great sex when the connection is both physical and emotional. Sex is amazing when it happens with someone you *know* loves you madly, passionately, and deeply, and who you love in that same way.

Can you have a great relationship without great sex? I don't think so. Can you have great sex without a great relationship? I don't think so either. In my opinion, one simply cannot exist without the other.

XX

Step #10

Even goddesses get angry. The fine art of handling conflict.

Wouldn't it be wonderful if relationships sailed along smoothly without arguments or disagreements? Wouldn't it be great if we always got along and were able to see things from the other's point of view? How fantastic would it be if "relationship bliss" meant our relationship was always "blissful?" Sadly, this is never the case.

Or maybe it's not so sad. As a wise woman once told me, "You can't have authenticity without conflict. Without disagreements, you'll never really know who the other person is." I think she was right.

The problem facing most relationships is not that there *is* conflict but rather *how* conflict is handled. Most people – men and women both – just don't know how to fight fair. And this is the death of many, many relationships.

DATING RULE #105:
How you fight is what will make or break your relationship.

Generally speaking, men are just more "agreeable" than women. They go along to get along and are less likely to "sweat the small stuff." It takes a lot to really piss them off, doesn't it? Women are different. For some of us, just a whiff of bad behavior will cause World War III. We have trouble distinguishing between the little things and the big things. And we're much more likely to get on our guy's case, nag him, or show him we disapprove of him. Look back on your own relationships. How many fights started because he was upset with you or something you did versus the number of fights which started because *you* were upset with *him*? I bet it's not even close.

The things that piss us off

Do you remember the Tazmanian Devil from cartoons? Remember how he would freak out and start spinning, destroying everything in his path? How often do women get like that as a result of feeling hurt by her guy? Much too much, in my opinion. She will yell, slam doors, and hurl insults. It's almost like fire is coming out of her mouth, isn't it?

Dear Jenn,

I'm having problems with my husband when it comes to our arguments. He'll do something that makes me angry and even if it's not a huge deal, I completely flip out on him. He doesn't like my temper and I know it's driving a wedge between us.

I feel like I can't help but blow up at him and when I'm upset I'm incapable of having a rational discussion. How can I learn to deal with conflict more appropriately? I don't want to ruin my marriage.

Keira

Even if we don't act like Keira and lose emotional control and flip out, a man can still make us see red. Maybe we don't yell at him, but we *seethe* instead. My friend Jaime didn't blow her top with her ex-boyfriend, but would give him the cold shoulder when he upset her. If he asked her what was wrong, she would tersely reply, "Nothing" and then shut him out. Of course, he knew it was "something" but because of her lack of communication, he would remain clueless until if and when she chose to share what was bothering her.

When a woman goes silent and gives her man the cold shoulder, he can immediately sense she is upset. In fact, whenever you disapprove of him, he is usually well aware of it. No, he might not realize exactly what it is he's done to cause your contempt (more often than not, he won't), but he sure feels it. Why? *Because men are dependent on their partner's admiration.* And when he's not getting it, he knows.

I think there are four main categories of things a man can do which will cause a woman to become angry. Here they are.

HOW TO MAKE HER HEAD SPIN IN FOUR EASY STEPS

If your guy really wants to piss you off, he just needs to accomplish one or more of the following:

- He fails to do what he says he'll do.
- He doesn't seem to understand or care about your emotional needs.
- He taps into your jealous nature.
- He appears to take you for granted.

When he fails to do what he says he'll do

In the early stages of a relationship, this usually manifests itself by not calling when he says he'll call or breaking plans at the last minute. Invariably, it will cause the woman to question how the man feels about her and where she stands in the relationship.

How to Be a Goddess

Dear Jenn,

I've been dating this guy for a few weeks and I'm learning he's not so great at keeping his promises. If he says he'll call the next day, some-times he does and sometimes he doesn't. He also told me he'd do things (help me with a school assignment, for example) and then didn't do them. It's making me really mad! I've called him out on it and he claims he sometimes forgets what he's said. It's only been a short time that we've been together and we've already gotten in a few fights about it. It makes me feel like I'm not that important to him. Am I completely wasting my time with this guy?

Gretchen

Here's the deal: If a man shows you early on he is not a man of his word, he is not a man you should get involved with. That's the bottom line.

If he forgets to call one time or needs to postpone a date because of an extenuating circumstance (but happily makes it up to you on his own), who cares? Let that kind of stuff go. People forget things. (Yes, even when they are important to us, we all let things slip from time to time.) We all make mistakes. Life happens and things don't always go according to plan. But a man who continually breaks promises? No, I'm sorry. That's not a man you want to have a relationship with.

One of the things I appreciated about my boyfriend when we first started dating was that he never ended a phone conversation by say-ing, "I'll call you tomorrow." Instead, he would say, "I'll talk to you soon." If I didn't hear from him the next day? No big deal. In fact, "L" has never one time promised me something and not delivered on it. If plans had to change, he explained that clearly and found an alternate arrangement. Finding a guy who is true to his word means finding a guy you can trust (respect). When that happens, appreci-ate him.

Even goddesses get angry. The fine art of handling conflict.

DATING RULE #106:
If he breaks his promises to you in the beginning, you can't very well expect him to start keeping them later on.

Later in your relationship, a broken promise usually means he forgets or neglects to do something you asked him to do. He doesn't bring home the milk. He lets a door handle remain broken. Stuff like that. How do you handle it? It depends. But what you never want to do is emasculate him or nag him. Acting in those ways will not bring the desired result.

WHEN HE FORGETS SOMETHING YOU ASK HIM TO DO

I'm sure you know the expression "There's no use crying over spilled milk." This means that we shouldn't get upset over the small stuff. I agree. Likewise, there's no use in crying if he *forgets* the milk.

- When he arrives home from the store, don't go through the bags and immediately say, "You forgot the milk." Instead say, "Thank you for picking up the groceries."
- Don't beat him up over it. When the mistake is realized say, "That's okay, honey. No biggie."
- Show him you can handle it yourself if you can. "I'll swing by the store tomorrow and pick some up." If he says okay, have toast instead of cereal for breakfast the next morning. Remember he's not your personal shopper. But chances are high he will happily run back to the store right then and there.
- Don't mention it again. Don't say, "Well, I *was* going to make scrambled eggs, but since *somebody* forgot the milk, fried will have to do!" This is emasculation at its finest. It will make him feel like a loser who can't even get the grocery list right.

> ■ The next time he goes to the store, don't remind him he forgot the milk on his last trip. "I just want to make sure that you get milk this time." This is emasculation *and* nagging. And he'll never want to go to the store for you again.

The milk analogy may seem silly. It's supposed to. It's silly to get upset over the silly stuff. When Corrine first started living with her boyfriend Matt, she found herself getting annoyed with his love of reality television. Corrine is a PBS kind of girl and thinks tabloid television featuring people behaving badly is a nonsensical waste of time. In addition, he would occasionally forget to record one of her favorite programs.

"It really bugged me," she said. "I found myself completely overreacting and getting angry even though in nearly every other way he's a model boyfriend. One day, he looked at me and said, 'Is it worth getting this upset with me?' It wasn't. After that, I quit harassing him about his television choices. If there was a program I didn't want to miss, I made sure I recorded it myself."

Let the little things go. If he's a great guy, it's not a big deal if he forgets things from time to time. If he's wonderful, who cares if he has bad taste in television?

DATING RULE #107:
A goddess doesn't fight over something which shouldn't be a battle in the first place.

More often than not, women get upset over "the little things" because her relationship is lacking in "the big things." Protection and trust have eroded. Cherishment and admiration have left the building. Or maybe those things were never there in the first place. If that's the case, you need to look at the deeper issues. Going to war over a minor transgression is not the answer.

Even goddesses get angry. The fine art of handling conflict.

WHEN HE NEGLECTS SOMETHING YOU ASK HIM TO DO

Forgetting isn't the same as neglecting. Forgetting is unintentional; neglecting is intentional. This is why it usually pisses us off more. Here's a common scenario.

- Oh, damn. The door handle breaks. It's time for Mr. Fix It to get out that fancy tool set he *had* to buy at Home Depot and get to work. But Mr. Fix It wants to act more like Mr. Couch Potato.
- You say, "Honey, the door handle is broken."
- He sighs, gets up, and lumbers over to the door. He begins to inspect it like he's about to perform surgery. You think, "Oh! Good sign! He's going to fix it right away!" Don't be fooled. This is an act. What he's trying to assess is just *how* broken it is. Maybe if he jiggles it a bit... it will snap back into place.
- No such luck. In fact, his jiggling has now caused it to hang from the door by one teeny, tiny piece of metal.
- You say, "Stop! You're making it worse!" Which makes the situation and how he feels even worse, by the way.
- He thinks, "This is too much for me to do right now. I just want to watch the game in peace, not spend my Sunday fixing a stupid door handle." (Side note: Have you ever noticed that home disasters always seem to occur on the weekends or late at night? When having someone come to fix it would either be impossible or cost the equivalent of one year of college tuition? I think it's a cosmic conspiracy. But I digress...)
- He says, "I'll fix it after the game."
- You say, "Really? Because the last time you said you'd fix something it took three months before you did it."

> (Emasculating.) He replies, "Yeah, yeah, yeah." Or something to that extent.
> - Of course it doesn't get fixed. Not that Sunday or the next. Or the next. No matter how many times you ask (nagging) there's always something which takes precedence over that dang door handle. "I'm tired." "My toe hurts." "I thought you wanted me to pick up milk today. How can I do that *and* fix the door handle?"
> - Eventually you get sick and tired of it and become angry. "You never fix things around the house!" "I always have to ask you to do something over and over before you do it!" And a fight ensues…

When a woman is faced with a man who is being neglectful with something she asked him to do, she has two choices.
- She can fix the problem herself

  or
- She can "threaten" to outsource; thereby giving him a choice

If you attempt to fix it yourself, I have two words of warning. First, it should be something you actually *can* do without making the situation worse. (Personally, I'm a wiz with door handles.) Second, be prepared this activity will now become one of "your" duties. If you touch his beloved tools and then make things a bigger mess, this will only make the situation worse. If it's something you can do, and don't mind doing it in the future, go for it. There's nothing wrong with a man thinking, "Wow. It's pretty cool my wife knows how to fix a door handle."

The most effective way to handle "neglect," is to give your guy a choice. Instead of nagging him daily, don't say anything about it for a week. Often, simply not feeling pressured into doing something

– combined with his own annoyance that the door handle is all messed up – will cause him to take action. If it doesn't, say something like this: "Babe, I know you've been dealing with that stupid door handle, too, and I think it's time we get it fixed." Present him with the names and numbers of a couple of handymen. "I spoke with Sue and she said Joe is really good and not terribly expensive. Should I call him or do you want to save some money and fix it yourself?"

Nine times out of ten he'll be horrified at the thought of giving his hard-earned cash to a stranger when he can solve the problem himself. That's when Mr. Couch Potato usually scurries into the garage to get his tools. If he says, "Call Joe." Fine. Grab the phone and immediately start dialing. See how that works? You didn't nag him. You didn't emasculate him. You gave him the opportunity to step up and make a decision. Sure, you might have pushed a bit, but who among us doesn't need a little nudge once in a while?

Once the handle is fixed – whether by Joe or by him – show your appreciation.

"Thank you so much for fixing the handle. You did such a great job and you saved us money!"

"Thank you so much for having Joe come out. I appreciate how hard you work to pay for stuff like that."

Make him feel like a hero and he'll want to be your hero. *That's* how you deal with "neglect," ladies.

DATING RULE #108:
Once he stops being "neglectful," make him feel like a hero.

When he doesn't seem to understand or care about your emotional needs

Ever notice how that guy who is reluctant to fix something around the house will be the first to try to "fix" your problems? In fact, the number one complaint women have about their men is that they try to solve their problems instead of just listening to them. It happens in almost every relationship. A funny example of this was portrayed in the movie "White Men Can't Jump." Rosie Perez is in bed with Woody Harrelson when she tells him she's thirsty. He offers to get her a glass of water. This is how she replies:

"If I'm thirsty, I don't want you to bring me a glass of water. I want you to sympathize. I want you to say: 'Gloria, I too know what it feels like to be thirsty. I, too, have had a dry mouth.' I want you to connect with me through understanding the concept of drymouthedness."

I only saw the movie one time, but I will never forget that scene.

Listen, I totally know this is hyperbole. If we say to our boyfriend or husband, "I'm thirsty," what we want is for him to get us a glass of water. (Or milk. But since he forgot the milk, water will have to suffice…) No woman in her right mind would want a guy to discuss "drymouthedness" with her. But it illustrates a good point.

DATING RULE #109:
Women want to connect over problems. Men want to solve them.

When we go on and on to our man about the woman who is out to get us at work, we don't want him to break out an Excel spread sheet and come up with the proper formula for keeping her in line. We want him to listen. We want him to empathize. We want him to nod his head and exclaim, "What a bitch!" when we get to the worst part. In short, we want him to act the way *we act* with other women. Does this happen? Usually not.

Instead, he's more likely to say, "Ignore her," "Forget about her," or "Do XYZ and that'll stop her." Then we feel slighted and as if our feelings don't matter. That's when "You don't care about me" and "You never listen to me" start to fly out of our mouths.

Even goddesses get angry. The fine art of handling conflict.

Dear Jenn,

What is wrong with guys? My boyfriend can't listen to me when I am having a problem without offering his advice. I tell him I want him to keep quiet and hear me out, but it's like he's incapable of it. How can I get him to listen to me without opening his mouth and telling me how I should do things differently?

Nicole

Here's the thing you have to remember about men: When they love someone, they don't want them hurting. The quickest way to hurt a man? Hurt someone he loves. By trying to solve your problems, he isn't dismissing you. He really does think he's helping! It isn't about him not caring how you feel. *It's that he doesn't want you to be upset and is attempting to help you out of that place.*

Doesn't that change your perspective at least a little bit? I hope so. When you realize he does this because he cares and not because he doesn't care, it should help minimize your hurt. You need to be heard, but he needs to feel that he is helping.

DATING RULE #110:
A man who loves you will always want to "fix" your problems.

So now that you have this piece of information, how do you handle it from here? How do you get your emotional needs met while still allowing him the opportunity to be your hero?

The best way to approach a man with a problem is not just to tell him the problem, but to also explain how he can solve it for you. "Honey, Jane really upset me at work today (problem). If you could just listen to me vent about it for ten minutes, I know that would make me feel better (solution)." Guess what? Your knight in shining armor will give you his undivided attention. Probably for more than ten minutes.

Or try this: "Honey, Jane is really making things tough for me (problem). Could you spend an hour tonight helping me strategize how to handle her? You're so good with people and I could really use your advice (solution + admiration = bonus points)." Dah dah dah dah! Here comes Superman to the rescue!

DATING RULE #111:
When presenting a problem to a man, also tell him how he can solve it for you. That way you both get your needs met.

Men often complain that women talk too much. I think that's a fair assessment. So be sure to give him an end point. No guy wants to hear you go on and on. He wants to know the problem, figure out how he can help, and then move on. There's absolutely nothing wrong with that.

> *Dear Jenn,*
> *You know how they say men can't listen to your problems without telling you the solution? I'm in a worse situation. My boyfriend won't even listen to me at all. If I have an issue I need help with or need a place to vent, he doesn't give me that opportunity. He usually cuts me off, changes the subject, or completely ignores the conversation. Does he even care about me?*
> *Marie*

I should note here that if a man is unwilling to help you with your problems, you might have an even bigger problem on your hands. If he loves you, he will want to help you. But even a guy who is crazy in love with his gal doesn't want to hear her drone on about how the shoes Jane was wearing today were "hideous" or how her new haircut makes her look like an elf. Save those conversations for your girlfriends.

When he taps into your jealous nature
This one's a doozy, isn't it? Show me a woman without jealousy and I'll show you... I won't show you anything because she doesn't exist. There is nothing – I repeat, nothing – that will make us crazier than when a

man causes us to feel jealousy. The green-eyed monster is a beast unlike any other. She strikes us at the root of all of our insecurities – that we aren't pretty enough, sexy enough, hot enough, smart enough, *whatever* enough – and that another woman is better. At least in our man's eyes.

Men totally know this. (Sneaky bastards.) If he's had just one girlfriend in his past, he is well aware of how competitive with and jealous of other women we can be. Unless he's a complete ignoramus, he knows the things that are likely to set us off. Here are a few examples.

HOW A MAN AWAKENS THE GREEN-EYED MONSTER

- He gawks at or comments on other women in our presence.
- He flirts with them in front of us.
- He talks about his ex. And not in a bad way.
- He offers details of his sexual past. Or engages in other "locker room" type of talk with us.

Jennifer's boyfriend Kirk had a knack for inciting her jealousy.

"He would comment on other women all of the time. We couldn't walk down the street without him saying something like, 'Wow, look at her' or 'She's in good shape.' It made me crazy and I was constantly wondering how he thought I compared to them.

Do men do this intentionally? I'm not sure. Most men definitely do test the boundaries in order to see what they can get away with and what they can't, especially in the beginning. I also think sometimes guys are just guys. They don't understand why we get so upset because it's not something they would do. Tell your boyfriend that your ex was handsome and he won't bat an eye. (Tell him that he was a CEO who drove a convertible Mercedes and that's a different story, however.)

Very often, the tone the woman sets in the beginning will determine if this behavior continues. Ask him how old he was when he lost his virginity, how many women he's slept with, or if he's had a threesome – congrats. You've just opened the door. Point out how big some girl's boobs are and he'll think it's okay to comment on the cleavage of every female he passes. I know we all want to seem cool. But it's important to remember that any behavior you encourage or accept will be behavior which continues.

When you're on a second date, it's not that big of a deal to tell him, "I just saw the new Katherine Heigl movie. She is sooo pretty!" Fast forward a few months when that guy is now our boyfriend and we're attached. He says, "Katherine Heigl is smoking hot!" and we want to blow a gasket. "How come you never tell me how hot I am anymore? Do you think she's prettier than me?" Watch your boyfriend become quickly confused. He was just playing by your rules, after all.

DATING RULE #112:
If you talk to him like you're one of the boys in the beginning, he doesn't expect that to change once you become his girlfriend.

So do yourself a favor. Know – in advance – what you will be okay with and what you won't. Don't engage in behavior which will ultimately bite you in the ass.

Maybe you haven't encouraged him in this manner. Maybe he's just one of those guys who talks about whatever comes into his head no matter who the audience is. If that's the case, I still think you need to check his behavior early on. If he comments on another woman, tell him, "Babe, I'm not one of the boys. How about saving that stuff for 'guy time?'" And then change the subject. If he's talking about his ex, calmly say, "Babe, I don't really need to hear about Jessica." And then change the subject. If he starts telling you about a wild night he had in Vegas, cut him off. "Babe, I'm sure it was fun. Where do you want to go to dinner?" Don't get mad, freak out, or make it a bigger deal than it is. Make your boundaries known loud and clear, but don't call him to the carpet over it.

If he's a cheater, that's a completely different story. There's a big distinction between a man who doesn't know when to keep his mouth closed and one who doesn't know how to keep his pants zipped. Try not to confuse the two. You can handle the first. You can't handle the second. If a man cheats on you when he's your boyfriend, I say that's a complete "deal breaker." Always. It's best to get out right away because that behavior will not change. If you take him back, you've essentially condoned what he did. But you will never trust him. Where can the relationship go after that? Surely you don't want to marry a man you don't trust.

If you've been married for a while and have a family, I realize this can be much, much more difficult. I won't even be so presumptuous as to offer advice here except to tell you that you need to get into marriage counseling. Pronto.

When he appears to take you for granted

Remember the good old days of courtship? The dinners and the flowers. The excitement of just being together. Aaaah, 'twas a splendid time indeed…

Now you're living under the same roof and things are, well, not so splendid. You're not at the top of his priority list. Your time together doesn't feel very special. You feel taken for granted.

THE WAYS A MAN MAKES YOU FEEL TAKEN FOR GRANTED

- He makes you feel more like his maid or his cook than his lover.
- He spends more "quality time" with his colleagues or his friends than with you.
- He stops with the romance.
- He often seems to be in a bad mood around you.

What do women usually do? They nag.

"You never take me out anymore."

"Do you even realize how much I do around here? Can't you ever help out?"

"How many times do I have to ask you to pick up your socks?"

"Why do I have to plan everything?"

When a woman nags, a man will do one of two things. He will either retreat (flight) or he will attack (fight).

DATING RULE #113:
When you nag a man, he goes on the defensive, which will cause his defense mechanisms – fight or flight – to go up.

One common complaint I hear from women is that their boyfriends and husbands are extremely messy and refuse to clean up after themselves. Here's a typical example of the questions I receive.

Dear Jenn,

I've been with my boyfriend for three years and living with him for two. He's a good guy with solid morals and a stable career. Here's the problem: He refuses to clean up after himself, wash dishes, or do laundry. I'm not his mom and I'm certainly not a maid! I've tried talking to him about it without nagging, but when it doesn't get done I can't help but nag. Which always causes a fight. What should I do?

Blair

Another common question comes from girls with boyfriends who rarely take them out.

Dear Jenn,

My boyfriend of nearly a year and a half has stopped with the romance and we hardly ever go on dates anymore. When we're together, he's perfectly happy sitting on the couch and watching DVDs. However, it's a different story when it comes to his friends. If they're involved, he makes sure he gets out of the house and does something fun with them. I've found myself becoming that girl I swore I would never be: a nagger, whiner, and complainer. It still doesn't work and we usually end up arguing.

I love him and he's really awesome in many, many ways. How can I make him see my point on this?

Cora

As relationships devolve into a nagging war, everything else suffers. Every minor transgression is a personal affront. Communication breaks down. Resentments flourish. The sex dies. Maybe you end up staying together – especially if you've been married for a long time – but these are not happy relationships. They're the kind where both parties are dissatisfied and miserable.

Men do not respond well to criticism. (None of us do, really.) And it's not an effective way to encourage him to change his behavior. What works? Try this magic formula.

HOW TO ENCOURAGE A POSITIVE RESPONSE

Clear Direction + Praise = Desired Result

These are the times when you say:

"I love that you have such a great group of friends. And I love how much fun you have when you're with them. I'd love to spend some fun time with you, too. Why don't we go out to a nice dinner this weekend? Just the two of us?"

"You are such a hard worker! I appreciate how much you do and I know you're tired when you get home. I'm tired at the end of the day, too. Do you think we could both make an effort to pick up after ourselves so neither one of us feels extra pressure?"

When he makes an effort to make you happy, be sure to notice it.

"Thank you so much for dinner, honey. It made me feel wonderful to spend some time together. You're the best."

DATING RULE #114:
If you want him to do more of something, praise him whenever he does it.

Serena learned this lesson when it came to dealing with her husband.

"When Jake and I were first married and I began to see all of his flaws up close and personal, I turned into a professional nagger in order to try to change him. Of course, he started to pull away and after a couple of years, I began to wonder if we were going to make it. A friend suggested I try a different approach. So instead of nagging, I started to make my needs and wants clear. If I wanted more help around the house, I asked for it. If I needed him to step up the romance, I told him. Of course, always in a nice and loving way and without being demanding! Nine times out of ten, he would accommodate my wishes and I made sure we had fun – whether it was painting the nursery or going to a movie – while we were doing it. Afterward, I would show my appreciation by thanking him and making him feel good.

Honestly, this approach totally transformed my marriage. Fifteen years later and we're still going strong. We're more in love now than we were when we first got married. That's the trick – growing your love instead of depleting it."

When he upsets you
Here's how it all boils down: In any type of conflict – whenever your man does something which upsets you – you have two choices of how to handle it: You can either accept his behavior or you can reject it. The trick is to know which behavior to accept and which to reject. This is

dependent on one thing only – what you can live with and what you cannot.

Perhaps he is always late and it bugs you. Maybe he makes off-color jokes and you find yourself wanting to roll your eyes. Whatever it is, it bothers you but it's not a "deal breaker." That is "imperfect" behavior you are willing to accept. Leave it alone. Let it slide. This is not sweating the small stuff in action. No one is perfect and you've got to get it out of your head that someone will be.

When Robin started dating Andrew, she thought he was as close to perfect as a man could be.

"He was absolutely wonderful and we had the best relationship I'd ever had. He was attentive and thoughtful. In contrast to all the 'bad boys' I'd gone out with, he truly was a good person. After about six months, I started noticing his imperfections. He talked a little bit too loudly when we were in public. He sometimes put his foot in his mouth. One time, he told my sister how he thought women's softball was a waste of a sport. Apparently he'd forgotten that she was on her college's softball team.

I found myself getting bothered at times – even angry. But I made a decision that I was going to overlook those annoyances. In my opinion, they weren't that big of a deal. If I can live with it, why get on him about it?"

Let's contrast this with the behavior you need to reject. This is the big stuff. Whatever it is, if it's important to you and you can't live with it, you need to address it.

Dear Jenn,

I'm not sure what I should do about my boyfriend. As a general rule, he's great and we have a good relationship. However, there is something I don't know if I can handle. You see, he's a single dad and has joint-custody of his twelve year-old daughter. She doesn't like me too much; I think she worries I'm trying to replace her mom. She's pretty vocal about this and tries to cut me down by saying nasty things.

My boyfriend doesn't defend me or tell her she can't talk to me the way she does. Personally, I think he feels guilty because of the divorce and he walks on eggshells around her. I love him and I'm trying to ignore it. But it hurts me and I think it will end up causing problems down the line.

In addition, I don't even know how to bring it up. I don't want to inter-fere with his father/ daughter relationship. Help me, please!

Candace

Many a well-meaning woman has made the mistake of trying to accept something her gut told her she should reject. She pushes it aside and tries to rationalize it away. She hopes that by ignoring it, it will either magically disappear or she will learn to live with it. If it is truly some-thing she needs to reject, this never happens. And sooner or later the resentment will build and that woman will end up yelling at her boy-friend because he chews with his mouth open. (An annoying behavior she had earlier decided to accept.)

Why do we do this? Because we don't want to cause conflict. Because we don't want to risk losing our relationship by saying something. Because we are afraid the man will say, "Tough luck, sweetie. I ain't changin'."

Here's the truth. Behavior that you should reject will always be a "deal breaker." It will end up ripping your relationship in two. If you keep your mouth shut, you have a 100% chance of it coming ruin. But if you address it? You stand a good chance of working through it, especially if the man really loves you and takes pride in making you happy.

Even goddesses get angry. The fine art of handling conflict.

DATING RULE #115:
A goddess does not try to accept behavior she knows she should reject, even if it means losing the relationship.

I explained this to Candace when I wrote back to her. I told her that if she didn't discuss the issue of her boyfriend's daughter with him, she would become resentful and angry. I had little doubt it would eventually cause the demise of her relationship. After a series of email exchanges where we strategized her approach and what she would say, Candace decided to talk to him about it. Much to her delight, her boyfriend acknowledged it was a problem and promised to handle it with his daughter. From that point on, she noticed a distinct change in the daughter's attitude toward her. And if she ever got out of line, her boyfriend corrected it right then and there.

Telling the difference between what to accept and what to reject can be difficult. But here's a good rule of thumb: If it bothers you every day for more than a couple of weeks – if it keeps you up at night – that is behavior you need to reject.

I, too, dealt with this fairly early on with my wonderful boyfriend. There was something he did – not knowing it hurt me – which I knew I could not live with; something that preyed on my deepest fears and insecurities and probably wouldn't bother 90% of women. For months, I agonized over it. In every other way, he was incredible and I didn't want to lose him and the best relationship I had ever had. I tried to change my thinking and how it made me feel. But in my gut, I knew I could not live with it permanently. So I told him. It was maybe my most vulnerable moment in my dating life and I was terrified of his reaction. But "L" listened. And then he said the most miraculous thing to me: "Jenn, I love you. And I would never want to hurt you. Thank you for telling me. I will stop."

It was at that moment I knew how it felt to be really, really loved by a man despite my own issues and insecurities. Yes, it's fabulous for a man to love you and all your great qualities. But there is an even bigger joy that comes from being completely authentic – revealing the most secret parts of yourself – and knowing that he loves you *anyway*.

DATING RULE #116:
You put your relationship in greater jeopardy if you hide from the things you should reject than if you confront them.

Helpful tips for handling conflict

It's no big secret that navigating through conflict is the most challenging aspect of any relationship. Relationships are made or broken depending on our conflict resolution skills.

> *Dear Jenn,*
>
> *I don't think I'm very good at this whole relationship thing. I can't seem to find one where I'm not butting heads with my boyfriend. I've never been able to have a relationship without a lot of fighting, which ends up causing us to break up.*
>
> *I know I'm not perfect and I know no man is perfect, either. Arguments are going to happen, right? How can I learn to deal better with conflict? How can I prevent disagreements from becoming a huge deal? Is there something seriously wrong with me?*
>
> *Whitney*

When it comes to conflict, it's usually not that there's something wrong with you so much as there's something wrong with the way you handle it. There are certain things you should always – and never – do when it comes to conflict. They apply to all of the scenarios discussed in this chapter and to anything else that might come your way. These are the secrets to "fighting fair."

Even goddesses get angry. The fine art of handling conflict.

THE SECRETS TO HANDLING CONFLICT EVERY GODDESS SHOULD KNOW

- Timing is everything. Don't confront him about something that's bothering you in the heat of an argument or while he's watching game seven of the World Series. Wait until you are both in a good mood and he's not distracted.
- Never start with "We need to talk." It will immediately put him on the defensive.
- If you begin to argue, take a breather. If one of you needs to cool off, say so. "I need to take a walk." However, the person who is leaving always needs to assure the person left behind that they'll be back. Give a time frame. Make it concrete. "I need fifteen minutes to compose myself."
- Talk slower and softer when you bring something up to him. Use your feminine charms. He will become disarmed and be more receptive to listening. If you yell or raise your voice, he will shut you out or yell back. Never go there.
- Don't be emotional. Screaming or stomping around is bad news. Men don't know how to deal with it. He'll think you're acting "psycho."
- Don't repress things that hurt you unless they're "the small stuff." Resentment is the only outcome if you do.
- Don't accuse or speak in generalities. "You always…" "You never…" These are no-no's.
- Keep it private. Don't argue with him, criticize him, or correct him in public and especially not in front of his friends or business associates. If he did something you need to address, do it after you get home.
- Be willing to forgive. If you work through an issue, never bring it up again. You don't get to say, "Remember that time six months ago when you…" Never hold anything over his head.

How to Be a Goddess

Stop! In the name of love

In almost every conflict, there is a moment where things can turn and get ugly. You know what I mean – the insults, the cussing, and the degrading remarks. Some women will even escalate it physically and will push, scratch, or throw something. It's completely unacceptable and it's essential to not let it go there. Even if it's just hurtful words, you can't take them back and they can do a lot of damage. Never allow an argument to stoop to that level.

I once asked Betty, an older and happily married woman, her secrets to dealing with the inevitable conflicts that occur in her marriage.

"Whenever I find myself getting upset, I take a deep breath and just… stop," she told me.

"How do you stop yourself when you're in the heat of the moment? How do you not let it go to 'the ugly place?'" I asked.

"It's funny, actually. I imagine a big, red stop sign in my mind. I put a hold on whatever I'm feeling and take a few seconds to calm myself. I try to process my feelings instead of simply reacting to them. I ask myself, 'Is this really that important? Does it really matter long-term? Do I really need to get angry about this?'

I also think about the good qualities my husband has and how much I love him. When you're upset with the other person's actions, it's usually because you don't feel very loved by them at that moment. What you need to focus on is *your* love for *them*. That usually calms me and I am able to take a rational and sane approach to dealing with my hurt. We've been married for nearly fifty years and we've both made a concentrated effort to not let things get nasty – no matter how upset we are."

I love the idea of picturing a stop sign when you're about to lose it and I've employed Betty's technique in my own life. Give it a try and see if it doesn't work for you, too. Loving someone means working toward being your best self. As my dear friend Dana once told me, "I don't think it's ever good to become ugly with the man you love. If it happens with any regularity, it always destroys the relationship."

Even goddesses get angry. The fine art of handling conflict.

"The bitch slap"

Have you ever been with your guy and things are going great and then all of a sudden he just snaps at you or says something kinda… rude? And you're like, "Whoa! Where did that come from?"

> Dear Jenn,
> Should I be upset? Earlier tonight, I was goofing around and did a little striptease for my boyfriend. I thought he'd get turned on and he totally did, but while I was dancing he said, "Don't give up your day job, babe." WTF?? I know he was joking, but it still hurt my feelings. Should it? I laughed and we ended up in bed, but it bugged me. I'm overreacting, right?
> Paige

I totally get where Paige is coming from and maybe you've been in a similar situation. Maybe you've cooked dinner and he says something snotty. "That smells awful," for example. Or maybe you've gotten all dressed up and are looking gorgeous and he says, "Why'd you put all that makeup on? We're just grabbing a pizza." Or maybe it's a distasteful joke at your expense. Whatever it is, it feels just a wee tad bit disrespectful and it stings. I like to call this "the bitch slap."

Of course I mean all this figuratively, not literally. (Hitting is never okay.) And I hope you'll see that I use the phrase "bitch slap" in a humorous way. But that's what it is; a jab – a poke – and given when you least expect it. And he needs to know right then and there that you've noticed his behavior and it's not cool. So what do you do? You "bitch slap" him back.

It's not about trading insult for insult; that's not the way to handle it. And you never want to blow it out of proportion or make a federal case about it. It shouldn't escalate into a full-fledged fight. Just say something like, "If you want to be nasty, save it for the bedroom." Or "Just so you know, mister, the *correct* response was 'You look beautiful.'" Or

"Babe, I didn't appreciate that comment." And then smile sweetly, give him a quick kiss, and drop it. That's usually enough to put him in his place and keep him on his toes for a bit.

DATING RULE #117:
It's okay to let a man know when he intentionally disrespects you; even if it's only a little bit. Just don't let it escalate into something bigger than it is.

When you're at fault

Every once in a while, it is our behavior that causes the conflict. We say or do something hurtful. We act in a way that upsets him. And he brings it up.

It's not that we don't make mistakes. We do. All the time. It's just that men are much more likely to let them slide than we are. So chances are if he gets angry about something, it's usually because it's a big deal to him.

Here's what you don't want to do. Don't argue back and tell him why he's wrong. What is actually happening is your man is expressing his feelings to you. And if you think about it, that's not such a bad thing. In fact, women often complain that men don't express their feelings enough. So why stifle him? Shut him down now and he'll feel much less comfortable talking about his feelings – bad or good – in the future.

Just like you want to feel heard, so does he. Listen to what he has to say. And don't be so quick to tell him that it's not that big of a deal. It is to him. Don't turn it around and make him out to be the bad guy.

There's a saying that I really like: "You can be happy or you can be right." If your goal is to be "right," then argue with him when you're the one at fault. If your goal is to be "happy," listen to him and be quick to apologize.

Even goddesses get angry. The fine art of handling conflict.

DATING RULE #118:
A goddess has no problem with owning up to her mistakes.

The upside of anger

It's a fantasy to think your relationship will be conflict-free. Just as there is no such thing as the perfect man, there's no such thing as the perfect relationship. And guess what? You're not perfect either. Perfection should never be the goal.

Remember that wise woman I mentioned in the beginning of this chapter who told me that conflict can actually be a good thing? She also told me something else that I think is important to note. She explained that when handled improperly, conflict can absolutely destroy relationships. But if you do it right, it has the ability to bring a couple even closer together. Learning how to successfully resolve conflict; how to deal with each other's flaws, is what makes for the strongest relationships.

DO AS I SAY, NOT AS I DID
(My Own Journey from Doormat to Goddess)

I am not proud of my history with conflict. Knowing how to deal with it has been something I've struggled with my entire dating career. If I wasn't sure that I was in good company – that most women have the same problems I've had – I'd probably feel more hesitant to share this with you. After all, I'm supposed to be an expert, right? But I think very few of us are really "experts" when being hurt is concerned. It's more of a trial and error thing. On the job training, if you will.

Looking back, I realize I tried different styles of conflict. When I was younger, I was always the aggressor. My boyfriend would do something which hurt me and I'd lash out and get angry. You know what? I usually had a right to be angry. Anger itself is rarely the problem; many times it's justified. It's how we express that anger that's the issue. Being aggressive, confrontational, and emotional isn't the answer, but for many years, that's the tactic I employed.

My marriage was very helpful in that it taught me to (somewhat) keep my angry outbursts in check. My ex-husband is a good man and I never wanted to go to "the ugly place" of insults and shouting matches. It's very hard to take back horrible words, even when they are said in the heat of passion. So I learned to retreat. Did I get angry? Yes. But I tried to stuff it down. I repressed it. Which, as I explained in this chapter, only caused resentment to grow. That's not handling anger well either.

One complaint I've heard from every single man I have been involved with in my "adult" life – from my ex-husband to "L" and everyone in between – is that I leave. I do. I get hurt and without explanation I say, "See ya," and walk out for a while. Why do I do this? Because I don't want my anger to express itself. And that is no more the correct response than pitching a fit.

There's something that happens when you are with someone you really love and who really loves you in return. I think Jack Nicholson's character in "As Good As It Gets" summed it up best when he said, "You make me want to be a better man." My relationship with "L" has made me want to be a "better woman" in the area of conflict. It's my big weakness and, for both him *and for me*, it's what I've worked on the most.

So that's where I'm at. Learning as I go and hopefully able to impart these lessons to you, my dear reader. Handling conflict properly isn't an instantaneous thing. You won't read this chapter and suddenly be the world's fairest "fighter." But you absolutely can get a whole heck of a lot better at it. And hopefully you're with someone who wants to improve right along with you.

XX

Step #11

Surviving and thriving in a long-term relationship.

Think about this for a moment: How many relationships do you know that are truly awesome? How many "seem" awesome but you suspect might not actually be so great? And how many are downright miserable? As I've researched this and have really started looking at the people around me and their love lives, I'm amazed by how few are in satisfying, healthy relationships. Is anyone truly happy anymore?

Dear Jenn,
Everywhere I look, I see people who are miserable in their rela-
tionships. My friends are all unhappy with their boyfriends and I
can't name more than a few couples who seem to have a healthy
relationship.

How to Be a Goddess

I'm single and would like to find someone. I really do want to get married and start a family eventually. However, it depresses me that so few people seem to be truly in love. Is there hope?
Erin

Erin's observations certainly seem accurate. Many relationships start off well enough. Two people meet and fall in love. Everything seems fabulous and they eventually get married or move in together. But as life wears on, the cracks begin to show. They begin to fight. Resentments build. The initial fires extinguish. And eventually each person is left with a feeling of disappointment and unmet expectations.

When this happens, many couples will stay together out of obligation or fear. They don't want to be alone. They don't want to break up their family. They figure what they have is better than not having anything at all. They may be surviving, but they certainly aren't thriving. I get it. But I don't think it's any way to live.

Mariah had this exact experience with her ex-boyfriend, Chase.

"After a couple of years, it seemed like we were fighting all of the time. Every difference between us that seemed small when we first started dating was now a glaring issue. All of the incompatibilities we'd ignored when we first fell in love began to rise to the surface. Since neither of us was happy, we both began to check out of the relationship and began to invest less and less to make it work. We didn't want to break up, but I don't think we wanted to be together either. After about six months of misery, we finally decided to part ways."

If this sounds familiar, it's because it's a typical scenario of what happens when relationships aren't built on a solid foundation. Amazing relationships are absolutely the exception rather than the rule. But they are possible. Maintaining and growing those initial feelings can happen. Love can increase rather than decrease.

DATING RULE #119:
Long-term relationships don't have to suck!

Dear Jenn,

My boyfriend and I have been together for over a year and a half. We've had some minor ups and downs, but so far it's great! We've even been discussing marriage recently. I want to make sure that if we do get married our relationship will continue to be as strong as it is now. Can you give me some tips on how to make that happen?

Lana

There are five components which are present in any successful relationship. And they must exist in order for your love to not just survive, but to thrive.

THE FIVE COMPONENTS OF A FANTASTIC LONG-TERM RELATIONSHIP

- Chemistry
- Compatibility
- Communication
- Compromise
- Commitment

Chemistry

I often receive questions from readers asking me what they should do when they meet a guy who is really nice, but they just don't feel that "spark." Have you ever been in a situation like the one Randy is in?

Dear Jenn,

One of my friends introduced me to this guy. He's very nice, successful, and polite. The problem is I just don't feel any sexual attraction to him. It's not that he's bad looking – he's not. But I just don't have any desire to kiss him!

I figured I should give him a chance and we have now been out three times. I was hoping my feelings for him would grow, but they haven't. He just doesn't do it for me! My friend says I should keep going out with him and see where it leads but I'm not sure. What do you think? Should I keep going out with him? Is it better to be with a guy who you might not feel a spark with but who is nice?

Randy

Ladies, it's not an either/or situation. Find a man who you are attracted to *and* who is a good guy. Whenever I receive a question like Randy's, my answer is always the same: Keep him as a friend but don't get romantically involved with him. Does this sound cruel? Shouldn't we give guys a chance even if we aren't that attracted to them? No way, Jose! Physical attraction is key. It must be present in the beginning for your relationship to have a chance in the future. That initial chemistry is essential to surviving the road ahead.

DATING RULE #120:
If you aren't physically attracted to him, he's a potential friend not a potential boyfriend.

Even if a relationship starts out with two people who are incredibly attracted to each other, the "spark" will diminish to some degree. The initial high will wear off and day-to-day life will set in. It just happens. But you've got to make sure the fire doesn't burn out completely.

So how do you keep the chemistry alive? When it comes to what a woman needs to do, it's really very simple: *She needs to maintain some mystery.*

Surviving and thriving in a long-term relationship.

DATING RULE #121:
A goddess always maintains some mystery.

> ### THE MAGIC FORMULA FOR KEEPING THE MYSTERY
> - Keep bathroom rituals to yourself.
> - Keep your own life.
> - Keep "dating."

I'm always skeptical when I hear women say, "My relationship is perfect. We share *everything*." Here's the truth: If you want to keep things passionate, you have to have things that are "yours" as well as things that are "ours." This is what creates excitement. In contrast, too much "togetherness" equals boredom. Or, as the famous saying goes, "Familiarity breeds contempt."

Dear Jenn,
I've heard you say that men like women who are mysterious. What does this mean? How can I be "mysterious" when we've been together for a million years? Does this mean I keep secrets or that I'm not transparent with him?
Kelsey

Being mysterious is not the same thing as being secretive, and it certainly isn't being deceptive. In fact, with just a few minor adjustments, you can seem mysterious to a man even if you've been together for many years.

When it comes to our daily routines, a man never needs to see you putting on deodorant, waxing your upper lip, or squeezing a zit. Don't follow him into the bathroom or keep the door open when either one of you is on the toilet. Don't talk about how bad your diarrhea is or

How to Be a Goddess

how you have the "taco shits." I know of one woman whose husband of over forty years has never witnessed her brushing her teeth. This may be the extreme, but I think you get my point. There are certain activities which should be done during "alone time" and certain things you don't need to discuss with your guy. Ever.

Likewise, maintaining your independence is also essential to maintaining your mystery. If he can predict where you'll be and what you'll be doing every moment of every day, there's an increased likelihood of boredom setting in. He shouldn't be able to set his watch by your comings and goings – no matter how long you've been together. Go out with your ladies, have a slumber party with your BFF once in a while, and take an occasional weekend trip with the girls.

My friend Bridgette realized the importance of maintaining the mystery with her long-term boyfriend, Paul.

"Throughout our relationship, I've placed a priority on having my own life and I refused to drop everything just because I had a boyfriend. For example, one night a week I have a 'girl's night out' with my friends. I never wanted to be that girl whose friends complain she's never around anymore because she spends all of her time with her boyfriend. It's funny – whenever I spend time apart from Paul, he seems to appreciate me more when I come back home. I think it's a good idea to let a man miss you from time to time."

Even more important is continuing with the hobbies and activities you enjoyed before you met him. I think every woman should have one thing that she is passionate about apart from her relationship and her career. Maybe it's Pilates. Maybe it's charity work. Whatever it is, it should be something that you love doing and that you do without your beloved. (Side note: Shopping doesn't count!) This is what makes us "well-rounded" and "balanced." And keep in mind that it is your "alone time" which will inspire a man to want to share romantic "together time" with you!

DATING RULE #122:
Maintaining your independence and some mystery not only helps to keep the chemistry alive, it's actually what encourages a man to keep courting his woman.

Speaking of "together time," I recently had a conversation with a married woman. She told me how she missed those pre-matrimonial days of dating her husband.

"It was so much fun to put on makeup and a pretty outfit. I remember how happy he would look when he picked me up. Now he sees every step of the process – from taking a shower to getting dressed. It's hard to have that 'special moment' when he sees you for the first time that evening looking beautiful. I think it takes away from the mystery and magic."

She's right. Once you are both living under the same roof, it can be difficult to truly continue "dating," but it is important that you do. It's a great idea to have a built-in "date night;" one night a week where you get a sitter (or alternate babysitting duties with a girlfriend) and leave the kids at home. Try to get ready separately or, better yet, when he's not even around. Do your best to give him that "ah-ha" moment of seeing you go from housewife to hottie. It will help you both to remember that you are still the same sexy woman he fell in love with.

Vacations – or if finances are tight "stay-cations" – are also important. I'm not talking about the family road trip to Disneyworld. Make it your goal that twice a year you ship any kids off to grandma's and get away – just the two of you. It doesn't have to be a trip that sets you back five figures. A short jaunt or a weekend where you lock yourselves in the house will do just fine. The important part is to spend some time together without the distractions of work, schedules, family, and your cell phones.

Sophia and Tim, a married couple I know, make sure they carve out time for their relationship even though they are often busy with the work of raising three boys.

"It can be extremely difficult to make our marriage a priority since our lives are packed full with different commitments and obligations.

A couple of years in, we realized that if our marriage was going to survive, we had to cultivate it and find the time to be together alone. Yes, we are parents, but we are also husband and wife.

We make sure we have one night a week where we let the kids stay with friends or with family members and we go out on a date. We also make sure to take a trip by ourselves once every six months. One year we took an amazing vacation to Jamaica. The next year, when money was tight, we stayed in town and went to a local hotel for the weekend. We've had periods of time where we thought we couldn't afford it – either financially or time-wise – but we came to the conclusion we couldn't afford *not* to do it. Having a strong marriage is that important to us. That solid bond also helps us to be better parents."

DATING RULE #123:
Create a feeling of newness in an old relationship by continuing to date.

Compatibility

Compatibility is an interesting thing isn't it? It's true you can't really have a successful relationship without it. But what makes two people truly "compatible?" More importantly, once life's ups and downs set in, how do you remain "compatible" over time?

Dear Jenn,

The longer I date my boyfriend, the less it seems that we have in common and it's starting to affect our relationship. Because we have different outlooks on life, we've started to` disagree more and more about things that might seem petty. We actually got into a big fight about whether basketball or football is the "better" sport. I'm serious!

Do you think it's true that "opposites attract?" Or is it better to be with someone who is similar to you? What should you look for when it comes to compatibility?

Autumn

Surviving and thriving in a long-term relationship.

We typically think that if we share similarities with our guy, that's what will make us compatible. This isn't totally untrue. There are certain fundamentals which, when shared, create the basis for a strong relationship. But it goes beyond that and encompasses more than just "getting along" with another person. In fact, there are three categories of compatibility.

THE CATEGORIES OF COMPATIBILITY

To have a successful, long-term relationship, you must be compatible in the following areas:

- **World View Compatibility:** How we are raised, our religious faiths, and our education levels are all examples of influences that shape how we look at life. Having similar backgrounds and beliefs can indeed translate into relational compatibility. Being in harmony on the "big things" – how to raise your family, financial matters, and faith – can help diffuse disagreements over the "little things." But even more important than agreement is respect. Seeking to understand where each of you is coming from and compromising when necessary is much more important. You and your guy aren't always going to be of like mind and it's ridiculous to think you will be.

- **Activity Compatibility:** I think there's truth to the old adage that "couples who play together, stay together." Yes, keeping your independence and "alone time" is important, but so is having a shared interest or hobby with your guy. It's not so important what it is – it could be wine tasting or going to the movies. What is important is you enjoy it as a couple and carve out time to make it a priority. If you don't have an interest or two in common, chances are high your relationship will get stale and eventually fizzle out.

> ■ **Negative Trait Compatibility:** I think women overlook this much too often. How do you feel about his worst habits or biggest piece of baggage? Is it something you can live with? If it never changes or gets any better, are you okay with that? As far as I see it, guys come with an "as-is" policy. Trying to change him into who or what you want him to be rarely works. Sure, we all go through transformations as we grow older and grow up. But while our lives and our relationships may refine us somewhat, who we fundamentally are usually doesn't change. So make sure his "negative qualities" work with your own faults. Remember that what is mildly annoying now will be ten times worse in ten years. Finding someone who you can live with and love through their worst moments makes for true compatibility.

One of the most frequently asked questions I receive about compatibility concerns religious views. Women ask me whether or not a relationship between people of different faiths can work.

Dear Jenn,

My boyfriend and I have been together for close to a year. We're at that point where we are deciding if we have what it takes to get married. So far, everything has been great with the exception of one major problem. You see, he's Hindu and I'm Muslim.

It doesn't bother us now, but I do wonder if this difference would affect our relationship should we end up getting married. In addition, neither of our parents is particularly enthusiastic about the idea of us marrying. I love him but I don't want to overlook something as important as this. What are your thoughts?

Farrah

Surviving and thriving in a long-term relationship.

Can a marriage work if the husband and wife have different religions? Yes, absolutely. However, it is one of those deeply personal belief systems that can be extremely difficult to navigate. Details such as what religion you will raise your children and whether you will observe your religions separately or together need to be discussed beforehand. It's also important to note Farrah's comment that both her potential future in-laws and her own parents might be unhappy about the union. While you shouldn't base your dating and marriage decisions solely on parental approval, inspiring their disapproval can be one more obstacle to relational compatibility. It's always a good thing to have families who support your marriage. Just ask any woman (or man) who's experienced a toxic mother-in-law!

Personally, I feel it is always preferable to have a common religious perspective. My boyfriend told me the story of a female friend of his who is Jewish and would only consider a Jewish man when it came to marriage.

"What if you met the perfect guy and the only problem was he wasn't Jewish?" he asked her.

"Then he wouldn't be the perfect guy for me," she said.

Great answer! If you and your guy have different faiths but you are both respectful of your individual beliefs and willing to work through any issues – go for it. However, if you are like my boyfriend's friend and have clear-cut deal breakers when it comes to religion – amen to that, too.

DATING RULE #124:
Never overlook the importance of finding someone you are compatible with.

Compromise
Here's what you *never* want to compromise: Yourself. Your goals, your morality, your sense of who you are – those are non-negotiable. No relationship is ever worth giving them up and trying to do so will only make for unhappiness and dysfunction. Any man who expects you to compromise yourself and the things that make your life complete is not a man worth having.

How to Be a Goddess

Tammy learned this lesson while dating Harrison. They weren't more than a few months into their relationship before he wanted her to transform various aspects of herself to better suit his preferences.

"He made me feel who I am wasn't enough for him. He was very critical and tried to influence my behavior and my way of thinking. He demanded things were done on his terms alone. He tried to tell me what I should eat, who I should vote for, and the type of music I should be listening to. It wasn't about compromise. It was about control."

DATING RULE #125:
A goddess never compromises herself.

However, fundamental to healthy relationships is the ability to compromise on the "little things." It's about learning to be okay with not always getting what you want right when and how you want it. It's about being able to see that another person's needs are just as important as your own. There's got to be some give with your take.

SOME EXAMPLES OF HEALTHY COMPROMISE

- He likes beef. You like fish. Compromise by cooking chicken a couple of times a week.
- Don't always drag him to see the latest "chick flick." Go with your girlfriends instead. If he sat through a couple of estrogen-driven tear jerkers with you, tell him you'd love to see an action movie with him next time. Similarly, take turns controlling the television remote.
- The weekends shouldn't be all about what you want to do. "Quality time" isn't you shopping while he dozes on a bench in the mall. Instead, come up with activities you both enjoy.
- If you disagree over how to spend money, talk it through. Make a budget together and come up with a solution that both of you are cool with.

No self-respecting woman would be content with a selfish guy who only cares about his own desires. Likewise, we shouldn't expect our man to be concerned with our happiness to the exclusion of his. That just isn't fair. If there's something you do which upsets or bothers him, look at it from his perspective and think about working on it. There's nothing wrong with allowing a relationship to help you to become a better person.

I've learned the joy of compromise in my own relationship. For example, I wasn't particularly fond of watching hockey on television. (Viewing it live from great seats is another matter, however.) My boyfriend, on the other hand, is a *huge* hockey fan. Although there are plenty of times that I'd rather put something else on the TV, I've made sure he has the opportunity to view the games that are important to him. Since he often indulges my obsession with true crime programs, it's the least I can do. You know what? I've started to love watching hockey with him. Some of our most fun times together have been spent watching a Los Angeles King's game at a sports bar while eating chicken wings and potato skins.

DATING RULE #126:
If compromise is healthy compromise, it will benefit both of you.

Communication

In an earlier chapter, I briefly mentioned that men often make the generalization that women talk too much. We do. Here is how one man I interviewed described his ex-wife:

"She never stopped talking. As soon as I'd get home from work, she'd start talking non-stop. She'd talk to me through the bathroom door. She'd talk all throughout dinner and wouldn't let me get a word in. She had an opinion on everything and never shut up. Sometimes I'd go to the gym just to get away from her voice and find some peace and quiet."

Another one of my male friends echoed his sentiment. He told me that most of the women he has dated recently have a hard time *not* communicating their every thought.

"Men don't want to know everything a woman is thinking right away. It's more intriguing if she keeps some things to herself. I find myself listening and nodding a lot on dates because I'm not given the opportunity to talk. They may think they are communicating but in reality they come off as needy for attention."

DATING RULE #127:
When it comes to communication, women need to focus on quality rather than on quantity.

Just because you are a "Chatty Cathy," doesn't mean you are a good communicator. In fact, the best communicators are often adept at listening more than they speak. Effective communication isn't about discussing every thought that pops into your head. Instead, it has to do with expressing your needs and desires to your partner in a way he can understand and be receptive to.

ARE YOU A BAD COMMUNICATOR OR A GOOD COMMUNICATOR?

- A bad communicator doesn't let the other person speak. A good communicator makes sure her partner has an opportunity to be heard.
- A bad communicator interrupts or plans what she's going to say while her guy is still talking. A good communicator knows how to truly listen.
- A bad communicator expects that her man will know what she wants or needs without having to say anything. (And then gets upset when he doesn't do it.) A good

communicator has no trouble expressing her expectations without being demanding.

- A bad communicator is afraid to bring up important issues for fear of rejection or criticism. A good communicator is not scared to address significant matters.
- A bad communicator often lets discussions become heated. A good communicator knows how to keep a cool head.
- A bad communicator goes off on tangents. A good communicator stays focused on the topic at hand.

Commitment

Very few relationships will survive if there's no end goal. Most couples can't keep dating for years and years with no thought of the future. For the vast majority of people this "ending point" is known as marriage.

I think it's a fallacy to believe that men are so averse to getting married. If that were true, marriage would not happen as often as it does. The fact is most people end up getting married at some point in their lives. How many of those men are led down the aisle while kicking and screaming? Not too many. In fact, the vast majority of weddings I've attended usually contain a groom who looks adoringly at his wife-to-be.

Dear Jenn,

My boyfriend and I have been together for nearly four years and living together for three of them. In the past, he told me I was someone he would consider marrying. However, he's no longer saying that. In fact, whenever I bring up the subject of marriage he says he doesn't want to talk about it.

This causes us to have a lot of arguments. He knows I want to get married and that I'm becoming impatient. What should I do? Is it time to tell him we're finished if he doesn't want to marry me?

Carly

How to Be a Goddess

All too often, women make the mistake of thinking that she somehow has to coerce or manipulate a man into proposing marriage. She thinks if she doesn't give him an ultimatum, he'll never get there on his own. Usually, the problem isn't the idea of marriage itself, it's that the woman isn't someone he wants to marry.

DATING RULE #128:
A goddess never has to force a man to marry her. Instead, he wants to marry her because she is someone he can't live without.

If you've followed this book, you should have no trouble moving to a place of long-term commitment. Why? Because you haven't wasted time on a guy who isn't serious about you. Because you've conducted yourself like a goddess throughout your relationship. And because he is so crazy about you that securing you for a lifetime is his only option.

There are, however, a few things you should keep in mind if marriage is your goal. These are additional tips to help you get the ring…

IF YOU WANT TO GET TO "I DO," DON'T DO THE FOLLOWING:

- Don't ever give the impression that marriage is your ultimate objective. Not on the first date or the fiftieth or the five hundredth. The less pressure he feels, the more likely he is to want to commit.
- Don't move in together if you want to get married. Couples who shack up are more likely to break up. Don't underestimate the "why buy the cow when you can get the milk for free" mentality. Living together can delay him wanting to get married.
- Don't even mention marriage until a year has passed and he's crazy in love. If he hasn't proposed within one to two

> years, tell him you'd like to get married at some point and ask him what his thoughts are. If he says he's not ready, take him at his word. Decide if you want to continue seeing him, but never try to force his hand.
> - Don't get knocked up hoping he will marry you. That's beyond wrong.

For others , marriage isn't even on their radar. Instead, many women today are looking for what I like to call "the committed partnership." On paper, it might very well look like a marriage, *but without "the papers."*

Johnna always thought that she would be devastated if she wasn't married by the time she was thirty. Now that she's closing in on thirty five, her views on having to be married are changing.

"I've started to realize I'm okay if I never get married. Don't get me wrong, I do want to share my life with someone. However, it doesn't have to be the whole white dress and horse-drawn carriage fairy tale."

The great thing about being alive today is there is no one-size-fits-all rule when it comes to how you want your life to look. There's no law which says you have to get married to have a full and satisfying life. If you want to emulate Oprah more than June Cleaver, that's well within your rights. Deciding not to get married (or remarried) doesn't make your relationship any less valid.

If you're one of those women looking for "the committed partnership" rather than a marriage, there still needs to be an articulated commitment. You both need to be on board for the long-haul. No, there's no marriage license keeping you there, but there's a promise nonetheless. And once you move in together (thereby embarking on your partnership), you're still going to need to negotiate the day-to-day terms of your lives – how to handle finances and household responsibilities, for example.

How to Be a Goddess

Regardless of how it's accomplished – either by marriage or a "committed partnership" – the vast majority of us need a long-term commitment in order to have a long-term relationship. Living separately and dating for years upon years is rarely a situation that works. We need to invest in something that has staying power, not merely spin our wheels.

Dear Jenn,

My boyfriend is confusing me! He has said he wants to get married and have kids someday, but lately he's been backing off of that statement. Whenever I simply mention the word "marriage," he gets an unhappy look on his face and tries to change the subject.

We've been together for almost two years now. I don't want to waste time with someone who isn't serious about me and I think it might be time to cut my losses. Do you have any suggestions on how I can tell if I'm with a guy who has no intention of ever marrying me without bringing up the subject of marriage? I feel like every time I talk about it, he shuts down and refuses to communicate.

Mahdvi

One of the biggest challenges a woman faces is figuring out if her guy is commitment-minded. Use this checklist to see if he's visualizing forever or focused on right now.

IS HE NEARSIGHTED?

People who are nearsighted have trouble seeing things in the distance; not unlike a man who isn't envisioning a long-term future with you.

- If words like marriage, wedding, and kids make him shudder…he's nearsighted.
- If he tells you he has no interest in *ever* getting married… he's nearsighted.

- If he hasn't introduced you to his family and friends after a few months...he's nearsighted.
- If he doesn't take his work or financial independence seriously...he's nearsighted.
- If he makes little effort to include you in his everyday life... he's nearsighted.
- If you suspect he's not quite done sowing his wild oats... he's nearsighted.

DATING RULE #129:

Unless there is some sort of long-term commitment, you won't be able to sustain a long-term relationship.

Your "LTR"

One of the biggest relationship myths is that when it's "right," your relationship will be easy. It won't be.

> *Dear Jenn,*
> *My friend recently got engaged and posted on her Facebook page, "When you know, you know." Do you think this is true? If a relationship is the right one does that mean there are no hard times? I've thought I've "known" with a couple of different guys but all of those relationships eventually ended. Will there be that one, special guy who will be different?*
> *Sharon*

Even the best relationships can be difficult at times and require energy and effort. The best relationships are those where both involved continually strive to cultivate and nurture it. Those are the relationships which survive and thrive. Unfortunately, this is a rare occurrence in today's era of disposable commitments where most people would rather jump ship than do the things necessary to grow their love.

How to Be a Goddess

So I say we need to alter our thinking. A great love doesn't mean your relationship won't require work. It totally will. But when you find it, it should inspire you to want to do the work. And that "work" will be more of a joy than a burden.

DO AS I SAY, NOT AS I DID
(My Own Journey from Doormat to Goddess)

I was always pretty skillful with getting guys to "like" me. But when it came to having a successful, long-term relationship? Not so much. In my younger years, I used to tell my friends that I was great at getting a boyfriend, but not so great at being a girlfriend.

I think most of this stemmed from the fact I bought into the whole "when it's right, it's easy" myth. Due to my immaturity and naivety, I had no idea what I was supposed to do in order to cultivate a relationship. Communication and compromise were not my strengths, to say the least. I had no idea how to sustain the chemistry. My level of commitment depended on the level of my other options. Combine all of this with the fact I didn't choose men I was truly compatible with or those who were the best candidates for an LTR themselves… Disaster alert!

As the divorce statistics prove, most people – both males and females – struggle when it comes to sustaining a long-term relationship. We often get such a rush from the early days of a romance, that we forget that what is new will eventually become old. We want to maintain those head-over-heels feelings and when they fade and the real work sets in, we become disillusioned. Many of us – me included – will bounce from relationship to relationship hoping to get that excitement once again.

Have you ever heard the expression "chasing the dragon?" It is usually used to describe heroin addicts who keep trying to get the high of the very first time they felt an opiate rush. I, too, have "chased the dragon" when it came to love. As soon as my relationships became too "difficult," I would move on to another, seemingly "better" one. Just like an addict, I wanted to recapture those earlier feelings and hoped things would be different the next time around. But it wasn't too long before the same old problems would rear their ugly heads. And my current relationship would become a carbon copy of the one that preceded it.

The bottom line is this: Until we really begin to do the work to sustain our relationships, we won't have successful relationships. Changing relationships is not the answer if we haven't tried changing our current relationship. For me, it took going through a divorce – and realizing I never wanted to go through another – to break my patterns and alter my thinking. Finding love is fantastic, but doing the work to grow it is even better.

Great relationships are not easy. But it shouldn't go without saying that having a relationship with a great man (who thinks that you are great in return) does indeed make it easier to work towards relationship greatness. After years of dealing with counterfeits, when you find the "real thing," you rarely want to let it go.

XX

Step #12

FAQs every goddess wonders.

I love the questions I receive from my readers. Not only is it rewarding to help others solve their relationship issues, but I learn things in the process. And because you trust me as an authority, I am absolutely encouraged to practice what I preach. My readers really do help me to be more goddess-like in my own life! So I thank you for that.

Most of the questions you ask fall into a few distinct categories. Many of them – "How do I know if he likes me?" or "Where do I meet guys?" for example – I've already tackled in this book. But some of them don't fit neatly and nicely into one of the preceding "steps." Some of them are unique situations which can occur at any point within a relationship. And I've been saving them for this last part of our journey together.

So without further ado, let me outline the last big relationship questions and issues that almost every goddess will have to deal with at some point in her romantic life. Master them and you'll have earned extra credit toward your "goddess degree."

> **BONUS POINTS IN ACHIEVING "GODDESS STATUS"**
> Congratulations! You're nearly there! Just a few more tips to help you fine tune your new-found skills and avoid some common pitfalls. In this "step" we're going to learn:
> - How to handle it when he does the "guy pull back."
> - How to deal with your hormones.
> - Why you shouldn't try to change a man.
> - How to prevent cheating (as much as possible).
> - How to get over heartbreak.
> - What to do if you *don't* like him.

Sound good? Let's get to it!

The "guy pull back"

I receive countless questions from confused women who want to know why their once loving and attentive guy seems like he's "cooling off." If you've experienced this, you're not alone. In fact, the "guy pull back" is one of the most common relationship problems. And it happens – to some degree or another – in almost every relationship.

> *Dear Jenn,*
> *What's up with guys who go after you like crazy and then, once they've "gotten" you, stop giving you as much attention? I've had this exact thing happen with almost every guy I've dated for more than a couple of months. It's so annoying!*
> *What I can I do to prevent this from happening in the future?*
> *Marcela*

Can you relate to Marcela's question? I know I can and I've been in her situation myself. Let's start by defining it so we all know what it is we are talking about. According to my dictionary, the "guy pull back" is:

When a man, who pursued you in the beginning of the relationship, eases up on the pursuit.

HOW TO SPOT THE "GUY PULL BACK"

At its most benign, the "guy pull back" will include (but is not limited to) the following behaviors:

- Calling (a little) less or not calling for a couple of days at a time.
- Wanting to see you (a little) less than he did in the beginning.
- Being (a little) cold, distant, or aloof.
- Acting (a little) less enthusiastic and certain of you and/or the relationship.

The "guy pull back" should not be confused with its more extreme cousin, the "guy pull out."

Dear Jenn,

Five months ago I began a relationship with a guy I've known for several years. He's been everything I could ask for. He's sweet, caring, and funny. I've completely fallen for him!

He recently told me his feelings were fading and he said he had no idea why. He didn't want to see me much after that and I barely heard from him. Then he just went completely silent. I've tried texting him a few times over the past couple of days, but he hasn't texted me back.

Is this the "guy pull back" you've written about? What should I do to get him interested again?

Isabelle

What Isabelle experienced is not the "guy pull back," but rather the "guy pull out." The "guy pull out" is basically a hop, skip, and a jump to a "break-up." Here's how the "guy pull out" might manifest itself.

IF IT'S THE "GUY PULL OUT," YOU'VE PRETTY MUCH BEEN DUMPED

I love the quote "If he was stupid enough to walk away, be smart enough to let him go." So if you experience one or more of the following, say "Ciao!" and wave buh-bye. He's sooo not worth your energy.

- He completely blows you off with little or no explanation.
- He disappears for a week (or more) at a time.
- He says things like, "I need space," "I'm not sure how I feel," or "It's not you, it's me."
- He puts forth little to no effort in sustaining the relationship or moving things along. Basically, he checks out and you're the only one doing any work.

If you've been following this book from the beginning, chances are your experience with the "guy pull back" will be minimal. Most men pull back when a relationship goes at lightning speed. So if you've been doing what you're supposed to be doing (i.e., going slowly), chances are great he won't pull back much, if at all.

DATING RULE #130:

The slower you go in the beginning, the less your guy will pull back.

Another occasion when a man might pull back is after you sleep with him for the first time.

After Jocelyn had sex with the man she'd been dating, she felt him grow a little distant.

How to Be a Goddess

"He backed off a bit. Not so much that I was alarmed, but I definitely noticed a slow down when it came to contacting me. It lasted for a couple of weeks before things went back to normal."

How did Jocelyn handle what I've termed the "post-sex pull back?" Like a goddess!

"I didn't even let him know I was aware of what was happening. I kept doing my thing and stayed busy. I didn't go psycho or start to act insecure. I think my 'coolness' was instrumental in him coming around again."

Again, the longer you wait to have sex, the less likely he is to pull back. But if it does happen, don't freak out! Don't become needy or clingy. Don't ask for reassurance that he still likes you. Act as if nothing has changed and go about your business. Show him you are still the same cool girl he has gotten to know up until this point. Once you do that, the "post-sex pull back" usually disappears quickly.

Sometimes when a man pulls back, it has nothing to do with us. Perhaps he has a work deadline looming, is dealing with a disappointment or setback, or is trying to handle a catastrophe. Here's an extreme example.

Dear Jenn,

My boyfriend is going through a really hard time. His mom recently (and unexpectedly) died which has understandably been tough on him. He's also been struggling at work. He has a new boss and the two of them don't exactly get along.

Since his mom's death, he's been acting a little bit distant. He still wants to see me but our time together is strained. I feel like I'm walking on eggshells and I don't want to upset him further.

I know his mom's death and his work situation is getting him down. I've asked him if I am doing anything wrong and he swears it has nothing to do with us. I want to be there for him but I feel like the *more I tell him this and offer my help, the more he backs away. I'm trying to let him know that I care but I don't think he sees that. What should I do?*

Kennedy

This is what I call the "crisis pull back." When it happens, you will usually know. Why? Because he cares enough about you to tell you about it. Sure, he'll probably still need his space; time to deal with it in his own way. Your job is to let him.

Here's how you deal with the "crisis pull back." Let him know you care and then let him handle it himself. Say something like this: "I know you're dealing with/going through___. I'm here for you if you need me. I want to help if you want me to." And then leave him alone. Depending on the circumstance, I might be hesitant to even ask about it again. (Use your own best judgment here.) Allow him his time alone and welcome him back without reproach when he returns. And never force him to discuss his "feelings" with you. If he wants to, he will. And he'll be much more likely to do so if he doesn't feel pressured.

If your guy is just pulling back for no reason in particular, how do you handle it?

Dear Jenn,

I've been seeing this guy for several weeks now. At first, he was extremely attentive and consistent with pursuing me. Once I went on a few dates with him, I noticed he didn't text as much. Suddenly, I was the one contacting him and asking him if he wanted to see me.

I don't understand what is going on. He still seems somewhat interested, but not as interested as he was in the beginning. Is there anything I can do to change this around?

Lucy

How to Be a Goddess

The first thing Lucy, and all other women in her situation, should do is stop believing the myths about it. Don't make the mistake of listening to well-meaning girlfriends who may say things like "He's just busy" or "He's scared." As my boyfriend likes to say, "Men make time for what is important to them." He's right. If he's smitten, a man won't go days without contacting you. It doesn't matter if he's sick, swamped at work, or studying for exams. No guy is too busy to send a quick text or to make a brief call to a woman he cares about. And men don't usually "get scared" because they feel intensely about us. Sure they "get scared," but it's usually because we've scared them away. So identify the "guy pull back." Call it out (in your mind, *not* to him please) and don't make excuses for him.

The worst thing you can do is to try to move toward him, which is exactly what non-goddesses (doormats) out there do. They'll ask their guy "What's wrong?" or "Are we okay?" They'll bake him cupcakes or buy him a gift. They'll start pursuing him. But not you, my dear goddess! Instead, you reciprocate and respond by pulling back, too.

DATING RULE #131:
If a man is acting like he wants space, you need to give him the galaxy.

Be busy. Be hard to get a hold of. Be just outside of his reach. Go out with your girlfriends and don't return his calls right away. When he does get in touch with you, you are friendly for sure. Don't act mad, hurt, or disappointed.

When Zoe noticed her boyfriend seemed to be a little less attentive and enthusiastic about her, she fought her natural instinct to chase after him.

"I wanted to be extra nice and loving, hoping that would warm him up again. I wanted to start calling him all the time just to make sure we were okay. Then my friend told me that approach would likely send him in the opposite direction. I was a little skeptical at first. I mean, shouldn't I make it overly clear how I feel about him? But I listened to her advice. Instead, I kept busy and tried not to obsess. I became so busy, in fact, that there were a couple of times I couldn't see him because I already had plans. Even though I wanted to break them, I stuck to my guns. Sure enough, my friend was right. After a week or so of me pulling away from him, he was *dying* to see me."

Generally speaking, men don't respond well to women behaving all emotional and pressuring them to reciprocate. They don't like to answer questions such as "What's going on with you?" and "Why are you acting like this?" What they *do* respond to is the fear they may lose something important to them. Show him just how important you indeed are. The way you do this is by giving him space, pulling back as well, and allowing him the opportunity to miss you. Pressuring him or even giving the illusion of heading toward him will cause him to shrink back further, and very possibly disappear altogether.

I like to think of the whole "guy pull back" thing as a kind of dating physics. What's that law of motion Newton came up with? Oh, right, here it is... "To every action there is always an equal and opposite reaction; or the forces of two bodies on each other are always equal and directed in opposite directions." (Thanks, Wikipedia!) Those science buffs out there may think this is a crude analogy, but it's one I can wrap my brain around and picture in my head.

Here's how it works out: He pulls back from you, you pull back from him. He moves away from you, you move away from him. It's simple, really. But here's what Isaac Newton didn't anticipate (at least when it comes to *human* bodies): Responding to his pull back with an equal pull back yourself will almost always cause another reaction – he will once again move toward you. And *that's* how you deal with the "guy pull back." Goddess-style.

How to Be a Goddess

How to handle your hormones

Many of the questions you ladies ask me have the following inserted as a side note: "I was totally hormonal," "I think I freaked out on him because I was having my period," or "I wasn't feeling like myself because it was that time of the month." Listen up. Hormones happen. They're real. And they can affect everything from our moods to our energy levels to our sex drives. It's time for us to "woman up" and accept it.

> *Dear Jenn,*
>
> *I'm starting to notice a pattern. Every time I'm about to get my period I become super sensitive and very emotional. If I'm single, it's not such a big deal. I'll just get a little sad. However, if I'm in a relationship – watch out! Everything my boyfriend says is likely to start a fight.*
>
> *This has caused major problems in my past. I've been single for nearly three years now but I've just started seeing a new guy. He seems really great and I think I like him! I want to prevent this from happening with him. Do you know if that's possible?*
>
> *Sophia*

Let me be honest here. I get Sophia's struggle. I, too, have had my fair share of hormone-driven outbursts. When I was younger, I don't know how much I correlated my "hyper-sensitivity" with PMS. But as I've gotten older (and hopefully wiser and more in tune with my body), I have definitely seen the connection. I wish I could tell you I've perfectly mastered the art of dealing with my hormones. I haven't. But I sure am getting better at it. Here's what I've learned.

YOUR BODY, YOUR PERIOD*
(*Everything you ever wanted to know about Aunt Flo but were afraid to ask)

■ **Know when it's happening.** When I was younger, my mom told me I should keep track of my periods. This seemed lame, annoying, and antiquated. Kinda like those weird and uncomfortably thick old-school Kotex maxi-pads. Ummm, no thanks. But as I've matured, I see the value of this advice. Isn't it better to know when crazy might be coming to town? Wouldn't this help us to somewhat prepare for it? I think so. So figure out the days when you might not be feeling your best. When our emotions sneak up on us, they become a lot harder to handle.

■ **Figure out how it affects you.** When I was in high school, I remember the following happening quite frequently: I'd receive less than an "A-" on a test and I'd start to fight back tears. (Yes, I was a somewhat gawky, not particularly popular nerd.) And the next day? Poof! I'd get my period. As I got older, a sappy "diamonds are forever" commercial would cause the water works to start. (Next day? Poof! Period.) A guy didn't do what I expected him to do? My eyes would spurt like Old Faithful. (Next day? Yeah, you guessed it...) I eventually realized that the day before my period, there's an increased likelihood of emotional sensitivity. How does it make *you* feel? Crabby, cranky, and irritable? Tired and fatigued? Bloated and therefore "fat?" All of the above? Once you identify it, you'll go a long way in being able to manage it.

■ **"Medicate" it.** Let me put on my "motherly advice" cap. During that time of the month, it's important to get lots of rest, drink plenty of water, exercise (this alleviates cramps and regulates hormones), and stay away from foods that may make it worse (caffeine for me). My mom (is she a period guru or what?) swears calcium-magnesium supplements help with all types of PMS symptoms.

■ **Be wary.** If you know when it's coming and how it will affect you, this final piece of advice may be easier to follow. When you're in the throes of hormonal chaos, it's never a good idea to make a big decision or get into a "heavy" conversation with your significant other. If you find yourself upset about something he does or says, take a breath and ask yourself if maybe (just maybe) your estrogen levels aren't affecting your judgment. Try to keep your life as easy and stress-free as possible. Hopefully you've got the type of relationship where you can say "Honey, I'm feeling a bit hormonal. Go easy on me." And hopefully he's the kind of man who will understand.

DATING RULE #132:
Even goddesses get hormonal!
Why you shouldn't try to change a man

How often do we meet a guy and think to ourselves:

"He's great.

If only he didn't _____ ."

"If only he was more _____ ."

"If only he wasn't _____ ."

And then we set out to change him; we try to mold him into the man we want him to be.

My friend Peyton tried to change her boyfriend, only to meet with disastrous results.

"I thought I really loved Joel, but there were a few things about him that I couldn't stand," she explained to me. "First off, there was the way he dressed. It was awful. He wore sweats and baseball caps every time we went to dinner. So I started off buying him a whole bunch of new clothes. He thanked me, but I could tell he wasn't overjoyed. The next thing I tried to fix was his bad grammar. If he said, 'I feel badly for her,' I would correct him by saying, 'You feel *bad* for her.' I think he tried to ignore me when I did that. When I attempted to tell him he should switch careers and get out of sales and into consulting he asked me, 'Do you really like me?' I told him I did and was only trying to help him improve. I'll never forget what he said to me: 'I'm looking for a woman who loves me, not someone she wants me to be.' He broke up with me right then and there."

I'm sure you've heard the saying "You can't change a man." Guess what? It's true. Yet, judging from the questions I receive from my readers, Peyton is not alone. Many of us have tried to change a man. We usually fail miserably.

Dear Jenn,

I've been dating a guy for a little over six months now and I think I'm in love with him. He's everything I've been looking for – smart, good looking, confident, and nice. There's just one problem. He is a huge partier. He goes out with his friends several times a week to bars and clubs. He's always out on the town and I'm not particularly crazy about the group of guys he hangs out with.

I've tried everything to get him to slow down. I told him that I don't want to be with a guy who is always going out and drinking. I've tried to encourage him to do things other than going to bars. He doesn't listen! Instead, he insists this is just "him" and that he's young and wants to have a good time.

Is there any way to change this part of him? I really think he could be "the one."

Mackenzie

Remember how men come with an "as-is" policy? If you decide to purchase him, you've got to live with both the good and the bad without expecting those things to change. In fact, there are very few things you can truly change about him. You might have a little pull with his hairstyle. And maybe, just maybe, with his wardrobe. But that is pretty much it. It all goes back to objectively analyzing his character from the first moment you meet him. Because his character is the one thing which will never change. Ever.

DATING RULE #133:
You can never change who a man is fundamentally.

Women also make a big mistake when they fall for a guy based on his "potential." It's fine to envision what he's realistically capable of becoming in the near future. For example, if he's in medical school, it's okay to see him as a *potential* doctor. But you should never fall in love with an out-of-work video game "creator" because of his genius level IQ. Yet women do this all the time. They see what they think a man could be doing and then they try to "help" him reach his (her) goals.

My friend Riley thought her boyfriend Todd could be much "greater" than what he currently was – a bike messenger.

"He was incredibly smart; a real genius when it came to numbers and figures. I thought for sure he'd make a killer accountant or actuary. I was in business school myself at the time, working hard to get my MBA. I wanted a partner who had equally high goals. I kept trying to push him into taking the GMAT and to apply to business schools, but he kept blowing me off. One day he finally told me, 'Listen, I like my job. I like not having enormous responsibility and riding around on my bike all day. If you want a business man, find one.' He was right. So instead of trying to make him into what I wanted him to be, we parted ways and I found someone better suited to me."

Falling in love with his potential or for what he's capable of rather than who is actually is invariably sets both the "changer" and the "changee" up for frustration, resentment, and disappointment. So instead, focus on the man he is in this present moment; not the one you think or hope he can be.

You can and should have plenty of opinions about your own life – your beliefs, choices, and boundaries. But most men don't want a woman who barks orders and tells them what to do when it comes to *their* lives. Guys like to feel they can make their own decisions without your unsolicited advice. They see such behavior as controlling and domineering and it's a big time turn-off, especially in the beginning of a relationship. As your partnership grows, it's not uncommon for a man to ask your input on everything from wardrobe choices to career advice. Congratulations! He values and trusts your opinion and is looking to include you in his decisions. Until that time, it's best to let him do his thing without offering your two cents.

If you've ever made the mistake of trying to change a man into who and what you want him to be, you know what it feels like. Kinda like hitting your head against a concrete block, right? So here's the bottom line: If there's enough about him that upsets you and that you want to change, then it's probably time to make an "ex-change" and find a new object of your affection.

DATING RULE #134:
Don't try to change a man you know you can't live with. Instead, "exchange" him for a new one!

How to prevent cheating (as much as possible)

I've received some criticism for my thoughts on preventing cheating. Women have written to inform me that you can't really prevent someone from cheating if they're just a cheater at heart. I completely agree. But let's cut to the chase. Cheating (and its effects) is far and away the number one most common question I receive.

How to Be a Goddess

Dear Jenn,

Why does it seem that all guys eventually cheat? Every single one of my boyfriends has cheated on me and I can't understand why.

My current boyfriend always promised me he would never cheat. He knew my issues with it and told me he would be different. Turns out, he wasn't. Last night I found out that he hooked up with a girl he met at a bar who happened to be a friend of a friend. Even though this took place almost a month ago, one of my friends just told me yesterday! I would have had no idea and I'm sure he never would have admitted to it.

When I confronted him, he did confess. He said they didn't have sex. (I'm still trying to confirm that.) When I asked him why he did it, he made up some lame excuse that it was because we'd been having problems and he felt like I was always upset with him.

I'm not sure what to do now. I love him but I don't think I can trust him again. Why does this always seem to happen to me ?

Olivia

If I were to put a number on it, I'd say that over 75% of us have been cheated on at one point or another. Is that because we picked bad guys? Sure, sometimes it's as simple as that. But I can't help but feel there are occasions when we bear part of the responsibility. Not that cheating is ever okay – it's not – but I do think there are things women can do to minimize the chances of it happening when we are in a healthy relationship with a healthy guy.

Are you ready for the truth? Because here it is: Unless he's a heartless jerk, men are not very likely to cheat if they are in a relationship where their needs are being met. When he's in a great relationship with a great woman, a great guy will easily pass on some easy sex. In fact, it's usually not even that big of a deal. When he's truly in love, no other woman will compare. In the words of Bruno Mars, "They got nothin' on you, baby."

All this being said, don't think for a second that if he cheats, it's your fault. It's not. It's his. No matter what prompted it (be it problems in your relationship or the mere fact he's an a-hole), it is much more about him than you. A real man would deal with the issues and end things before he strays. Even so, I know without a doubt that employing the following strategies will cause him to believe he's got the greatest woman ever. Which will make both of you pretty darn happy and your entire relationship that much stronger.

So how do you prevent cheating? Let's take a look. Remember that most of it has already been discussed throughout this book. Just by being a goddess, you'll go a long way in making sure that – with a quality guy – it doesn't happen. But it never hurts to take a refresher course.

DATING RULE #135:
It's absolutely possible to prevent cheating.

AFFAIR-PROOFING YOUR RELATIONSHIP
Keeping the home fires burning makes him flame retardant to outside temptations.

- **Pick your men carefully.** Players, commitment-phobes, and guys who think life's rules don't apply to them are bad choices. Guys with good character and strong morals are less likely to cheat. It's as simple as that.
- **Don't push him into a commitment.** A lot of guys will acquiesce to a woman's wish for monogamy because he likes her and doesn't want to lose her. Great. But what you really want is a guy who is so crazy about you that the thought of you with another makes him miserable. When a man works to win a woman's heart, he becomes much less likely to throw it all away for a meaningless fling.
- **Don't take away his freedom.** Let's review. What is the number one thing men are afraid to lose? Correct! Their freedom. They need to maintain their independence and "guy activities." This is why you've got to let him do his thing, not

---

intrude on "guy time," and maintain your own life and interests besides him. If you try to keep him on a short leash, he's going to want to pull away. And some men will "pull away" and attempt to assert their independence by cheating.

- **Trust him.** Living in fear or accusing a man of infidelity without cause is a big time no-no. Think about it. Would you want a boyfriend who never wanted you to go out with friends, asked you to call hourly to "check in," or was always thinking you were up to no good? Would you want him looking at your texts or snooping in your personal space? I doubt it. Yet women engage in this type of behavior all the time. Acting as if you don't trust him can actually encourage him to prove you right. If you show you have faith in him, he's much more likely to want to honor that faith.

- **Treat him like he's your hero.** Remember that whole "respect" thing we talked about? It absolutely comes into play here. Bitching at him, nagging, or pointing out all his faults will tear him down. Instead praise him, encourage him, and let him know how wonderful you think he is. Appreciate him and tell him he's the best. If you consistently knock a man down, it won't be long before he's looking for someone to build him back up.

- **Keep him satisfied.** Guess what else makes him feel like a stud? Sex. So once you are in a committed relationship, you need to see to it that he's getting it often and he's getting it good. If he's like 99.9% of men, he needs sex. I'm no biologist (or would it be physiologist?), but I'm pretty sure this is a scientific fact. And not only does he want and need it regularly, he also wants and needs you to be into it. If you have any further questions on this subject, please reread Step #9 in its entirety. That should help you to figure it out.

When I wrote an article on preventing cheating for GirlsGuideTo.com, one reader commented that she and her husband had great success in their marriage by implementing the techniques I'd suggested. Here's part of her feedback:

"Yes, yes, and yes! We're going to celebrate our 25th anniversary in March and those are exactly the things I did. We are closer now than ever!"

How encouraging is that?

How to get over heartbreak

After issues of infidelity, the second most common question I am asked is how to get over a broken heart. We've all been there, haven't we? And we all know how badly it can suck. Whenever I receive a question from a reader whose heart has been split in half, I immediately want to give her a huge hug and let her cry on my shoulder for at least a day or two.

Dear Jenn,

I feel like my world is crashing down around me. My boyfriend broke up with me two weeks ago and I am completely devastated.

I still have strong feelings for him even though I know deep down that he isn't the guy for me. It is so hard to move on. I can't eat, can't sleep, and can barely move.

How do I begin to heal? I can't take this pain much longer.

Brooklyn

I am sure we'd all love to have a magic pill that would instantly remove all traces of heartbreak. I wish I had one for you, but unfortunately I don't. In fact, there have been many times I would have loved to have one myself. The truth is that getting over having your heart crushed takes time. It just does.

One of the things that is so fabulous about the goddess way of life is it truly minimizes your chances of getting dumped. Instead of going after bad guys who will ultimately hurt you, you're taking the time to truly make sure a man is high quality. You go slowly and don't give your heart away to any old guy who will borrow it for a bit. You keep your emotions in check by waiting to have sex. You work on being the best woman you can be in a relationship. Any man who would toss that away is surely crazy!

But heartbreak does happen. Couples realize they aren't right for each other and go their separate ways. Relationships do fall apart. Not everything concludes with a fairy tale ending. That's just the way life works sometimes.

Maybe you're reading this book because you haven't totally gotten over the last guy who sliced and diced your heart to bits. Maybe you're still clinging to the fantasy of a former love and are having trouble fully letting go and moving on. Maybe you're not ready for a new relationship because you aren't really over an old one. Yeah, I get it. And I've been there, too.

> *Dear Jenn,*
> *Why am I still pining for my ex? He is so totally wrong for me and our relationship was toxic. I know for a fact he is bad news and yet I still miss him!*
> *I keep hoping I find someone who makes me forget him, but I can't seem to let him go. I think my feelings are preventing me from truly moving on. How in the hell do I get over him???*
> *Amelia*

So for all my girls who are nursing a broken heart, this one's for you. I can't totally take away all of your pain. But hopefully these tips will help to get you through it.

DATING RULE #136:
Heartbreak sucks.

DATING RULE #137:
But you will, eventually, get over it.

HOW TO GET OVER THAT BASTARD WHO BROKE YOUR HEART

- **You grieve.** God invented cookie dough ice cream for a reason. I suggest taking a one week period of lying in bed (as much as your work or school schedule will permit) and crying your eyes out. A break up survival kit is not a bad idea. Make sure to have the following items close by at all times: Kleenex, take-out menus, a pint of Ben n Jerry's (don't forget a spoon), and your BFF on speed dial. But one week and no more, okay? Any longer and you'll be adding the ten pounds you gained to the list of things you're depressed about.

- **You cut him out of your life.** Don't pull up his Facebook page, check your phone every twenty seconds to see if he's called or texted, or do anything that reminds you of him. Do not contact him. Try to stay away from all social media outlets (no snarky status updates allowed) and email accounts. Immediately remove his contact info from your phone.

- **You avoid alcohol.** Don't go out and get drunk with your girls. More than likely you'll end up falling in the middle of the street, making out with a complete troll, drunk dialing your ex, and waking up feeling even worse. So when you get home from work, put your hair in a ponytail, wear your pajamas like they're the latest fashion, and be very, very thankful that Lifetime Movie Network has programming nearly 24/7.

- **You decide to feel better.** You've gotten to the point where you have no tears left, you're beginning to get bed sores, and the mere thought of ice cream makes you nauseous. Good! So put a comb through that rat's nest, trade your fuzzy slippers for some running shoes, and rejoin the land of the living! So much of our life is determined by our attitude and perspective. Start believing life will go on (it will), you will heal (you will), and someone will love you again (they will). I believe physical exercise is a great mood elevator (and it will help shed that break-up weight). So take long walks, go for a jog, or pull that dusty gym membership card out of your wallet. Train your body and your mind. When you find yourself thinking (obsessing) about him – stop. Just stop. Replace those thoughts by doing something positive that you enjoy. Let him go to boyfriend heaven and determine to move on. (Side note: If you must think about him, be sure to focus on all of his nasty qualities. One of my girlfriends kept repeating "Oddly shaped head when viewed from behind" to herself during her recent break-up.)

■ **You lean on your girlfriends.** There are many reasons why losing touch with your friends during a relationship is a bad idea. And, as any girl who's done exactly that and gone through a break-up will tell you, surviving heartbreak without strong female support is a very lonely experience. So after a break-up, it's imperative that you gather what I like to call your "Army of Bitches." Here's what you are looking for in your troops:

- A Sergeant: She's the one who will tell you straight up he was a loser/ugly/not worthy of you. She'll give you tough love when you find yourself wanting to slip back into the "grieving period."

- A Chaplain: This is the girl who will say profound and spiritual things. She should have the ability to guide you to your Zen place with her wisdom.

- A Private: Don't let the fact she has the "lowest" rank fool you. Your Private is (maybe) your biggest defense. She'll let you go on non-stop about every bad thing your bad guy did. She won't offer a lot of advice, but she will give a lot of sympathy. And as a result, you'll end up working through a lot of your misery just by talking her ear off.

■ **You rediscover (or discover) you.** Have you ever noticed how we women often lose ourselves in our relationships? It is much too common that we melt into a man to the point that we have little remaining self-identity. I think this is why break-ups are often so hard on us girls. Once he's gone, he's probably left a pretty big void, right? So now is your opportunity to find yourself – maybe even for the first time. What do you want your life to look like? What's important to you? Figuring it out – and pursuing it – will help you to come alive. It will renew your purpose. And it will help strengthen future relationships. Being whole and complete as a person (or as whole and complete as any of us can ever be) is a good thing. A man can't fix and fill our broken or missing pieces. We have to do it ourselves.

■ **You get back out there.** It's time to put back on your party dress and stilettos. Update your profile page. Start online dating (if you are so inclined). Let people know you are ready to be set up and accept any and all dates. Meeting an interesting new prospect (or ten) is exciting. (Side note: It never hurts if at least one of them is cuter, funnier, smarter, and richer than your last guy.) And it helps to put your ex where he belongs – in the past. At the very least, it will give you hope for the future. It's pretty hard to imagine yourself as the crazy cat lady who spends her days sitting on the bus stop while wearing a plastic shower cap when you're dating up a storm.

How to Be a Goddess

Getting over heartbreak takes time. How long, you ask? I wish I knew. Some break-ups are brutal while others aren't so bad. Some people leave scars that will – over time – heal, but will possibly never fully fade. (I have two myself.) What I do know is the horrible pain eventually becomes a dull ache which – at worst – turns into a minor pang every so often. And no matter how badly you feel in this present moment, it does indeed get much, much better.

What to do if you DON'T like him

Since we've dealt with everything from hormones to guys pulling back to cheating to heartbreak, I thought we'd conclude the FAQ portion of this chapter on a lighter note. How does that sound? So let's discuss what a goddess would do when faced with a man who is smitten and she's, ummm, not.

> *Dear Jenn,*
> *I was recently set up on a blind date by a guy friend of mine. My date turned out to be very nice, but he wasn't my type. Even though we had fun together, I didn't feel the need to pursue things further with him. A second date was definitely not needed!*
>
> *My problem is this guy is totally into me. He told my friend he likes me a lot and wants to see me again. I've told my friend I'm not interested, but he said it was up to me to tell him. He's made a few attempts to contact me but I haven't returned his calls. I don't want to hurt his feelings and I don't want to seem like a bitch. How would a goddess handle this?*
> *Miranda*

I'm a firm believer that honesty is always the best policy. There's no sense in continuing things when you're sure there's no future. It's not respectful to either the man or to your own desires.

What would a goddess do when she's confronted when a man is hot after her and she's feeling ice cold about him? Great question! Listen up ladies, because the more goddess-like you become, the more you will be faced with this situation.

LETTING HIM DOWN GENTLY (YET FIRMLY)

- Never say, "I'm not interested in a serious relationship right now." He'll see that as a challenge and usually pursue you harder. Politely thank him for the date (or the invitation to go on a date). Follow it up by saying something like, "I didn't feel a strong connection and I don't want to waste your time." Thank him again, wish him well, and then end the conversation.

- Some women like the "fake boyfriend" excuse. "Thanks so much, but I've started seeing someone." If it's the truth, there's no harm, but if it's not, I think it's the coward's way out.

- Don't pull a Houdini. We hate it when men disappear on us, so don't do it to him. When I was much younger I went on a few dates with a man who told me, "If you don't want to see me anymore, just tell me. Please don't stop returning my calls." Guess what I did? I stopped returning his calls. I still feel bad about that.

- Be honest with him. Don't tell your mutual friend or the person who set you up you're not into him. Tell him directly! I went out on a Match.com date with a man who I was positive wasn't for me. When he asked me out again, I wanted to dodge his calls as to not hurt his feelings. My friend Sheridan said to me, "Jenn, just tell him. He's paying a monthly fee to find someone." I took her advice. He was a complete gentleman and thanked me for being candid.

- If all else fails, break the "mystery" rules. Remember how you're not supposed to discuss details of your bodily functions with men? That's true unless you're dealing with a guy who won't leave you alone. When I was in this situation, I "casually" mentioned to a man who used to follow me around that I had the "worst diarrhea" and was about to shit my pants. He looked at me like I was the most disgusting woman on earth and never talked to me again. Mission accomplished.

DATING RULE #138:
A goddess is not afraid to be honest!

Why it's up to us

Of all of the emails, Facebook messages, and direct tweets I receive, my favorites are the ones where my readers share their success stories with me. I cannot even explain the joy I feel when one of you lets me know you have found a wonderful relationship. Helping you to find success in your love lives is both my purpose and my passion.

"Thank you so much, Jenn! I've been following your advice and I have found an amazing boyfriend."

"Just wanted to share with you that I now have the world's best boyfriend. And I owe a lot of that to you."

"You've completely changed my life. I just got engaged and I'm not sure it would have happened if it wasn't for you."

Many others have written to tell me that my advice has inspired them to move on and clear the path for better things.

"For the past several years, I have been involved in an affair with a married man. After reading your last article, I found the courage to end things with him. Thank you for giving me the strength to do it."

"I recently went through a major heartbreak. Your blog has given me hope and it has made me laugh. Sometimes I reread your posts over and over. Thank you for making me feel better."

FAQs every goddess wonders.

"After finding 'Jenn X: 30Something & Single,' I realized my boyfriend wasn't treating me the way I deserve to be treated. I'd thought about breaking up with him for a while now. Thank you for showing me that I was settling for less than I should and confirming my thoughts."

And still others let me know that they are in the process of transforming from doormat to goddess and loving every minute of it.

"I have been a doormat my whole life. Now, thanks to you, I am learning to be a goddess. I feel like a whole new person."

"Thank you for showing me the things I was doing wrong with men. I'm listening to you, Jenn! It is making a huge difference."

"I've never had this much confidence! I really am becoming a goddess!"

Congratulations, ladies. I am so proud of each and every one of you for taking the steps to improve your romantic relationships and your entire lives.

I love the image of the "goddess" and I am so happy that women all over the world are learning about the goddess way of life. I love the idea a woman can be strong without being a bitch or a ball-buster. I love that she respects herself and makes good choices when it comes to men and her relationships. I also love that she is soft and that she knows how to love a man in the right way. To me, being a goddess is to be the best a woman can be; it's living how we were created to live.

Listen, if I could write a relationship book for men they would actually buy and (more importantly) *read*, I would. But the truth is most men don't care too much about "relationship advice." The extent of what they're interested in pretty much consists of titles like "How to Get Laid" or "An Idiot's Guide to Picking Up Chicks." And maybe once every blue moon he might mention to a buddy that his girlfriend is acting completely "psycho." But that is pretty much it.

Don't get me wrong, I get a lot of emails from guys. But here's what they usually say: "Will you marry me?" or "I totally agree with what you said in that article."

How to Be a Goddess

So you see, taking the initiative to improve our relationships is up to us. And there's absolutely nothing wrong with that. If every woman worked to improve her relationships, the world would probably be a much better place. So instead of criticizing men for being lazy, let's give ourselves a round of applause for being so proactive.

I think we all want to have a more satisfying love life. I think we all want the secrets on how to find and keep an amazing relationship. Isn't that the truly important part of life? At the end of the day, we aren't measured by how big our house was or how designer our labels were. When we evaluate the true "successes" of our lives, don't we judge ourselves (and others) by how well we gave and received love? Isn't that what really counts? I think it is. In the deepest parts of ourselves, it is what we all ultimately want.

Maybe when you started this book, you thought being a goddess was way beyond your reach. Maybe you've been an utter mess when it came to your relationships. I hope I've shown you from my own failures and successes – and everything I've learned as a result – that goddess-status is absolutely possible. I hope I've given you encouragement, motivation, and the tools to get it done. I hope you're as excited to be a goddess as I am for you!

Now that you've completed this book and are putting it into action, I must congratulate you! You, my dear, are officially a goddess! You know what it takes to be successful in love and in almost every aspect of your life. You've got at your fingertips all the skills and resources to make your dreams a reality. And don't ever let anyone tell you otherwise! Which brings me to my final dating rule…

DATING RULE #139:
Never give up on your dreams. Never compromise yourself. And don't be afraid to hold out for your best life possible.

Epilogue

Do As I Do...Now

There have been three experiences in my life which have encouraged me to pursue goddess-status. In the beginning of the book, I told you about the quote from Pablo Picasso which inspired "Jenn X: 30Something & Single" and my whole philosophy about being a goddess. That's one of them. But I have never shared the other two. So let me use this opportunity to fill you in.

I will never forget the time when one of my boyfriends told me the following story. He described a conversation he had with his beloved mother. She'd been divorced for a long time and out of the blue she said to him, "You know, I have never known what it feels like to be loved by a man. I mean really, really loved. I don't want to live the rest of my life without ever knowing that feeling."

I knew his mother well and I loved her dearly. She was beautiful, smart, and funny. She was an amazing woman in every way and I still think about her. But I've thought about that story even more. It made me so incredibly sad. And it often made me wonder about myself and my own life. Would I ever know what it feels like to be loved by a man? *I mean really, really loved?*

The second instance came when I spoke to an old friend for the first time in a while. I asked how her four-year relationship was going. "It's *incredible*, Jenn," she said.

Wow. What must that be like, I thought? How does it feel to have an "*incredible*" relationship? Honestly, at the time, I was unable to imagine it. But, it gets better! After my divorce, I spent a few days with this couple. I watched how they interacted and treated each other. It was amazing. When I told her boyfriend I was so happy they had found each other, he said something to me I will never forget:

"She is *awesome*."

And the *way* he said it completely blew my mind. He said it from his gut and with every fiber of his being. It was one of the truest things I have ever heard a man say.

I thought about what the men in my past had probably said about me.

"She's a cool girl."

"She's fun."

"She's cute."

But "She is *awesome?*" No way. Not a chance. And it was at that moment I knew I wanted a man to say that about me someday. In that exact way.

On one particularly self-reflective day right before I started "Jenn X: 30Something & Single," I thought about these experiences and insights. I decided to make a "bucket list." I wrote down everything I wanted to accomplish in my lifetime. Some of them were "silly" – like hike the Grand Canyon and play paintball. But the first two were my really big goals – the things I knew I had to do or my life would be incomplete. Here's what I wrote:

1. I will become a professional writer.
2. I will know what it is like to really, really be loved by a man. And to really, really love him, too.

I think the first one is self-explanatory. It's why I went public with my blog. It's why I do what I do. What was amazing is how quickly everything happened. Within a couple of weeks of pursuing that goal, I began writing for websites. After a month, I was approached by a magazine to be a columnist. And here I sit, accomplishing my life-long dream of writing a book. It's rather cool what happens when you work to turn your fantasies into your reality.

As for the second…

If you've read my blog, you'll know I've been pretty transparent about my relationship with "L." What you might not know, however, is that he came into my life at the exact right moment. I've often wondered if I hadn't gone through everything I did, would I have been ready for a guy like him? As Mae West said, "A woman has got to love a bad man once or twice in her life to be thankful for a good one." I think there's truth in that. If I hadn't made bad choices with men, would I have learned to make good choices? If I hadn't done things wrong, would I have learned how to do them right? I don't think so.

By the time "L," an old business associate, appeared on my voicemail to wish me "Happy Birthday," I was ready for him. And I am so thankful for God's timing in all of it. One moment earlier would have been too soon.

From our first date, I wanted to do things differently with "L." I wanted to conduct myself in the way I always knew I should, but had never done. In essence, I wanted to be a goddess…

Part of it was due to him. As I got to know him (slowly), I learned he has the qualities I was looking for in a mate. He is strong. He has good morals. He has a really cool job. He's handsome, tall, and in great shape. He's super smart. He's honest. Yes, he is fun, funny, and outgoing. But he isn't a boy in a man's body. He is actually a *man*. He is someone I can truly respect.

But mostly I wanted to become a goddess for myself. I wanted to be that woman I knew I could be; that lady who is successful in her relationships and in her life. I wanted to be my best self. No matter what happened with "L," I wanted to be able to look back on it and say, "I did it right."

As I began the relationship process with "L," it was amazing how my life mirrored my writing. And vice versa. Every lesson I imparted to my readers was also a lesson for me. Everything I wrote, I took to heart and tried to implement myself. As my writing grew and took shape, so did my own love life. It was an unbelievable journey and one which brought me to this place; this exact moment of typing my final thoughts to you. Today, I can honestly tell you that yes, I am a goddess and still working to become more and more goddess-like. And as a result, I have found a truly *"incredible"* relationship.

There is no doubt in my mind that "L" really, really loves me. And he loves me in the way a woman needs to be loved – the way in which *I've* always needed to be loved. And he is the first man to ever do that. In return, I really, really love him the way a man needs to be loved; the way in which *he* needs to be loved. Guess what? He's the first man I've ever done that with. And I know that when he talks about me to other people, "She is *awesome*" is exactly how he describes me.

I have no idea where I'll be in a year. My life has shown me it's never wise to predict the future. But when I think about it, I hope it's not too dissimilar from where I am right now – finishing up another book and excited to spend my life with my true love. But no matter what happens, at least I'll be able to say that I was able to accomplish the first two items on my bucket list.

XX

Appendix
The dating rules at a glance.

Dating Rule #1: The higher quality you are, the higher quality of men you'll attract.

Dating Rule #2: Confidence is the most attractive attribute a woman can possess.

Dating Rule #3: The less you seek other's approval, the more confident you are.

Dating Rule #4: Men want a woman who needs them, not a woman who is needy.

Dating Rule #5: A man wants a partner, not a daughter.

Dating Rule #6: We can all be bitter about something. But a goddess knows that bitterness will only end up hurting her.

Dating Rule #7: Men are attracted to what they see.

Dating Rule #8: Real men want a woman who is a woman.

Dating Rule #9: If you want a man to behave like a gentleman, you have to behave like a lady.

Dating Rule #10: Men who are relationship material want a woman who is a bit of a challenge.

Dating Rule #11: A quality man who loves you will always try to treat you with respect.

Dating Rule #12: A goddess has the strength to stand up for herself… even if it means walking away.

Dating Rule #13: It's in a man's nature to want to pursue a woman. And it's in a woman's nature to want to be pursued by a man.

Dating Rule #14: A goddess never chases after a man.

Dating Rule #15: Sex is truly great sex when the connection is both physical and emotional.

Dating Rule #16: Throw away your fantasy lists and focus on what's really important in a guy!

Dating Rule #17: He can change his haircut, his job, and his friends. But his character will never change.

Dating Rule #18: You'll never find happiness with a man whose words and actions do not match.

Dating Rule #19: The more you show him you respect yourself, the more a man will respect you in return.

Dating Rule #20: Surround yourself with people who support you.

Dating Rule #21: Guys who are selfish with their time, energy, and money will also be selfish with their emotions.

Dating Rule #22: You can't have a mature relationship with a guy who is immature.

Dating Rule #23: Before you fall for what's on the outside, make sure he's good enough on the inside.

Dating Rule #24: If a player really wants to stop being a player, he will stop acting like one.

Dating Rule #25: If he cheats on you in the beginning of a relationship, he'll cheat on you until the end of it.

Dating Rule #26: If he cheats with you, he'll cheat on you.

Dating Rule #27: Anyone who treats you badly, disrespects you, manipulates you, or continually hurts you – no matter how they do it – is a total "deal breaker."

Dating Rule #28: Never try to make a "Mr. Wrong" your "Mr. Right."

Dating Rule #29: If he's hot and cold, he doesn't feel more than lukewarm about you.

Dating Rule #30: Emotional unavailability means he is unavailable.

Dating Rule #31: Watch closely how he treats his mother. It will probably be similar to how he treats you.

Dating Rule #32: Reruns are for television, not for relationships!

Dating Rule #33: If he's casually using you for sex, he'll never give you anything more than casual sex.

Dating Rule #34: If you want to meet men, you have to put yourself in a position to meet them.

Dating Rule #35: A goddess knows that it's better to be single than in a bad relationship.

Dating Rule #36: More than anything else, your attitude will determine how successful you are with meeting guys.

Dating Rule #37: Your smile is critical when it comes to attracting a man.

Dating Rule #38: Always be ready to meet someone. Anywhere you go, there "he" could be.

Dating Rule #39: Online dating is a great addition to an already active social life, but it shouldn't be your entire social life.

Dating Rule #40: Where you meet men is not nearly as important as your attitude while you are there.

Dating Rule #41: If he isn't attracted to you romantically, he will never see you with long term potential.

Dating Rule #42: A goddess is only interested in men who are attracted to her.

Dating Rule #43: If you approach men, they have the power, not you.

Dating Rule #44: Just because women can approach men, doesn't mean we should.

Dating Rule #45: If you're constantly wondering if he likes you romantically, he probably doesn't.

Dating Rule #46: A goddess never makes it obvious she's into a guy. Instead, she flirts a bit and waits for him to make it obvious he's into her.

Dating Rule #47: A goddess flirts in a way that is both natural and classy.

Dating Rule #48: Online dating is still dating!

How to Be a Goddess

Dating Rule #49: A goddess knows there is great reward in letting a man come to her and be the one to ask her out.

Dating Rule #50: A goddess has the mindset she is a "selector," not merely a "selectee."

Dating Rule #51: A goddess does not make an emotional or financial investment in a man she does not know. No matter how hot he is.

Dating Rule #52: The more we invest in something, the more invested we become in its outcome.

Dating Rule #53: Always keep the restaurant he's taking you to in mind when choosing your first date outfit. And dress slightly dressier.

Dating Rule #54: A goddess is a classy woman. As a result, men see her as high status.

Dating Rule #55: If you want to be interesting, you have to give him something while leaving him to wonder about the rest.

Dating Rule #56: A goddess starts every man off with a clean slate. She does not hold a new man accountable for the sins of an old one.

Dating Rule #57: A woman who radiates warmth and friendliness is a woman men want to be around.

Dating Rule #58: A goddess never acts like a "Begging Puppy."

Dating Rule #59: When sex happens at an accelerated speed, the chance of a real relationship hits the skids.

Dating Rule #60: If you pay attention, a man will tell you almost everything you need to decide if he's got boyfriend potential on the first couple of dates.

Dating Rule #61: Analyze his behavior to see if he's worth more of your time and emotions. If he's not, cut your losses and run.

Dating Rule #62: Even if it was the best first date you've ever had, he still isn't necessarily your soul mate.

Dating Rule #63: Do not deprive yourself of a proper courtship!

Dating Rule #64: The more you let him show you what he's capable of and willing to do, the more you will know how he feels about you.

Dating Rule #65: If a man is the hunter, the woman is the gatherer. So gather all the necessary information, analyze his character, and act accordingly.

Dating Rule #66: When you challenge a quality man who truly likes you, he will want to rise to the occasion.

Dating Rule #67: It's a lot easier to negotiate the terms of how you want to be treated upfront, rather than attempting to fight for them later.

Dating Rule #68: Keeping a level head will protect your heart.

Dating Rule #69: No matter what your friends, MTV, or the magazines say, you absolutely cannot have sex with a man you like without becoming even more emotionally attached.

Dating Rule #70: You want a relationship and he wants sex. The way for both of you to get what you want is through a proper courtship.

Dating Rule #71: If he's properly courting you, he will act like a boyfriend without being your boyfriend. Which will make him want to be your boyfriend.

Dating Rule #72: If your goal is to have a lot of sex with a lot of guys, sleep with men quickly. If your goal is to have a relationship, don't sleep with them for a while.

Dating Rule #73: The amount of time it takes for him to get to "commitment" is directly proportionate to how proper your courtship period is.

Dating Rule #74: A goddess never puts pressure on a man to commit. But because she is so desirable, a quality man will want a commitment on his very own.

Dating Rule #75: You can only have a healthy relationship with a man who is relationship material.

Dating Rule #76: A goddess watches to see whether he's truly open to a relationship. If he's not, she moves on and doesn't try to convince him otherwise.

Dating Rule #77: Don't act like a girlfriend before you're his girlfriend!

How to Be a Goddess

Dating Rule #78: Sex does not equal a commitment, at least not in his mind.

Dating Rule #79: A quality man commits to a woman who can confidently handle her life whether or not he's a part of it.

Dating Rule #80: A goddess never initiates "the talk." In fact, words like "commitment" and "exclusivity" are not uttered during courtship.

Dating Rule #81: Women feel loved when they are adored. Men, however, feel loved when they are respected.

Dating Rule #82: You should only respect a man who is worthy of your respect. And you should only love a man who is worthy of your love.

Dating Rule #83: If you emasculate him, not only will you lose respect for him, but he will lose respect for himself. And it won't be long before he finds something or someone who builds him back up.

Dating Rule #84: A man needs to feel admired by the woman he is with. It's what makes him feel like a man.

Dating Rule #85: When you show a quality man that you trust him, he will want to honor that trust.

Dating Rule #86: When a man cherishes and protects a woman, she feels adored. In her mind, that translates into being loved.

Dating Rule #87: If he didn't act like a boyfriend during courtship, he will not act like one once he actually becomes your boyfriend.

Dating Rule #88: When he is cherishing you, respond to it by letting him know you cherish him and appreciate him, too.

Dating Rule #89: You need to reciprocate in order to be fair, but not as a means to get more love.

Dating Rule #90: As long as he's feeling respected (admired and trusted), a quality guy who is crazy about you will always strive to make you feel cherished.

Dating Rule #91: Unless he is a trustworthy man, you will never know what it is like to feel protected, and therefore truly loved.

Dating Rule #92: Needing a man doesn't make you needy. It demonstrates you trust him to protect you.

Dating Rule #93: A goddess waits for a man to say "I love you" first. That way, she knows he really, really means it. And she only says it back if he's a quality guy and she really, really means it, too.

Dating Rule #94: Your "wedding night" should be a physical culmination of everything that's been built throughout your relationship.

Dating Rule #95: Good girls do. But they only do after a certain level of commitment and trust is established.

Dating Rule #96: As the modern version of the famous saying goes, a man needs his woman to be a lady in the streets and a freak in the sheets.

Dating Rule #97: A goddess knows there is a time to be a "lady" and a time to be a "freak." And she has no trouble moving from one to the other.

Dating Rule #98: A goddess is confident with her sexuality.

Dating Rule #99: Because he works to keep her satisfied, a goddess has no trouble wanting to keep her man satisfied in return.

Dating Rule #100: Don't deal him your wildest card upfront. Instead, keep the fires going by starting off with a slow burn.

Dating Rule #101: A goddess is "dirty." In a totally good way.

Dating Rule #102: You don't necessarily have to have sex with him to figure out what kind of lover he will be.

Dating Rule #103: Very often the "safer" you feel with a man, the hotter the sex will become.

Dating Rule #104: A goddess only has a sexual relationship with a man who meets both her physical and emotional needs.

Dating Rule #105: How you fight is what will make or break your relationship.

Dating Rule #106: If he breaks his promises to you in the beginning, you can't very well expect him to start keeping them later on.

Dating Rule #107: A goddess doesn't fight over something that shouldn't be a battle in the first place.

Dating Rule #108: Once he stops being "neglectful," make him feel like a hero.

Dating Rule #109: Women want to connect over problems. Men want to solve them.

Dating Rule #110: A man who loves you will always want to "fix" your problems.

Dating Rule #111: When presenting a problem to a man, also tell him how he can solve it for you. That way you both get your needs met.

Dating Rule #112: If you talk to him like you're one of the boys in the beginning, he doesn't expect that to change once you become his girlfriend.

Dating Rule #113: When you nag a man, he goes on the defensive, which will cause his defense mechanisms – fight or flight – to go up.

Dating Rule #114: If you want him to do more of something, praise him whenever he does it.

Dating Rule #115: A goddess does not try to accept behavior she knows she should reject, even if it means losing the relationship.

Dating Rule #116: You put your relationship in greater jeopardy if you hide from the things you should reject than if you confront them.

Dating Rule #117: It's okay to let a man know when he intentionally disrespects you; even if it's only a little bit. Just don't let it escalate into something bigger than it is.

Dating Rule #118: A goddess has no problem with owning up to her mistakes.

Dating Rule #119: Long-term relationships don't have to suck!

Dating Rule #120: If you aren't physically attracted to him, he's a potential friend not a potential boyfriend.

Dating Rule #121: A goddess always maintains some mystery.

Dating Rule #122: Maintaining your independence and some mystery not only helps to keep the chemistry alive, it's actually what encourages a man to keep courting his woman.

Dating Rule #123: Create a feeling of newness in an old relationship by continuing to date.

Dating Rule #124: Never overlook the importance of finding someone you are compatible with.

Dating Rule #125: A goddess never compromises herself.

Dating Rule #126: If compromise is healthy compromise, it will ultimately benefit both of you.

Dating Rule #127: When it comes to communication, women need to focus on quality rather than on quantity.

Dating Rule #128: A goddess never has to force a man to marry her. Instead, he wants to marry her because she is someone he can't live without.

Dating Rule #129: Unless there is some sort of long-term commitment, you won't be able to sustain a long-term relationship.

Dating Rule #130: The slower you go in the beginning, the less your guy will pull back.

Dating Rule #131: If a man is acting like he wants space, you need to give him the galaxy.

Dating Rule #132: Even goddesses get hormonal!

Dating Rule #133: You can never change who a man fundamentally is.

Dating Rule #134: Don't try to change a man you know you can't live with. Instead, "ex-change" him for a new one!

Dating Rule #135: It's absolutely possible to prevent cheating.

Dating Rule #136: Heartbreak sucks.

Dating Rule #137: But you will, eventually, get over it.

Dating Rule #138: A goddess is not afraid to be honest!

Dating Rule #139: Never give up on your dreams. Never compromise yourself. And don't be afraid to hold out for your best life possible.

Acknowledgements

First and foremost to my parents who have always supported my dreams and helped me to achieve my goals. It was my mother who once told me, "You think you need someone to believe in you, but what you really need is to have more belief in yourself." Mom, you were right. But every kid should have parents who believe in them. I am very grateful I do.

To my girl, Dana Salston, who sent me Picasso's quote right when I needed to hear it. It was that quote that inspired "Jenn X," the subsequent article, and this book.

Thank you to Brette Borow and GirlsGuideTo.com. Without you finding me and asking me to write for your website, I wouldn't have a fraction of the following I do. And you're also a great friend.

To Cortney Kizirian for being the test audience for "How to Be a Goddess." Thank you for all of your input and advice, my dear girl!

To William Sudah and the entire staff of Expert Subjects. Thank you for all of your hard work in making my book shine.

To all of my resources, both male and female, who never seem to get too annoyed by my incessant texts asking their opinion on love and dating issues.

To my beloved readers and every girl who has written to me, asked my advice, or commented on one of my articles. I'm honored you trust me with something so important as your love lives.

And finally to the woman of Proverbs 31, who in my opinion is the ultimate goddess. "A wife of noble character who can find? She is worth far more than rubies. Her husband has full confidence in her and lacks nothing of value. She brings him good, not harm, all the days of her life. She selects wool and flax and works with eager hands. She is like the merchant ships, bringing her food from afar. She gets up while it is still night; she provides food for her family and portions for her female servants. She considers a field and buys it; out of her earnings she plants a vineyard. She sets about her work vigorously; her arms are strong for her tasks. She sees that her trading is profitable, and her lamp does not go out at night....She opens her arms to the poor and extends her hands to the needy. When it snows, she has no fear for her household; for all of them are clothed in scarlet. She makes coverings for her bed; she is clothed in fine linen and purple. Her husband is respected at the city gate, where he takes his seat among the elders of the land....She is clothed with strength and dignity; she can laugh at the days to come. She speaks with wisdom, and faithful instruction is on her tongue. She watches over the affairs of her household and does not eat the bread of idleness. Her children arise and call her blessed; her husband also, and he praises her: 'Many women do noble things, but you surpass them all.' Charm is deceptive, and beauty is fleeting; but a woman who fears the Lord is to be praised. Honor her for all that her hands have done, and let her works bring her praise at the city gate." (NIV)

About the Author

Jenn Clark is a writer, relationship coach, and dating expert. She is a monthly columnist for "The 9s" – a men's lifestyle magazine. In addition, Jenn is a featured relationship advice writer for a variety of websites including DigitalRomanceInc and GirlsGuideTo, and an expert for the online dating site SinglesWarehouse. She was recently named one of the top ten dating bloggers by DatingAdvice.com.

Jenn lives in Los Angeles with her new husband, "L," and their adopted Rottweiler, Lili. You can find her at www.beingagoddess.com and on her Facebook page "Jenn X: 30Something & Single."